PENGUIN BOOKS

GREAT DAY COMING

R. Serge Denisoff is associate professor of sociology at Bowling Green State University and editor of the *Journal of Popular Music and Society*. He received his B.A. and M.A. degrees from San Francisco State College and, in 1969, his Ph.D. from Simon Fraser University in British Columbia. He has written for *Rolling Stone, Creem, Broadside, Journal of American Folklore, American Quarterly*, and numerous other magazines and journals. Books to his credit include *Social and Political Movements* (with Gary B. Rush), *Sing a Song of Social Significance*, and *The Controversies and Polemics of Sociology*.

Great Day Coming

*FOLK MUSIC
AND THE AMERICAN LEFT*

R. Serge Denisoff

 PENGUIN BOOKS INC · Baltimore, Maryland

Penguin Books Inc
7110 Ambassador Road
Baltimore, Maryland 21207, U.S.A.

First published by the University of Illinois Press 1971
Published in Penguin Books 1973

Acknowledgments are made to the following organizations
for permission to reprint verses from songs.
For "Love Me I'm a Liberal": Copyright 1965, Barricade
Music, Inc., New York, N.Y. International copyright
secured. Made in U.S.A. All rights reserved.
For "One Big Union for Two" and "Sing Me a Song with
Social Significance": Copyright 1937. Mills Music, Inc.
Copyright renewed, assigned to Florence Music Company,
Inc.

Foreword

Charles Seeger is fond of telling the story of two government security agents entering the Library of Congress and demanding the source of "all those subversive folk songs." To a very minor extent this work asks a similar question. The quest here is not for subversive ballads, if there are such things, or their composers, but rather for some light on a beclouded, murky, and historically unclear subject: the relationship of the American Left to folk music. While most Americans know that this relationship existed and the chroniclers of the recent revival hint at some correlation between urban folk singers and progressive movements of the 1930s and '40s, little in the way of objective data is presently available. Despite treatments of this kind in drama and literature, any inquiry into the subject very soon becomes hampered by political ghosts and super-Americans. The mere mention of the topic to a handful of individuals elicits a Pavlovian response of "Red baiting." Certainly, this reaction does have some merit, as any cursory examination of *Rhythm, Riots, and Revolution* and other anti-Communist tracts would suggest. Media blacklists, which now appear a thing of the past, also have created obstacles. Time has placed many a barrier before the researcher: memories dim and fade, the grim reaper and illness are never far away. Yet a great deal of material still remains for the sociologist to examine.

The purpose of this book is to examine the use of folk music by the American Left, especially the Communist party, during the thirties and forties. More specifically, it is an analysis of the use of folk material as a weapon to achieve particular sociopolitical ends. In doing this, we ask a fundamental question: "Why folk music in an industrial urban setting?" It is an attempt to trace a political-intellectual fad of the sectarian Left into the mass media, where it emerged as a commodity to be sold in the marketplace of popular music.

The book is an endeavor to answer labor historian Archie Green's request for an objective treatment of the role of Communists in the so-called urban folk music "movement." Total objectivity, as Julian Huxley has suggested, is impossible. This is especially true for students of social movements and related phenomena. In this vein I have attempted to avoid using inflammatory statements and identifications made before congressional investigating committees where outside material is not available. However, in the following pages it is well to remember that individuals and organizations mentioned here were not necessarily card-carrying Communists. Membership in People's Songs Inc. does not *ipso facto* point to support for William Z. Foster. Views expressed in Communist publications can be assumed to reflect political policy and implicit support, since political editors, either Communist or Bircher, rarely give space to views at variance with their own.

Acknowledgments

This presentation would not have been possible without the substantial help given me by a hardy band of participants in the events to be discussed. I am especially indebted to Bess Hawes, Maurice Sugar, Malvina Reynolds, Gordon Friesen, Bill Mandel, and several others who preferred anonymity. Such students of protest songs as Bill Friedland, Archie Green, and Richard A. Reuss supplemented and corrected many parts of this work. I am especially grateful to Dick Reuss for supplying esoteric references and historical facts when needed. Professors T. B. Bottomore, Norman Friedman, Gary B. Rush, Frank Collinge, and particularly Andrew P. Phillips are to be thanked for their guidance in both sociological and editorial spheres. Julie Zambetti, Kay Houston, Jean Butts, Dorothy Darr, and Mary Williams provided invaluable help in the preparation of the manuscript. I would also like to express my appreciation to the American Folklore Society for allowing me to reprint in Chapter IV sections of a paper originally published in the *Journal of American Folklore*.

Finally, I wish to acknowledge the role my wife, Carol, played in the undertaking. Without her help, presence, and encouragement this work would have remained in a desk drawer, half finished.

R. Serge Denisoff

Contents

ix

I heard a man play a five-string banjo at a crowded
    street corner meeting—
And his eyes were shining with a tomorrow light
    as he sang of a "Great Day coming."
I listened carefully and I heard myself singing
    with him.

IRWIN SILBER
July 24, 1949

1

Folk Consciousness as Utopian Ideology

Beginning with Plato, social observers have pointed to the power of song to achieve political ends. The Greek philosopher in *The Republic* cautioned that ". . . any musical innovation is full of danger to the whole State, and ought to be prohibited [because it] imperceptively penetrates into manners and customs; whence, issuing with greater force, it invades contracts between man and man and . . . goes on to laws and constitutions, in utter recklessness, ending at last . . . by an overthrow of all rights, private as well as public." This admonition, it appears, was received quite seriously, for political princes frequently outlawed rhymes opposing their personages and philosophies. Such English monarchs as Henry VIII, Mary I, and Elizabeth I all took great pains to control ballads and broadsides. Mary I issued a proclamation barring the painting and distribution of "books, ballads, rhymes and interludes" without royal authorization. Elizabeth was no more tolerant of papist ballads. Andrew Fletcher, the eighteenth-century English political writer, echoed "the power of song" thesis: "Give me the making of the songs of a nation, and I care not who makes its laws."

In America similar sentiments have been expressed by presidents and ministers, popular singers and political radicals. The engineer-turned-beleaguered-president, Herbert Hoover, during the throes of the depression remarked to crooner Rudy Vallee, "If you can sing a song that would make people forget their troubles . . . I'll give you a medal." Enjoying the heady fruits of the folk music revival in 1964,

Peter, Paul, and Mary told an interviewer: "Do you realize the power of PP and M? We could mobilize the youth of America today in a way that nobody else could. We could conceivably travel with a presidential candidate, and maybe even sway an election." In 1968 they put this boast to the test. Their candidate, Senator Eugene McCarthy, lost in his bid to be the Democratic standard-bearer in the presidential election.

Several performers have pictured their musical instruments as weapons. Woody Guthrie inscribed "This Machine Kills Fascists" on his guitar. A decade later Pete Seeger printed a less ambitious slogan on his banjo, "This Machine Surrounds Hate and Forces It to Surrender." Heeding the words of Plato, the radical Right has launched several campaigns to combat the influence of song, particularly upon the young. Such contemporary critics as entertainer Art Linkletter and David Noebel of the Christian Crusade have charged folk singers and rock 'n' roll artists with implementing a Machiavellian plot to hypnotize and subvert the youth of America.

The belief that art is a weapon and music a key to political success is an old one. Throughout history this proposition has flourished in many quarters but never as strongly or widely as in left-wing political movements, especially those following the tenets of Marxism-Leninism. Marxism, being an offshoot of Hegelianism, placed great stress upon the creation and emergence of true or class consciousness. Lenin, desiring to arouse the Russian peasants, underlined the need for agitational and propaganda work among the exploited in order to facilitate political consciousness. Art and music were to play an important part in the plan for revolutionary change. In the United States the zenith of the "art is a weapon" tenet occurred during the 1930s when the Marxian millennium was believed by many to be close at hand. In intellectual circles proletarian culture was exalted; books and paintings focused on factory workers and displaced migrants. Drama and literature became socially significant, and songs of protest, rarely heard since the heyday of the Industrial Workers of the World, once again were bellowed by unemployed street marchers. In Communist party circles folk music became a cry for justice.

The relationship of folk music to the Communist party of the United States (CPUSA) and several of its satellite organizations makes for a fascinating study in the sociology of political and ideological radicalism or nonconformity. The proposition that folk songs are a cry for justice was a unique one generally confined to the American

Communist party (or the Stalinist movement, as it was frequently called because of its allegiance to the Kremlin and to Stalin's view of Marxist doctrine) and its sphere of influence. This view was not shared by its rival Marxists, the Trotskyists or the Socialists led by Norman Thomas. Indeed, the idealization of the folk song by the CPUSA nearly paralleled that of the Nazi movement in Germany. Moreover, the glorification of a rural musical genre by an urban-based political movement was even more curious, since social crusaders historically have relied upon songs that were familiar to their potential audiences. Agricultural reformers, the Grangers and Populists, absorbed the musical style and fervor of fundamentalist religious hymns. The syndicalist Industrial Workers of the World utilized hymns and hobo jungle tunes to convert the masses to their One Big Union.

City dwellers, the main supporters of the Stalinist movement, were not part of the *Gemeinschaft* or folk community, which anthropologist Robert Redfield, in the *American Journal of Sociology,* characterized as "small, isolated, non-literate, and homogeneous with a strong sense of group solidarity." While few anthropologists today would use this definition of "folk," there is little doubt that the urban culture of New York was a giant step away from the rural hamlets of the South or the oil boom towns of the West. The offerings of Rudy Vallee, Russ Columbo, Buddy Rogers, and the big bands were the musical preference of the cosmopolitan during the 1930s. For the highbrow the master works of Bach, Brahms, and Beethoven represented the zenith in symphonic art. Aaron Copland's compositions symbolized the avant-garde in formal music circles. The Stalinists, while aware of these musical trends, rejected them. History would suggest that the Communists used material from the Broadway stage, Tin Pan Alley, and the swing bands to inculcate class consciousness. Instead, they turned to a basically rural genre, folk music, and created the "song of persuasion."

A song of persuasion may be thought of as a propaganda song which employs the instrumental and stylistic techniques generally associated with folk songs. The music itself is relatively simple when contrasted to symphonic orchestrations. Guitars and banjoes are the instruments customarily used. The structure of the music frequently is tied to a three-chord progression such as G-C-G-C-G-D^7 or E-A-E-A-E-B^7, with the lyrics being stressed. This latter feature makes it ideal for propaganda purposes, since the music does not detract from the message. Equally, the lyrics in many cases are easily adapted to contemporary situations. For example, Woody Guthrie simply changed "You've got to walk that lonesome valley" to "You've gotta go down and join the union." Another Guthrie lyric, "Round and Round Hitler's Grave," based on the square-dance tune "Old Joe Clark," is a "zipper song," which allows almost total improvisation, always returning to the basic chorus. To illustrate a zipper song, we need look no further than "We Shall Not Be Moved"; its line "Jesus is our savior, we shall not be moved" can be used to state that Lenin, Thomas, or whoever "is our leader, we shall not be moved." Despite these obvious advantages for the political propagandist, the song of persuasion, until its popularization, had exhibited a number of limitations.

The major restriction of the song of persuasion, at least prior to the folk music revival of the 1960s, was its tie to rural America. After 1920 an ever-increasing portion of the population resided in metropolitan areas. Many of these urban inhabitants were first-, second-, or even third-generation offspring of foreign immigrants who had little knowledge or appreciation of rural America. Consequently, the song of persuasion during the 1930s and later lost a great deal of its effectiveness when directed to most urban dwellers. The unfamiliarity of this musical genre presented many related difficulties. Folk music as a genre did not draw outsiders to political rallies. The fact that Woody Guthrie was billed to appear at a union rally did not exactly generate any unexpected activity or heightened interest in the union. The word "hootenanny" until the late 1950s was meaningless except to those in the Stalinist orbit. Folk singing in the urban milieu was tied to a picket line, a political rally, or a summer camp meeting attended by supporters rather than by the neutral or open-minded outsiders to whom the musical political message might be addressed. Within the Stalinist camp in New York City the song of persuasion as a weapon was directed to maintaining the moral affirmation of the adherents. Its ability to serve as a recruiting device was greatly hampered by its esoteric nature. We can now ask the question, "Why would a movement dedicated to the education and politicization of the urban proletariat pick folk song as a propaganda tool?"

The answer to this question is perhaps best introduced by referring to the work of German sociologist Max Weber. In his classic economic treatise *The Protestant Ethic and the Spirit of Capitalism* Weber argued that rational ideas explain social action, or, individuals act the way they do because of their state of awareness or consciousness. The Protestant ethic with its emphasis on the duty of work and deferred gratification leads to an understanding (*Verstehen*) of the actions of the capitalist. In other writings Weber expanded his method of *Verstehen* to political affairs. Politicans, he wrote, seek power within the framework of their belief systems. In the process of pursuing political office, noble ideas are reified; that is, ideology becomes real to the political actor. It is the rare politician who does not present himself as a man with the highest of ideals, seeking *only* to be a servant of the people. For Weber men act upon ideas; therefore, social phenomena can be understood by examining the actor's level of rational consciousness.

Another German sociologist, Karl Mannheim, can be credited with expanding Weber's argument with his notion of "relationism." Relationism at its most simplified means that consciousness is determined by the social location of an individual. The individual's class position, education, associations, and occupation all contribute to his consciousness and his definition of what is real. What is reality for one person or group may be false to someone not in a similar social situation. Ideology, one form of consciousness, is correct or incorrect on the basis of societal position. For example, the consciousness of the businessman will differ from that of a politician on the basis of such factors as education and class. These states of awareness, of course, are by no means totally exclusive, since both political and economic men may find many of their interests mutually rewarding. On the other hand, when individual interests and their pursuant forms of consciousness conflict, then open struggle can emerge. This occurs when the world view of one group is brought into direct, irreconcilable confrontation with that of another. A conflict group in the political-economic sphere of social action is a social movement. A social movement presents itself as an alternative to existent social organizations. The key feature of a social movement is, as Weber and Mannheim suggest, its unique form of social consciousness. One aspect of this particular consciousness Mannheim calls utopian mentality; facts, events, even history are ordered in such a way as to take on the character of destiny in keeping with the fundamental directions, wishes, or goals of a movement.

Egon Bittner, in the *American Sociological Review*, recently has elaborated upon this interpretation, redefining utopian mentality to mean "doctrines and beliefs that seek to impose a unified internally consistent schema of interpretation upon a world of heterogeneous meanings." This form of radical consciousness transcends the everyday meanings of life and leads to social action. If, as Max Weber wrote in "Politics as Vocation," "an action of good intent leads to bad results then, in the actor's eyes, not he but the world, or the stupidity of other men, or God's will who made them thus, is responsible for the evil."

In short, by examining the consciousness of the members of a social movement and the strictures of the organization, its actions can be understood. In keeping with Weber, Mannheim, and Bittner we will attempt to answer the rhetorical query "Why folk music" by probing the consciousness and ideology of the CPUSA and its spheres of influence. More specifically, this investigation will center upon those aspects of Stalinist consciousness and experience which led to the adoption of such slogans as "a cry for justice" and "people's songs" to describe folk music. This view of reality will be called folk consciousness.

Folk consciousness is defined as a gestalt of factors which predisposes those sharing it to act in a certain manner under specified conditions. It motivated its adherents to present rural music as the genre of the urban proletariat; to emulate Okie attire; and to define middle-class intellectuals as folk singers and genuine rural songsters as people's artists. In tracing the development and emergence of folk consciousness, we shall also be concerned with the relationship of the political radical to his society. Can a man not of the world succeed in it? The Communist fascination with folk music is an example of the difficulties of converting those with common sense—the amount of knowledge necessary for the average man to solve his everyday problems and protect his interests in a socially understandable manner—to a radical political prospective.

The Roots of Folk Consciousness

Arlene Kaplan, in a study of urban folk singing which appeared in *Sociologus*, suggests that the political use of the genre gains impetus "from Marxist doctrine with its emphasis on the importance of the proletariat." At first glance this assertion appears plausible, since the Communist party of America did play a significant role in the development of urban folk singing during the 1930s and particularly the 1940s. But upon closer examination, Marxist or left-wing ideology alone is not sufficient to explain the Stalinist idealization of folk music. Most American left-wing movements avoided folk material in favor of the songs they had learned in the home, the church, or especially in the "old country." The Socialist party of America, for example, drew upon both European and Populist sources and sang lyrics added to well-known religious melodies at their quasi-evangelical camp meetings. Prior to World War I the Socialist party published several songbooks which circulated widely but contained few folk songs. Two such songbooks were *Socialist Songs with Music* (1901) and *Songs of Socialism for Local Branch and Campagin Work Public Meetings, Labor, Fraternal and Religious Organizations, Social Gatherings and the Home* (1911). American followers of Leon Trotsky in the Workers party, Independent Socialist League, and Socialist Workers party had little to do with folk songs. The most proletarian of all the American leftist movements, the Industrial Workers of the World, who used songs extensively, primarily adapted the songs of the streets and the church. Greenway in his pioneer work, *American Folksongs of Protest,* indicates that the Industrial Workers resorted to the use of song as a means of combating the street bands of the Salvation Army and the Volunteers of America, who frequently would drown out Wobbly speakers in a "cacophony of cornets and tambourines." IWW organizers performed parodies of religious hymns and practices, such as being required literally to sing for your supper by the "starvation army," as Wobbly bards labeled the religious movement. Using the Army for a model, the IWW published a songbook to fan the flames of discontent. Each song was designed to "illustrate and dramatize some phase of the struggle." While Wobbly songs mirrored both the European ideologies of Marx and the French anarchists, folk songs were not idealized in the slightest. As one observer reported, "The absence of commentary [on folk song] in Socialist and IWW writings, of course, does not preclude individual members from having been exposed to folksong, consciously or unconsciously, but it does suggest that it was not part of the collective thinking of either group." Given the absence of folk singing or the awareness of this genre by most American Marxist movements, the original correlation of idealization of the proletariat and folk music does not appear to be correct. Upon examination, the teachings and example of V. I. Lenin and the Bolsheviks appear to have pointed the American Communists in the direction of folk material.

Lenin's fundamental tenet of revolutionary ideology was that "consciousness determines being." The revolutionary leader time and again stressed the need for a vanguard to educate the populace, thereby mobilizing a unified group willing to carry out the political actions necessary for social change. In *What Is to Be Done?* he suggested that "it is not sufficient to explain the political oppression of the workers (as it was not sufficient to explain to them the antagonism between their interests and the interests of the employers). It is necessary to agitate in connection with every concrete manifestation of such oppression." The agitator is essential to political action, since "he will . . . arouse mass dissatisfaction and indignation at the crying injustices of capitalism."

The communication of ideas is not limited to pamphleteering or speechmaking. Art, literature, posters, proverbs, music—all are as effective, if not more so. In czarist Russia propaganda could not be simply a task of printing copies of the *Manifesto* or *Iskra,* assuming that these works could escape detection, since the masses by and large were illiterate. Consequently, it became necessary to use the art and argot of the people to create political consciousness. One Soviet art scholar notes that the Bolsheviks "found a fountain of inspiration in folk songs and fairy tales, in proverbs and adages." In pre-Soviet Russia folk music was in fact the music of the people. Bolsheviks utilized folk music because it was *the* music the illiterate *muzcik* or peasant knew. The Russian peasant was familiar with political themes being inserted into his music. Russian propaganda songs performed in the style of the folk were analogous to those found in Elizabethan England. Many historical topical ballads were written about the czars, particularly Ivan the Terrible; the Bolsheviks only expanded upon this tradition. The Soviet folklorist, Y. M. Sokolov, indicates in *Russian Folklore* that the usage of peasant or folk tunes was highly successful: "The revolutionary fighting ardor at the time of the October Revolution, the revolutionary enthusiasm, the heroic moods at the time of the civil war sought expression for themselves. The chief means of such expression were . . . the popular, widely diffused revolutionary hymns, marches, and songs of the proletariat."

The impact of the October Revolution upon the entire American Left cannot be overstated. All the theories, dreams, hopes, and expectations had finally come true. As Howe and Coser have noted in *The American Communist Party: A Critical History,* "This was how it happened; this is how it's done." Many of the practices and techniques of the October Revolution, including propaganda songs, were superimposed upon American society. The propaganda songs favored by American Bolsheviks were Soviet, especially those from the revolutionary period and, of course, the "Internationale." Many of the Soviet songs were not generically based on folk material but were idealizations of rural culture, which in Soviet Russia was deemed proletarian. Maxim Gorky, the leading Soviet proponent of socialist realism, or proletarian realism as it was called in the United States, saw folk art as the true expression of the working class. The Proletarian Musicians Association of Moscow in 1929 is reported to have characterized folk music as suitable for the "ultimate victory of the working class." From the 1917 Russian Revolution American Communists learned the value of political agitation. But they applied the lesson rather indiscriminately, since the conditions which led to the Soviet victory did not exist in the United States. The United States was not predominately an agrarian society, nor was illiteracy a major barrier to communications. Indeed, the whole application of Leninist techniques was doomed to failure. For our purposes, however, the idealization of Soviet culture by American Stalinists is highly significant, since it is here that rural *qua* proletarian culture emerges. In time, when the Stalinists were directed away from their nearly total emulation of Soviet culture, the rural or folk tradition of art would remain.

In 1927 the Communist Academy in Moscow was told that "there is no revolutionary situation in America." The Marxist vanguard was not circumventing the false class consciousness engendered by the Roaring Twenties. This lack of success was primarily due to the composition of the American Communist movement and the ideological disputes of the period, and not to the false glitter of the Age of Normalcy.

The CPUSA until the late 1930s was a movement of the foreign-born. Only one-seventh of the 20,000 American Communists spoke English. One party organizer bitterly stated, "We had great difficulties . . . because most of our members could not write English." A comrade wrote of the Freiheit Gesang Ferein (a Yiddish chorus), ". . . we have so many comrades who do not happen to be born Jews and they simply do not understand Yiddish." Meetings to attract the native American proletariat were frequently conducted in Eastern European languages or Yiddish.

The lack of ability to speak or sing in English was but one difficulty stemming from the foreign composition of the party. Another consequence was that newly immigrated party members were reluctant to move outside their own ethnic groups. Jewish migrants with a tradition of ghetto life in many European countries were particularly susceptible to this social distance factor. Other ethnic or language groups also found the security of nationality to be more important than the mobilization of the American worker. The problem of assimilation was not ignored in the Kremlin. According to the Comintern, the CPUSA was to be "a vanguard of the American people," not a sub-culture. International Communist leaders were highly critical of the American movement and the social base of the organization. The reasons for this strong disapprobation were twofold: Lenin's concept of a solidified party, and the lack of concrete results in the largest capitalist country in the world. Lenin argued that a strong unified movement was necessary to achieve social change. The language sections of the American party were far from unified. In fact, the intraparty disputes of the late 1920s over Lenin's grave were intensified by Communist nationality groups.

Moscow's major irritation with American Communists was the movement's isolation from the masses. As early as 1920 the Comintern had stated: ". . . with the rapid development of the class struggle, and when the American proletariat is faced with an extremely complicated problem, the language federations will only be in a position to fulfill their duty if they amalgamate as closely as possible with the organizations of the American worker." Several years later the Comintern restated this position in much stronger language: "The Communist immigrants have brought many virtues with them to America. . . . At the same time, however, their greatest weakness lies in the fact that they desire to apply the experience they have acquired in the various countries of Europe mechanically to American conditions." This note ended by ordering those comrades who could not conform to these tactics and policies to leave the party.

Other directives dealing with this question followed from the International. Why, asked Moscow, was there not an English-language newspaper when there were dozens of foreign-language publications? In 1929 the International issued an open letter to its American affiliate, in part stating, "The Workers Party of America has been for many years an organization of foreign workers *not much connected with the political life of the country*." Musically, the party did not reflect American culture either. The genesis of Communist songs was European, especially Soviet. French, Yiddish, Chartist, and Eastern European songs were frequently sung at party functions. One letter to the *Daily Worker* in 1927 amply outlined the situation: ". . . our comrades can't sing. They sing half bad the Internationale and the English Boatman song, further they are deaf and dumb." Indeed, it was not until the advent of the Daily Worker Chorus in the early 1930s that a Communist chorus sang primarily in English.

The language question was not the only handicap plaguing the movement. The intraparty disputes of the late 1920s also diverted the Communists from their historical mission. During the return to normalcy the party was hampered by the same polemic that ripped the international movement over the succession in the Soviet Union. American party members and leaders, following the left, right, or middle positions as manifested by Trotsky, Bukharin, and Stalin, rose and declined in the reflected light of their Soviet models. Supporters of the Trotskyist position of permanent revolution, such as James Cannon, were expelled. Such adherents to the moderate Bukharin school as Gitlow and Lovestone were removed after Stalin had consolidated his power. The party devoted much of its time and energy to internecine warfare, resolving ideological and structural questions rather than recruiting and organizing the masses. Its major program during that period was the Trade Union Educational League (TUEL), which was primarily concerned with propagandizing union members.

In time, as a means of overcoming its lack of success in the twenties, the party employed the tactical approach which Lowenthal and Guterman describe as the "simple Americans" technique. This technique was designed to appeal to the masses, transcending class and political divisions. These authors, in their *Prophets of Deceit: A Study of the Techniques of the American Agitator,* describe the method: ". . . the agitator describes his American-Americans as a people of sound instincts and, he is happy to say, little sophistication." This approach, partially suggested by Communist campaigns during dual unionism (the creation of party-controlled unions in opposition to the AFL), was designed to ameliorate the segregation of the party. It also capitalized upon the quasi nationalism found in intellectual circles. This technique involved many symbols of Americanism and helped reinforce the identification of party members with the proletariat. Functionally, this method somewhat reduced the isolation of the movement because the Stalinists were able to appeal to some non-Marxists. The membership, which until 1936 was still predominantly foreign-born, falsely felt that it was finally a part of the American working class. The slogan "Communism Is 20th Century Jeffersonianism" added another element to the folk consciousness of the party. The ideation of rural culture and the Kremlin-ordered Americanization of the party pointed the movement toward the folk genre. The Marxist-Leninist view of art added yet another dimension to the gestalt of folk consciousness.

For ideological adherents to Marxism-Leninism there exists a class struggle. Every form of art becomes a weapon in the conflict and each artist is a soldier. The artistic taste of each social class must reflect its own status interests. As Albert Rhys Williams has observed in *The Soviets,* "The old composers, whether they knew it or not, were upholding a political theory—for the most part bolstering the rule of the upper class." Instead, music must be used to combat the false consciousness of the ruling class.

Charles Seeger in a tone-setting article "On Proletarian Music" noted that "music is one of the cultural forms through which the work of humanizing and preparation operates. Thus it becomes a weapon in the class struggle." Some idioms of musical expression, according to leftist reviewers, had previous class commitments. Another Marxist theorist, Sidney Finkelstein, wrote, in his *How Music Expresses Ideas,* "Under capitalism, symphony and opera, chamber music are commercial and esthetic rivals . . . the form and content of the music are controlled by the hirer of talents. These talents, however skilled, have to obey a dictation which disguises itself in the form of 'box office' and profits." And in his *Jazz: A People's Music,* Finkelstein states that classical music is especially profitable to promoters, for they fit classical music easily into standardized patterns of performance, make minimal demands on mind or technique, and "challenge no prejudice or hidebound ways of thinking." Formal music was interpreted as obscuring the Marxist-Leninist system of reality. Lenin is reported to have said that "classical music was too nice" and only mellowed the political consciousness of the masses. He did not wish to soothe the people but rather to incite, arouse, or hit them on the head. Classical music was viewed as being appreciated only by the ruling class and not by the broad mass of the people. Only the intelligentsia could see the class struggle in Beethoven's *Eroica.* Lenin observed, "Art belongs to the people. It must penetrate with its deepest roots into the very midst of the laboring masses. It must be *intelligible* to these masses and be loved by them. It must unite the feeling, thought, and will of these masses; it must elevate them." Stalin, a folk music enthusiast, proclaimed that ". . . folklore does not separate itself from the people."* Louis Harap in *Social Roots of the Arts* elaborated this position. Folk art serves the interests of the masses: its subject matter is based on

---

* Stalin's personal interest in folk music may have been a factor in Communist minds. However, there is little to substantiate the view that folk consciousness was a product created and approved in Moscow.

their everyday lives, it is practiced by the people as participants, and its individual exponents spring from the people themselves. For Harap "folk songs exhibit . . . the general characteristics of a genuine people's art in class societies." For these commentators culture must be that of the people; that is, art must be of a style that can be communicated to the working class.

Similar statements are to be found in the literature of the American Communist party. Michael Gold, a leading proponent of socialist realism and the use of folk music, remarked that art must be for "lumberjacks, hoboes, clerks, sectionhands, machinists, harvesthands, waiters—the people who should count more to us than the paid scribblers." One paid scribbler, an Almanac Singer, outlined the ideological aspect of folk consciousness in this manner: ". . . I consider myself a writer, and would sit on the outside of a group and say, 'Why don't you write such and such a line?' Once I quoted a line and somebody turned to me and said it was over-intellectualism and proceeded right then and there to deliver me a lecture on how such things had to be done in a certain way—and I should use my talent for writing in a party functional sort of way instead of trying to write like Beethoven."

In short, the ideological stance of Marxist movements embraced the view that popular and classical music were tools of the ruling class and therefore unworthy and unrepresentative of the cultural orientations of the proletariat. Millard Lampell, one of the original members of the Almanac Singers, while discussing the relative merits of musical media, commented, "I am all in favor of Boogie Woogie . . . the form is excellent but the bourgeoisie have taken that form and used it in a different way for a wrong purpose. That form can be and has been used for genuine *music of protest*. It was no fault of early Negro jazz players that the form they evolved was taken over and commercialized." In the early thirties several writers, such as Richard Frank, waxed especially enthusiastic about the possibilities of Negro music. Because of its caste origins they viewed it as being free of the taint of commercialism or Tin Pan Alley. ". . . the American Revolutionary Movement [CPUSA] finds expression in Negro music," wrote Frank in the *New Masses*. Music, therefore, was viewed as a means of production; the dominant question became, "For whom is the music working?"

The theme of music monopoly is one frequently cited in such left-wing publications as the *New Masses, Mainstream, People's Songs Bulletin,* the early issues of *Sing Out!,* and, in the thirties, *Modern Music.* The fundamental motif is that musical entertainment, as well as other sectors of the social structure, is under the controlling thumb of the capitalists. Writing in *Masses and Mainstream* Finkelstein has described this phenomenon as "the power of monopoly-produced, pseudo-popular art." The social movements oriented to Marxist doctrine saw the music of American society as being utilized for eliciting profits from the masses and obscuring the class struggle. Their answer to this was a music reflecting socialist realism which in Lenin's words would "unify broad masses of people" and "reflect reality and not obscure the struggle." Vivian Howard, also in *Masses and Mainstream,* said of the People's Artists that they could "free a certain number of artists from the censorship and hampering control of the monopolies." Pete Seeger cites the creation of People's Songs Inc. as a means of combating the "heavy hand of entertainment monopoly." Woody Guthrie, in explaining the usage of folk songs by the labor movement and the Left, conveys basically the same argument. Musically, socialist realism for Marxists was to be "national in form: revolutionary in content." In this context Mike Gold urged that the role of the artist was more than mere creation; he was to radicalize his audience.

The three primary ideological features of folk consciousness were derived from Marxist-Leninist ideology, the lessons of the Russian Revolution, and the directive of the Kremlin pointing to or creating a disposition toward the folk genre. However, as we will see in the following chapters, the evolution of folk consciousness required nearly a decade of economic hardship, ideological polemic, and, finally, another Kremlin directive. Only then could American Marxist Sidney Finkelstein, writing in *The Composer and the Nation,* describe folk song as "a voice of its own time. It is distinguished by its combination of simplicity and artistic truth or immediate relation to life [and it represents] in its simplest form, social consciousness, the experiences and thought held in common by people who labor, suffer, and triumph together." This reflection of folk consciousness was unique. It was not shared, or even entertained, by other Marxist movements or, most important, by the urban proletariat. Despite this fact Stalinists and fellow travelers argued that folk music was truly the people's music.

2

The Rural
Roots of
Folk Consciousness

American leftists originally stumbled upon the folk-styled protest song in the hamlets of the rural South. In the southeast United States folk songs frequently addressed every phase of life and experience. These ditties in many instances were conservative and escapist in nature, condemning the "atheistic" John Scopes, drinking, and right of women to vote. Songs like "No Depression in Heaven" treated the hardship of life philosophically, arguing the pie in the sky theme. These ballads were general and rhetorical, rarely offering a serious solution to the social problems beleaguering the South. One observer remarked in the early thirties, "Most songs of industrial sections expressed abject hopelessness and are howled in tones more woe-be-gone than the wails of Negro Blues." These woe-be-gone wails customarily were couched in the symbolic rhetoric of the blues, which rarely offered solutions outside of a good woman, a bottle on Saturday night, or going to Heaven (as in "lay my burden down"). The heightened immiseration of southern workers found their songs focusing increasingly on economic and political conditions. However, it took northern ideologies to add the social panacea to the perceived dilemmas. The major catalyst for this growing consciousness was the Great Depression of 1929.

Overnight, it seemed, the nation was plunged into economic misery wherein credit vanished, companies collapsed, millions became unemployed. The impact on the shaky economic order of the region was devastating. The belt-tightening policies of some company towns and the closing of others forced miners and textile workers from their

15

homes as well as from their jobs. Jobless miners by the thousands depended on available charity as their means of survival. Mill and mine operations which did remain open attempted in many cases to pass the losses of the depression on to the workers. Company stores cut off credit and raised prices. The maintenance costs of company-owned equipment were shifted to the deduction columns of the miners' already thinner pay envelopes. The diminution of urban purchasing power affected agrarian workers and tenant farmers, some of whom were removed from the land. The socioeconomic conditions of the southern states triggered many undirected outbursts of violence and industrial conflict, which sharpened the focus of numerous radicals and reformers.

Prior to the depression urban activists had not been oblivious to the plight of the South and the opportunities for class movements. To illustrate, Communists and Socialists realized that the United Mine Workers Union was experiencing both internal and external troubles. Internally, a group of industrial unionists attempted to take over the Lewis-led organization. The dissidents were opposed to the union leaders, who were frequently charged with ignorance and corruption, and who had led the miners to a series of agonizing strike defeats. Outside the union a large segment of the mining community was totally alienated from the miners' union. To take advantage of this situation, elements of "Save the Union," a lobby within the United Mine Workers, and the Stalinists created the first dual union, the National Miners Union (NMU), to challenge the United Mine Workers. The NMU at its peak was to claim 15,000 adherents. In response to difficulties encountered in the textile industry, the Trade Union Unity League (TUUL), the prime vehicle for Communist dualism, formed the National Textile Workers. It was in the framework of dual unionism that the Stalinists discovered American folk music as a political tool.

Southern Labor Stirs: Gastonia

The Gastonia-Loray strikes began the Communist flirtation with folk music which would culminate in the proletarian revival of the late 1930s. The Loray strike appears to have been the first significant contact the urban-centered Communists had with folk material as a propaganda form. The Gastonia textile strike, like other confrontations in southern company towns, was interpreted as a classical "Marxian vision of an exploited and suffering proletariat in opposition to heartless capitalists." The Communist-led National Textile Workers responded to the situation, believing it to be the "first shot in a battle which will be heard around the world." Organizers from the parent movement and other groups arrived in force. The Communist party had an elaborate setup of auxillary organizations which aided the Loray workers. One participant, cited in Tom Tippett's *When Southern Labor Stirs,* described the Stalinist role in the following terms:

> The Workers' International Relief collected funds . . . and sent trained administrators to the mill village. The International Labor Defense Press Service dispatched experienced publicity men to the strike zone who kept Gastonia news in the radical press and got much space in the general labor and capitalistic papers. The International Labor Defense provided excellent legal talent to defend the strikers in the North Carolina courts. The Young Communists sent their representatives . . . to organize the children into strike activity.

One victim of the strike was Ella May Wiggins. As a child Ella May had acquired a reputation as a balladress, and during the strike, Greenway reports, "she joined to the rich tradition of mountain song composition . . . songs about the workers' plight, their hopes, and their determination to remedy intolerable conditions." At a union meeting an audience of 500 workers and northern organizers stood together in an oak grove and listened to Ella May render such "ballets" as "Come and Join the I.L.D.-ye" in tones of fervent exhortation. Mrs. Wiggins's singing career was to be ended abruptly by the gunfire of local vigilantes. A jury dominated by mine owners refused to indict any of the men arrested for the murder. Her violent demise made her a martyr in the eyes of the left-wing press, with some Communists planning to take the five Wiggins children north as "Southern Textile Exhibit No. 1." This move was circumvented by local ministers.

But the songs of Ella May did not remain in Gastonia. Upon leaving the area, Communist organizers brought them north. A number of her compositions were published in the *Nation* and the *New Masses* by Margaret Larkin. Larkin, a singer of cowboy and Wobbly songs in her own right, confirmed Mrs. Wiggins as a true proletarian in keeping with the notion expressed by Sidney Finkelstein in *How*

Music Expresses Ideas that "the artist has the power to move people and thus to accelerate the forward movement of history itself. . . ." Having established these credentials, the Larkin articles went on to argue the usefulness of folk song as a weapon: ". . . what propaganda could better describe the infamy of the bosses . . ." or ". . . truly revolutionary words, bare of all ornament, full of earnestness, and feeling. . . ." Upon returning to New York, Larkin continued to sing the songs and praises of Ella May Wiggins. Ella May's songs did not survive in the North after interest in Gastonia was replaced by other areas of class struggle. Though quickly forgotten, Gastonia historically was the Stalinists' introduction to folk material. The Communists would invoke this initial field contact later in 1938 as a model for the use of folk music.

Harlan County

Another struggle, which both served as a model and provided personnel for the proletarian renaissance, took place in the coal fields of Bell and Harlan counties in Kentucky.

The coal strikes of Kentucky were nearly identical to the one in Gastonia. Only the location and the degree of violence were dissimilar. In Kentucky the Communist apparatus for organizing was the National Miners Union, formed under the auspices of William Z. Foster. The organizational leadership was generally Communist; a good proportion of the membership was not. Yet there was enough smoke to convince the mine owners that the union and its members were all Reds. The operators saw their adamancy as part of a "holy crusade," while Communists and others saw it as a skirmish in a much larger class struggle. Communists and labor militants alike descended upon the coal fields of Kentucky. William Z. Foster recalled the conflict later, writing in his *History of the Communist Party of the United States:*

> The fierce struggle, with its slogan of "Strike Against Starvation," was conducted by the National Miners Union—T.U.U.L. The miners, whose U.M.W. union had been destroyed locally in the great strike of 1927–28, were at the last extreme of hunger and desperation. The strikers fought in the face of violence from the mine operators, the government and the U.M.W.A. leaders.

After a desperate struggle of four months the strike was broken. An aftermath of the bitter fight was a strike of 8,000 Kentucky miners, on January 1, 1932, also under the leadership of the N.M.U. Guerrilla war conditions prevailed, with the whole union leadership arrested in Pineville. This strike, too, was beaten. Harry Simms, Y.C.L. organizer, was killed in this Kentucky strike.

Harlan County, barring the violence, was an archetype of the rural struggles of the opening years of the "Red decade." The issues were clear and simple, fitting into a neat pattern of black and white. It was the rich against the poor, the Third International against such capitalists as mine owners Blair and Mellon. The exploiters and the exploited appeared clearly visible and definable. The capitalists were the mine operators, the professionals, and the merchants employed by them, protected and supported by police officials. On the other side were the miners. Malcolm Cowley described the situation to the readers of the *New Republic:* "It is a battle in which everyone must take his stand; there is no compromise. Whatever is black to one class is white to the other; whoever brings relief to the miners is an enemy of the operators—and they run him out of town." The basic issue in Harlan was the profit margins of the operators, pinched by the depression, the demands of their social position, and the miners' bid for a living wage. Even farmers in the area were drawn into the struggle either by their friendship with mine workers or by working for the operators as mine guards. Operators had a monopoly on the legal and social resources; miners mustered what resources were left, a handful of outside allies and guns.

Propaganda on both sides ran rampant. The mine operators once again charged a Soviet takeover. The rationale was that the National Miners Union was affiliated with the Communist party and that all of the membership and its supporters were Russian revolutionaries bent on destroying the "Christian southern way of life." Cowley, visiting Harlan, noted in the same article that the operators felt that "the Communists do not believe in God and seek to overthrow the United States government; therefore the operators are performing their duty as patriotic American citizens when they combat the miners by every means in their power, legal or illegal." An attorney for the operators proclaimed, "No Communist has any constitutional rights in Bell County," referring to union officials and miners alike. As if to enforce this statement, thirteen writers and professional people, attempting to distribute food to the miners, were beaten and sent forcibly from the state amidst cries of "Run Reds out of Kentucky." At this point the definition of "Red" was expanded to include "all who sympathize with the miners' struggle against starvation wages; impartial investigators, newspaper reporters, and physicians. . . ." In "I Am a Union Woman" Molly Jackson described the effects of the operators' publicity campaign:

> . . . and when I joined the union, they called me a Rooshian Red. When my husband asked the boss for a job these is the words he said: Bill Jackson, I can't work you, sir, your wife's a Rooshian Red.

The charges of "communism in coal" did more than just smear the miners and their supporters. In part, the indiscriminate use of the term Red minimized its effect. More significantly, the propaganda campaign legitimized the radical organizers. Anyone the operators were against, the miners were generally for. "Which Side Are You On" was a more pervasive force than fears of a Bolshevik conspiracy. As in Gastonia the miners saw urban radicals as their compatriots, a perception which was later to manifest itself in the alliance of several traditional singers with urban leftist movements. The fact that a person was for the workers was more important in southern labor conflicts than his ideological or political commitments. One southern organizer remarked: "For a long time I didn't know the difference between a Communist and a Socialist—just so they were on my side . . . any one who was on the workers' side was welcome."

Howe and Coser report similar reactions in Gastonia: "Among the textile workers . . . the initial response to the Communist leadership was enthusiastic, for many of them were clearly unaware of the differences between the TUUL and any other kind of union, while the older ones remembered how dismally the AFL had failed in an organization drive a decade earlier." One Gastonia striker responded in anger to the vilification of Communists: ". . . listen to me. These people are helping us. They are feeding us. . . ." A Harlan miner explained his party membership as follows: "I joined the C.P. because I seen that they are the only ones leading the workers to better conditions. I tried out everything UMVA, A.F.L. etc. . . . I found out that none of them was for the workers."

Bloody Harlan produced a number of songs and singers, some of whom were to become famous in northern Communist circles. The ballad-makers of Kentucky employed traditional songs to comment on the battles in which they participated. For example, Mrs. Florence Reece, following a number of attacks by "gun thugs" and the local sheriff, one day ripped a sheet from a wall calendar and wrote a song about the combatants of Harlan:

They say in Harlan County,
There are no neutrals there:
You'll either be a union man
Or a thug for J. H. Blair. . . .

Don't scab for the bosses,
Don't listen to their lies.
Us poor folks haven't got a chance
Unless we organize.

Aunt Molly Jackson, a songstress since her early childhood, expressed a similar theme in an organizing song written in 1931 entitled "I Am a Union Woman." One verse is illustrative:

If you want to join a union as strong as one can be,
Join the dear old NMU and come along with me.

The bosses ride fine horses while we walk in the mud.
Their banner is a dollar sign while ours is striped with blood.

The ballads from Harlan County took on a consciousness not previously found in folk material. Ralph Linton, in *The Cultural Background of Personality,* has argued that the last thing a fish in the ocean would discover is water: "He would become conscious of its existence only if some accident brought him to the surface and introduced him to air." The accident in Harlan County was the encounter of the Third International with Cumberland culture. In the words of Archie Green, quoted in Sarah Ogan Gunning's *Girl of Constant Sorrow* (Folk-Legacy Records), "In a sense, Piedmont mill villages and Cumberland mine camps became meeting grounds for the ideologies of Andrew Jackson and Karl Marx, Abraham Lincoln and Mikhail Bakunin. Few of the mill hands or coal miners were able to synthesize traditional and modern values into lasting literature, but some managed to compose folk-

Aunt Molly Jackson

Courtesy of John Greenway

like songs which fused timeworn melodies with strange, revolutionary lyrics."

These songs reflected a fusion of social movement technique, ideology, and traditional folk material. As Richard Reuss has noted in *Labor History:* ". . . the agitprop songs created on the basis of traditional music reflected the combined virtues and defects of American folksong. Lyrics were apt to be rough, unpolished, sentimental, and uncomplicated. . . ." Nevertheless, the songs were no longer folk songs but, rather, examples of folk consciousness. Folk songs had become "songs with *conscious messages,* composed with calculated awareness." Such ballads as Sarah Ogan's "I Hate the Capitalist System" and Jim Garland's "Ballad of Harry Simms" are illustrations of folk consciousness overtly applied to traditional material. These songs, particularly the Ogan composition, were sung in a traditional style and invoked folk themes with an urban ideology. One verse of the Ogan ballad is as follows:

> *I hate the capitalist system.*
> *I'll tell you the reason why.*
> *They cause me so much suffering*
> *And my dearest friends to die.*

This song continues to document the privations experienced by the composer and ends by invoking an organizational solution: join the union or the CPUSA. The verses were repetitive and easy to sing. The style was, as Reuss notes, uncomplicated and in the typical folk structure. Yet the terminology was politically sophisticated. Such language as "capitalistic system," "bourgeois," and "YCL" was foreign to the Cumberlands. These terms were conscious additions to folk material, thus altering the definition of both song and singer. D. K. Wilgus has observed in his *Anglo-American Folksong Scholarship since 1898:* "The recognition that singing has a direct and reciprocal relation to social, economic, and political issues has led to an equation of the 'cry for justice' and folksong. The discovery of folksongs of social protest has led some to the conclusion that a protest song is ipso facto a folksong, and to the postulation of a 'new folk community' composed of progressives, anti-fascists, and union members."

Folk material taken from Harlan County and other highland hamlets became part of the culture of the middle-class-intellectual-turned-worker who helped fulfill the prophecy made by Larkin after Gastonia: "These songs that begin 'Come all ye workers' and end 'Let's stand together, workers, and have a union here' are destined to be the battle songs of the coming industrial struggle."

The Labor Colleges

Another and more important source of protest song was the labor college, organized to mobilize rural workers into the industrial union movement. Such schools as Brookwood, Highlander, and especially Commonwealth Labor College all made some contribution to the folk consciousness of the North.

Prior to the program of dual unionism in the Communist party, radicals and progressives were involved in educational work complementary to existing AFL unions. Radicals, following the words of Lenin, saw the splitting up of any trade union as a "blow to the entire trade union movement." Progressives, including in their ranks Socialists, Communists (before dual unionism), and reformers, believed that organizations must be set up to train "labor leaders with 'ideals,' men and women who would 'take hold of things' and who would be guided in their leadership by 'social thinking' rather than by 'business psychology' of typical laborites," according to James O. Morris, in his *Conflict within the AFL*. The function of educating workers during the twenties, either in Lenin's sense of "political consciousness" or in the more pragmatic approach of socially oriented union leadership, was performed by numerous labor schools located in the East. Commonwealth Labor College and Brookwood Labor College, although different in their ideological and geographical bases, were the two most prominent institutions of this period.

Commonwealth Labor College was the end product of the New Llano Colony, a cooperative which had begun in northern Louisiana. A segment of the original group left the confines of utopianism and moved to Arkansas, where they purchased a site at Mena in the late 1920s. Lucian Koch was the first director of the school. According to one activist, Koch was not a Communist but he was "certainly far to the Left." The college was situated on a large farm, and a massive wooden edifice, heated by a wood stove, served as the recreational and educational center. The style of life was communal, reflecting the origins of the school. Both faculty and students spent four hours a day on farm chores. The teachers and staff received no pay and most of the students, radicals, and revolutionaries from New York paid $40 a quarter for instruction. The majority of the training was from a Marxist point of view. One Commonwealth publication listed the curriculum as including Marxian economics, working-class history, labor problems, creative writing, labor journalism (the short story, labor drama), labor dramatics, farm problems, and "other subjects of interest to those who are preparing for an active career in the labor movement." A participant described the school as an "intellectual menagerie." The propaganda songs originally used at Commonwealth were best symbolized by a Russian engineer who would wake the students each morning with off-key renditions of Soviet revolutionary songs. The most popular song at the college was the "Internationale." Other songs which were of interest to the residents came from Wobbly and Chartist collections. Such songs in support of the Soviet Union as "Bankers and Bosses Hate Soviet Stars" and the "Song of the Red Air Fleet" enjoyed considerable popularity. However, the appeal of these tunes did not extend to the local residents. H. L. Mitchell, one of the founders of the Southern Tenant Farmers Union, recalls in the *Oral History of the Southern Tenant Farmers Union* that "the young Communist organizer arrived with the delegation from Commonwealth College in 1935, he had radical song books with him and tried to teach the union members to sing the 'Internationale.' . . . *That song just didn't go over with the share-croppers."*

Other materials, such as the agitprop play *Waiting for Lefty* presented at Commonwealth, were viewed as being in the worst possible taste by the residents of the Mena community. Agnes "Sis" Cunningham, a teacher at the school, stated frankly, "There was some talk about there being some songs in the neighborhood, but nobody was particularly interested to go out and get them. . . ." The college issued such songbooks as *Six Labor Songs* containing ballads entitled "I Sing the Battle," "Song of the Lower Classes," "March of the Hungry Men," and "Cry of the People." None of these songs had any roots in the musical traditions of the South. One verse of "Song of the Lower Classes" by Ernest Jones gives the flavor of this collection:

> *We're low, we're low,*
> *Our place we know,*
> *We're only the rank and file.*
> *We're not too low to kill the foe,*
> *But too low to touch the spoil.*

The romantic motif of the material appealed to intellectuals, perhaps, but went over the heads of the hill people. In the closing years of Commonwealth College, due to the influence of Claude Williams, a Negro preacher, the school belatedly began to borrow traditional folk songs, primarily spirituals, to communicate themes of social protest. Ironically, these "political spirituals" were originally introduced to rural residents within the framework of agitational drama. Williams reportedly had a great impact upon two songwriters who would later move north: Lee Hays of Commonwealth College and John Handcox of the Southern Tenant Farmers Union.

Hays described the Williams technique of politicizing the southern spiritual in a report to the *New Masses* entitled "Let the Will . . . ":

> In Cotton Plant, Ark., I heard a Negro congregation singing an old hymn, "Let the will of the Lord be done."
>
> It is a fine song, what we call a "singout" song: the leader sings out each new verse and the congregation joins in. There is only

one line change in each verse, and the pattern of each verse is the same.

I began to think, "Here's a good union song. Let's see—let the will of the union—let the will of the people—"

The song leader, an old Negro man, interrupted me. He had heard several of my parodies and knew what I was up to.

"Now, wait a minute. Don't you go changing that song. It's all right just like it stands. 'Let the will of the Lord be done'—that says just exactly what we want it to say. What do you think the Lord's will is, anyhow? It's freedom! You leave that song alone!"

Here is how we compromised. . . .

> *Organize! (Organize—)*
> *Organize! (Organize—)*
> *Organize! (Organize—)*
> *Let the will of the Lord be done. . . .*

Hays transformed a number of other hymns into secular messages of protest, songs like "Jesus Is My Captain" and others which he learned from the Southern Tenant Farmers Union, a movement to be discussed shortly. Many of these "parodies" were to make their way north: "The parody of 'Jesus Is My Captain' has traveled from a North Carolina textile strike throughout the agricultural movements of the South and even unto the far reaches of New York City's May Day parades. . . ."

In the early years Commonwealth possessed a definite preconception of what proletarian culture ought to be rather than what it was. The school was ideologically segregated. The teachers and students reinforced and furthered their own sense of reality. In short, they talked to themselves. Only repeated tactical errors altered their consciousness of the situation. In 1940 Commonwealth College closed its doors for the last time, to be replaced by the Southern New Theatre School. Lee Hays came north and injected many of the songs he learned at Commonwealth into the songbag of the Almanac Singers. An Almanac Singer credited a good portion of the group's approach to music to the pioneering efforts of Commonwealth College and particularly Claude Williams. Lee Hays in *People's Songs Bulletin* acknowledged this indebtedness: "A good many of the Almanac union songs and certainly the spirit of all of them derived largely from Claude's work in this field."

Brookwood Labor College was founded in 1921 at the site of the Christian Socialist School for Children in Katonah, some forty miles from New York City. The previous occupants, William and Helen Fincke, pacifist members of the Fellowship of Reconciliation, decided to donate their property to be used for the general welfare. Toward this end the Finckes sponsored a conference of educators and union leaders. The organizational product of the conference was the labor college. The purpose of Brookwood was originally outlined as one of communicating and cooperating "with the national and international labor groups, also with the various local colleges and schools that send to it [Brookwood] working men and women who show promise and need further education in order to serve the labor movement and through it society." This educational goal was to be accomplished through a two-year residence program (later reduced to one year) in the social sciences, featuring courses in labor problems and economics.

The style of life here was similar to that of Commonwealth College, despite the ideological and geographical distances. One Brookwood faculty member recalled that "everyone who came here the first year, even as visitors, was pressed into service. Before he had his first meal, he was expected to cut up enough wood for the fires." Both faculty and students engaged in many extracurricular activities centering upon the physical maintenance of the school and its residents. Numerically, there was an average of about forty pupils per term. Admission to the school was on the basis of a quota system in order to get a broad spectrum of students. In spite of this selection process most of the students at Brookwood had trade union backgrounds, particularly in the garment and coal mining industries. Nonetheless, the caliber and intellectual backgrounds of the students varied greatly. As A. J. Muste, educational director of Brookwood, told his biographer, Nat Hentoff, as reported in *Peace Agitator: The Story of A. J. Muste,* "They ranged from devout church members from isolated and backward villages to extremely sophisticated people who read Marx and the Russian novelists . . . and went to avant-garde dances in Greenwich Village on weekends." Most of the students at Brookwood were generally left of center. May Day was celebrated annually by the students with pictures of

Marx, Debs, Lenin, and Gompers being prominently displayed. The inclusion of the latter portrait caused much dismay among the conservative AFL leadership, which contributed economic support to the school.

The school's social philosophy was more reflective of its educational director than of Marx or Lenin. Muste was a pragmatist. He once described the ideological role of Brookwood as follows: "The man with 'right' tendencies who goes out of Brookwood thinking that every 'left' is necessarily a destructive fool, or the man with 'left' tendencies who goes out thinking a 'right' is merely a yellow coward, has utterly failed to get the Brookwood point of view." The school's pragmatism invited criticism from both the Left and the Right in American labor. William Z. Foster, chairman of the CPUSA, characterized Brookwooders as "little brothers of the big labor fakirs." A *Daily Worker* columnist saw Brookwood graduates as carriers of false class consciousness, not fit "for anything better than lecturing before the left wing of the National Woman's [*sic*] Party." The directorate of the school was further denounced as catering to trade unions and as opportunists in search of "dough and Respectability." The American Federation of Labor, arch foes of the Left, pictured Brookwood Labor College as maintaining an antireligious and pro-Soviet posture. While not able to please either the conservative wing of the AFL or the Communist movement, enamored with its dual union program, the representatives of the labor college did rather well in their organizing forays into southern states. Once again pragmatism was the major coloration of their organizing drives. They rarely utilized the language or flamboyance of their Communist counterparts. Yet they possessed, as Edmund Wilson indicated in *The American Jitters* "the courage and will which carries them into industrial battles and makes them do thankless work and take chances which few middle-class people care to face."

Their employment of music was likewise practical in nature, songs being used that would appeal to their anticipated audiences. Outside cultural influences were purposely kept to a minimum. One of the major catalysts for this strategy was Tom Tippett, a former coal miner and United Mine Workers official, who came to Brookwood as an instructor. Tippett participated in the textile strikes of Elizabeth, Marion, Gastonia, and Greenville, North Carolina, prior to turning his attention to the coal industry. In the mining camps Tippett worked for the Frank Keeney–led West Virginia Mine Workers Union, which used propaganda songs extensively.

Tippett's role at Brookwood was not dissimilar to that of Lee Hays in the last years of Commonwealth in that he provided urban organizers with musical guidelines for the mobilization of southern workers. "The Marion Massacre" and "The Death of Mother Jones" were two songs he introduced to labor students. Archie Green in his insightful study, "The Death of Mother Jones," provides an excellent illustration of Tippett's educational function:

> In his constant travel between southern textile and mining areas and Brookwood Labor College, Tom Tippett carried hill-billy records north and union songbooks south. He brought the Gene Autry record "Mother Jones" to Katonah in the spring of 1931, and in the fall Seacrist and three fellow strikers went north to college. . . . Brookwooders were teaching "Solidarity Forever" in West Virginia in 1931; Seacrist in turn moved "The Death of Mother Jones" into urban circles.

In his instructional text, *When Southern Labor Stirs*, Tippett stressed the use of mountain culture for organizational ends. Hymns, spirituals, and hill-billy music are cited as the genre of protest. Some of these songs later were to find their way into the New York Garment Workers Union, which rarely used them.

Despite some of the organizational successes of the school, the impact of the depression steadily decreased its enrollment. Other problems also began to develop within the school, particularly in the role it should play in the growing economic turmoil in American labor. One faction, led by Muste, espoused the traditional educational purpose of the school, while another advocated militant physical involvement in labor situations. After a number of the internecine skirmishes so common to the American Left, Muste, two faculty members, and nineteen of the twenty-eight remaining students withdrew from the school in March, 1933. The school folded three years later. Brookwood indirectly introduced some songs into the American labor movement and to the New York–based Socialists, although Brookwooders rarely used rural songs in urban environments.

The significance of these labor colleges is that they served as transfer points by which songs and personnel were directed from one movement to another. Many graduates of Brookwood and Commonwealth joined the CIO and more ideological movements and used songs that they had learned and observed in use at their institutions.

A handful of instructors and students made their presence felt in the ranks of the Almanac Singers and later at New York "hoots." An example of a labor school using native folk material for social and economic purposes is Highlander Folk School, which, unlike the urban-directed educational endeavors discussed above, was a local enterprise created during the depression. The school was founded in November, 1932, by Myles Horton (a former Chicago theology student), Don West, and Dr. John Thompson. The site of the school was a 200-acre tract in Monteagle, Tennessee, donated by a leader in the cooperative movement. The organization of the institution was cooperative, owned by the staff and financed by contributors. Students and staff alike shared in the maintenance of the school, everyone assisting with repairs and food gathering. While unions were the major donors, as at Brookwood, other funds in later years came from such private philanthropists as Eleanor Roosevelt. The concept of a cooperative commonwealth gave way to a labor orientation after the school became involved in a coal mining strike in Wilder, Tennessee. Following the mine conflict Highlander became one of the focal points for labor education. According to one writer, "As the school grew, it found that it could help working people most effectively by helping them in the organizations they were building for themselves, and therefore the regular courses are now primarily for union people and for the training of union leaders."

As an educational institution Highlander was not visually impressive. The physical plant consisted of a simple frame building with a vine-covered stone porch. Despite the physical limitations the school produced many "responsible informed people, active union members of educational and cultural committees, teachers in labor schools, leaders of co-operatives, farm organizations and community life." James G. Patton of the National Farmers Union was later to comment that Highlander possessed "a most significant program in training rural leaders to build a new people's movement in the rural section of the south."

The educational goal at Highlander, based on the Danish model, was to allow individuals to pool their experiences and knowledge, learn from history, sociology, and practice, and seek solutions to social problems. The classroom addressed such seminar topics as "Union Problems" or "Economic Problems," standard educational issues. In this manner students were to learn problem-solving techniques and future solutions. Like Brookwood, the school was pragmatic and saw union organization as the solution to starvation and deprivation. One participant wrote, ". . . they [the students] want to find out how to build these unions, as their contribution to democratic living. They come to help solve the number one problem, the South, for themselves and for the rest of us."

One tactic to help solve the problem was the utilization of the aesthetic values and culture of the South. A member of the staff noted that "singing goes on most of the time, for fun and to learn new songs that may be taken back to local union meetings." Most of the singing was sparked by Mrs. Zilphia Horton, "the singing heart of the school." Zilphia was raised in a coal mining community in Arkansas and attended the College of the Ozarks, where she was a music major. In 1935 she came to Highlander as a student and married the director, Myles Horton. Because of her educational background she became director of music at the school. In this capacity she collected and compiled 1,300 songs from unions, left-wing groups, and Negro and white southern tradition. The songs ranged from "Barbara Allen" to a denunciation of Vice-President John Garner, "The Ballad of an Evil Old Man." She then disseminated these songs for organizational work. One example of this process is her edition of *Labor Songs,* compiled for the urban-based Textile Workers Union of America, which supported Highlander during the late thirties. In all, the folk school published eleven songbooks. The best-known song emanating from Highlander was "We Shall Overcome," collected by Mrs. Horton from the CIO Food and Tobacco Workers and later revised by her, Guy Carawan, and Pete Seeger. An examination of the Horton collection, consisting of 800 items, at the Tennessee State Archives at Nashville suggests that many of the songs originated in urban social movements, especially those in New York City. Nevertheless, the relationship between Highlander and the North had little resemblance to that of Commonwealth College and the Communist movement.

The significance of the rural labor colleges was in their role as models for northern movements. The schools exposed many people to songs of persuasion. Tippett, for example, greatly influenced the Garment Workers Union in New York. Lee Hays and other members of Commonwealth College provided musical direction for the Almanac Singers. The impact of these labor schools on northern movements was not equal. Brookwood influenced a dying Socialist party whose thunder had been stolen by the New Deal. The Socialists had little to sing about except their hated Communist rivals. Highlander did assist in publishing several songbooks for the labor movement, and these books were advertised and used by more militant Marxist groups. The most direct link between the labor colleges and the Communist party, of course, was to be found at Commonwealth College, which supplied both songs and personnel for the Marxist movement.

The Southern Tenant Farmers Union

Ironically, another rural musical source for the Communist party was the Socialist-led Southern Tenant Farmers Union (STFU). The STFU arose after a survey of 378 sharecroppers and their families in April, 1934. The study, conducted by the League for Industrial Democracy, found that the average family was subsisting on less than $250 per year. The league, under the aegis of Norman Thomas, later to be called the grandfather of the STFU, organized a union to combat rural poverty. Organizationally, the Tenant Farmers were an offshoot of the Socialist party in the South. H. L. Mitchell commented in Columbia's *Oral History* that "because of some of the educational work the Socialists did preliminary to forming a union, the sharecroppers were willing . . . to unite and form one union."

The STFU was racially integrated, a factor which during its early years created organizational problems similar to those of the Bolsheviks and United Mine Workers. Coupled with racial heterogeneity was the problem of illiteracy. To overcome these difficulties, the STFU used propaganda from idioms known to both black and white, literate and illiterate. STFU meetings were characterized by religious fervor, singing, and biblical phrases used as slogans. The meetings opened with prayers, a practice which was in accordance with the customs of the people. Mitchell further recalled that "there was a lot of singing, especially among the Negro members who were quite good singers. They would sing the old Negro spirituals. Many of them are songs of protest that grew out of conditions that existed before slavery was abolished. Some of the spirituals seemed to fit in with the union program. One of them for instance, was selected as the official union song. It was 'We Shall Not Be Moved.'" One factor leading to the popularity of this piece was its generality. Mitchell stated: "When Norman Thomas paid his second visit to Arkansas in 1935, A. B. Brookins came out with a new version 'Norman Thomas is our leader, we shall not be moved.' Thereafter, any outside speaker who addressed a meeting was likely to hear himself referred to in song as the leader of the union."

The STFU drew upon its immediate environment and Socialist-Populist tradition for song material, rejecting many of the songs made available to it by Commonwealth College. The voices of the movement were two local preachers, A. B. Brookins and John Handcox. Brookins was similar to nineteenth-century camp-meeting evangelists who had the ability to get people to sing. One of the major catalysts for the growth of the songbag of the Tenant Farmers was John Handcox. Handcox, a Negro sharecropper and preacher, was born and raised on an Arkansas plantation. Following in the footsteps of Claude Williams, he wrote and sang ballads based on religious material for the movement. Some of his better-known compositions included "Raggedy," "There Are Mean Things Happening in This Land," and "The Man Frank Weems." His most popular song was "We're Going to Roll the Union On," based on the gospel hymn "Roll the Chariot On." The original version by Handcox referred to the 1936 strike during which Governor Futrell ordered out the Arkansas National Guard:

> *If the governor is in the way,*
> *We're going to roll it over him,*
> *We're goin' to roll the union on. . . .*

The song was later revised by the Almanac Singers:

> *If the boss is in the way,*
> *We're going to roll it over him,*
> *We're goin' roll the union on.*

Upon leaving the STFU, Handcox traveled around the country singing his songs at various gatherings and rallies sponsored by urban radical and Communist groups.

Both Handcox and Harlan refugee Jim Garland provided artifacts of proletarian culture, not contaminated by commercialism, which fitted into the folk consciousness of the late 1930s. The musical forms or vehicles both employed were from their natural genre. It was only when both perceived themselves as *conscious* spokesmen of the "folk" that their traditional role was transformed into that of a folk entrepreneur (one who exploits a market outside the original folk group). This is an essential point. When Handcox sang his songs in the ranks of the STFU, he was not using folk song to be a proletarian. Rather, the Negro preacher was singing the tunes he and his listeners were born and raised with. Handcox was expressing his social indignation in a genre endemic and natural to his community. This is a far cry from his role in the North; there he became, in the eyes of Marxists, a spokesman for proletarian culture.

As we have seen, the labor colleges and the STFU relied heavily upon Negro culture for their propaganda songs. The American Communist party was both directly and indirectly affected by the same Negro culture as found in the shantytowns and frame churches of the South. In the late 1920s and 1930s the Communist party perceived the American Negro as the most oppressed member of the capitalist social structure and therefore a very likely candidate for its revolutionary cause. Within this wishful framework the artifacts of black culture were idealized. One reviewer of Em Jo Basshe's drama *Earth,* which dealt with a small, poverty-ridden Negro hamlet in the Reconstruction era of the South, wrote, "Is this proletarian drama? Is 'Earth' good for workers because it deals with simple people, because it isn't cluttered with intellectual patter, because it goes out in the fields and huts and mountain tops, into a community of people, a mass?" In time the answer to this semirhetorical question would be a resounding, collective "yes." Spirituals, hymns, and other forms of Negro music began to be treated as true indicators of class consciousness. Articles in the Communist press began to extol the music of the black man. His music was described as an effective and ideologically pure tool in the mobilization of the unorganized masses, both black and white. In the *New Masses* Richard Frank expounded this idea:

> When the American Revolutionary Movement finds expression in Negro music it is expressing itself in a medium capable of arousing not only the twelve or fifteen million Negroes of America, but also all the toiling masses of America, who for generations in one form or another have made Negro music their own . . . among the Negroes, it will be to a great extent through singing that recruiting will be done for the masses of Negro workers are held at illiteracy. Leaflets cannot appeal to them. But singing is their great form of artistic expression. In order to win the Negro people most effectively the revolutionary movement will have to make use of this instrument.

This exhortation was generally correct. Most Americans, both black and white, were familiar with various forms of Negro music, particularly the hymns and spirituals which were taught in elementary schools throughout the United States. Jazz in the 1930s was popular. Recitals featuring hymns and spirituals were not uncommon. Most important, many protest songs were based on religious models. In Communist circles the spiritual was one of the first folk forms to be treated as a genre of protest. In 1930 Lawrence Gellert began a series of articles in the *New Masses* dealing with "protest songs." Several years later Mike Gold, writing in the *Daily Worker*, lauded the transformation of "Old Time Religion" into "Gimme That New Communist Spirit." In 1933 the *Daily Worker* applauded when the spiritual "My Mother's Got a Stone That Was Hewn out of the Mountain" was altered in Birmingham, Alabama, as follows:

> *The workers need that stone that was hewn out of history,*
> *That was hewn out of history,*
> *Come a-rollin' thru Dixie,*
> *Come a-rollin' thru Dixie,*
> *A-tearin' down the kingdom of the boss.*

But the political use of the spiritual was sporadic prior to the Popular Front era. Occasional articles in the Communist press before 1936 reported hymns being used in specific areas of class struggle. Like the songs of Gastonia and Harlan, altered spirituals also were forgotten as the Stalinists' focus of attention shifted to such other campaigns as the defense of the Scottsboro Boys and the imprisonment of Communist party leaders in Germany. In the early 1930s spirituals remained primarily a form of entertainment rather than agitprop fare.

In the latter half of the decade the Communist press waxed enthusiastic over the spiritual as a form of protest, noting a number of hymns which were suitable for the mobilization of the masses. Lee Collier reported in "Portrait of New South," in the *Daily Worker*, that "Joshua" was parodied:

> *Black and white together we'll win the vote.* (3)
> *The Communist Party will lead the fight.* (3)

Spirituals were even changed to attack the role of religion in the life of the southern Negro. Gellert and Siegmeister in *Negro Songs of Protest* reprinted a song entitled "The Preacher's Belly," which outlined the exploitive nature of some Negro clergymen:

Religion is something fo' de soul,
But preacher's belly done git it all. . . .

He eat yo' dinner an' take yo' lamb,
Givin' you pay in de promised lan'. . . .

Given the content of these lyrics, their appeal was limited primarily to left-wing circles. As Elie Siegmeister was to observe, in the *Music Lover's Handbook:* ". . . *Negro Songs of Protest* has been received with tremendous enthusiasm by certain audiences as 'good' because they express the deepest feelings of an oppressed people." Such singers as Paul Robeson, who sang unaltered spirituals, also were viewed as "people's artists," since many spirituals did contain symbolic statements of protest. For example, as Greenway suggests in *American Folksongs of Protest,* many hymns contain covert sentiments of rebellion against slavery and "the man." Such songs as "Run to Jesus," "Didn't the Lord Deliver Daniel," "Steal Away," "Free My Lord," and "Go Down Moses" are the more obvious illustrations of spirituals containing declarations of discontent and dissent. These hymns fit nicely into the Communist theory of the Negro as the most exploited member of American society.

The role of the spiritual in the context of folk consciousness was both direct and indirect. Many of the songs of persuasion used by the Communists were based on spirituals. On the other hand, spirituals which were not overt assertions of protest were placed within an ideological framework and considered true expressions of people's art.

3

Urban
Folk
Consciousness

" 'Tis the final conflict, let each stand in his place" was a stanza
which appealed to many people in the dark years of the thirties. A
majority of Americans, of course, did not subscribe to the last line of
the "Internationale," which prophesied that communism would save
the human race. At this time, nevertheless, a good number of intellectuals, artists, academics, bohemians, and others believed that the Great
Depression was the last breath of the old order and the heralding in
of the new. Throughout the land the Marxian law of immiseration, or
increasing misery, was, as predicted, creating an industrial and rural
legion of unemployed. Certainly, the bank closings, the endless soup
lines, and the cluttered streets supporting an army of neophyte fruit
peddlers would usher in a political consciousness which in turn might
lead to class struggle. Communist and nonpolitical tabloids frequently
reported incidents of dispossessed workers fighting to resist eviction
from their homes and farms. Some American scholars and opinion-
makers were pointing to the Soviet Union, "the one socialist state," as
the land of full employment. Celebrated comic and front-porch social
commentator Will Rogers quipped, "In Russia along with all their
cuckoo stuff, they have got some mighty good ideas." Radicals of a host
of persuasions in the 1930s agreed that myths and stereotypes were
beginning to melt away and a national re-examination was being
generated. Pete Seeger recalled in an interview, ". . . when I was a
teenager, around 1932–3–4, I suddenly found out what unemployment
could do to people. The whole country was arguing. People got so mad
they thought of radical solutions to it."

It was within this historical context that the song of persuasion was introduced. In discussing the growth of urban folk consciousness, the prime focus will be upon the Communist subculture of New York City, where the proletarian renaissance was to flourish. The impact of "folkness" or people's music was generated here and filtered into the radical hinterlands only with the tours of the Almanac Singers and other so-called people's artists.

The Quest for Proletarian Music

The first half of the "Red decade" in New York Communist circles can best be characterized as a quest for proletarianism. In describing music, Mike Gold lamented, "Why don't American workers sing? The Wobblies knew how, but we still have to develop a Communist Joe Hill." Edwin Rolfe, in welcoming the publication of the *Red Song Book,* in the *Daily Worker* outlined the situation by noting that the book was "a definite accomplishment in a much-neglected field of workers' cultural activity. Since the days of Joe Hill . . . who wrote his words to fit the music of current popular tunes, no effort has been spent in the writing and composition of new workers' songs; and very little effort has been made, despite casual attempts now and then, to collect scattered pieces." This reviewer went on to laud the collection for its inclusion of several native "workers'" songs from Detroit, Gastonia, and Harlan County, along with the "songs which are sung throughout the world, songs which are an intimate part of the revolutionary movement."

Despite the introduction of folk-styled "revolutionary songs," the major musical activity at this time was mass singing, as manifested by the workers' choruses. The chorus, based partially on the Russian model, was seen as "one of the most popular mediums for reaching the masses. The capitalist class, through the churches and so-called People's choruses, uses this medium for lulling the workers. The revolutionary movement uses it for resolving the workers against the oppressors." In the early 1930s choruses were as common as folk-singing trios and quartets were to be several decades later. A few of these many groups were the American Workers' Chorus, the Daily Worker Chorus, the Freiheit Chorus, and the I.L.D. Song Group under the direction of Elie Siegmeister. These singing associations performed mostly traditional European material and songs supplied by the Workers Music

League (WML), the musical apparatus of the movement, with which they were affiliated. The Music League, formed in 1931 under the slogan "Music for the Masses," was a local federation of approximately twenty New York City choruses, bands, and orchestras of various party groups and language sections. In keeping with its dictum of standing "ready with advice and help to all workers and their organizations," the league published songbooks and single compositions, most of which appeared first on the cultural page of the *Daily Worker*. The league provided entertainment at rallies and other gatherings sponsored by the movement.

The function of song writing and serious work was delegated to the Composers' Collective of the Pierre Degeyter Club, named after the co-author of the "Internationale." The Degeyter Club was comprised of twenty-four professional musicians who developed a chorus and an orchestra, gave concerts, courses, and lectures on music, and attempted to stimulate the founding of a new proletarian music. The league nearly always encouraged "workers" to set up music groups. One article suggested that choruses be formed around a number of "simplistic" instruments such as (1) harmonica, (2) accordion, (3) bugle and drum, or (4) fife and drum. The Composers' Collective, more concerned with creating music, recurrently appealed for lyrics to songs: "Serious efforts are being made to write more songs by the Composers' Collective of the Pierre Degeyter Club (revolutionary musicians). However, they are handicapped by an almost total lack of suitable words to be fitted to music . . . the need of new proletarian songs is only too well known."

Despite this lack of suitable lyrics, a number of songs did spring from the members of the Degeyter Club, especially from "L. E. Swift," Jacob Schaefer, Elie Siegmeister, and Lahn Adohmyan. Swift's "The Scottsboro Boys Shall Not Die," Adohmyan's "Stand Guard," and "The Comintern" by German composer Hans Eisler were the most popular compositions of this period. Members also experimented with more complex presentations such as Siegmeister's first attempt at proletarian music, "May Day." These efforts by the Degeyter Club and the Music League, while seen as filling a cultural gap, were criticized on the grounds of musical complexity and over-intellectualism, charges which increased as the decade progressed. Charles Seeger pointed out that while Swift's material could be sung by dedicated workers' choruses, it would cause difficulty for other choruses. In a letter to Mike Gold, Swift concurred that the material Seeger cited was "too difficult" and "quite stilted, un-American, old-fashioned, difficult to sing, politically vague." Gold responded by suggesting that the proletarian music presented by the league was "sterile, cerebral music," "distant from the revolution."

For individuals concerned with the musical style of the Stalinist movement, the singing Wobblies were viewed as a model, with several ideological qualifications. Wobbly songs were seen as a "force which helped them fight and grow," but Communist songs had to have greater "class consciousness." The major objection to Joe Hill's songs was their class origin. Rolfe said, in his *Daily Worker* review: "Instead of the old hobo, lumpen proletarian songs, which made up the bulk of the I.W.W. collections, the *Red Song Book* reveals a greater class consciousness. . . ." Mike Gold repeatedly echoed this position: "One of the basic faults of the old Socialist and Wobbly songs was that they were generally written to hymn tunes. This was also true of the workers' songs in Europe. It is a mark of the theoretical advance of the workers' movement that today the revolutionary musicians are trying to create a *new kind of song,* which will be so identified with the workers that nobody can take it from them." Yet another Communist, in prescribing a program for proletarian composers, suggested, "There is still some room for occasional parodies of old songs such as 'Pie in the Sky' and 'Soup' but not for many of them. The revolutionary movement will have its own music. We shall keep as much as we like of the old, but build better upon it." The fundamental belief of proletarian musicians at the beginning of the decade was that a new musical form had to be *handed down* to the workers as their own, since the previous pattern of songs, given their class genesis, was unacceptable. Other native musical forms were equally ignored or were viewed as ideologically beyond consideration. In the course of the search for working-class music, the lyrical fare continued to consist of scattered Wobbly songs, rousing chorales from such Soviet and European revolutionary composers as Eisler, and the topical efforts of the Workers Music League.

This outlook is illustrated by the "workers'" songbooks distributed by the Communist movement in the early 1930s. The 1932 *Red Song Book* was published to fill the need for propaganda songs and to "act as an incentive toward the organization of choruses and singing groups, according to the stated purpose of the book itself." In the main the book was a collection of many musical styles, generally departing from the familiarity format of the Wobblies. Music for the songs was included in the collection as well as instructions for teaching people how to sing. More than a fourth of the songs were Russian in origin, with other contributions coming from Germany, France, and England. Of the twenty-six pieces collected, only three American songs reflected familiarity or folk themes in origin or composition, and two of these were folk-styled tunes from the Gastonia and Harlan campaigns: "ILD Song" and "Poor Miner's Farewell." The following excerpts are representative of early "folkish" propaganda songs:

> *Only a miner killed under the ground,*
> *Only a miner and one more is found;*
> *Killed by some accident, there's no one can tell,*
> *Your mining's all over, poor miner, farewell.*

> *Poor orphaned children, thrown out on the street,*
> *Ragged and hungry, with nothing to eat;*
> *Their mothers are jobless and their fathers are dead,*
> *Poor fatherless children, left crying for bread.*
>
> ("Poor Miner's Farewell")

> *When the bosses cut your wages,*
> *And you toil and labor free,*
> *Come and join the textile union,*
> *Also join the ILD.*

> *Come and join the ILD. (2)*
> *It will help to win the victory*
> *If you will join the ILD.*
>
> ("International Labor Defense Song")

In 1934 the Degeyter Club issued the *New Workers Song Book,* compiled by Adohmyan and Sand. Most of the compositions combined classical structures with proletarian lyrics. This book, as Gold later pointed out, was cumbersome, based on the European model, and designed for trained choruses. During the same year the *International Collection of Revolutionary Songs* was introduced into the Communist movement. In many respects this book was indicative of the state of proletarian song in America. The songbook was viewed as an alternative to national patriotic songs and consisted of thirteen songs from eight countries. These songs in turn were translated into three languages—English, German, and Russian.

Another songbook of the period, directed at the children of urban Communists, was the *Pioneer Song Book,* composed by Harry Alan Potamkin. The songbook was issued the day of Potamkin's death and was a collection of revolutionary songs put to Mother Goose rhymes. Illustrative of the type of song included is "Mother Goose on the Breadline" or "Sing a Song of Six Percent," based on "Sing a Song of Six Pence." After numerous verses the piece concludes:

What are we waiting for some day,
When set before them with many a groan and cry,
They'll find a hammer and sickle
Is carved on every pie.

With its illustrations, the songbook was very similar to the children's music books used in elementary classrooms. One Communist critic proudly noted that "the PSB [*Pioneer Song Book*] is made up attractively enough to rival any of the expensive, fancy books published for pampered rich kids." This children's songbook was one of the few propaganda vehicles employed by the Stalinists which contained themes known to the American people. The lyrics, however, made the work totally unacceptable except to those already committed. These songbooks, designed for diversified audiences, exhibited little awareness of folk material.

In the course of the Communists' odyssey toward proletarian musical fare, the folk song received some passing recognition. Margaret Larkin, after returning to New York from Gastonia, performed the "ballets" she had learned there at various functions for the Stalinist movement. During the Harlan County strike Jim Garland fled to New York to escape the legal charges filed against him, and Aunt Molly Jackson was brought to the city by the Drieser Committee to raise money for the miners' struggle. Aunt Molly appeared at a benefit for the miners before an estimated 21,000 people. But her compositions were rejected by the Workers Music League, which at that time was not interested in traditional material. Only Edwin Rolfe cited "Poor Miner's Farewell" and "The ILD Song" by Ella May Wiggins as "our songs in the fullest sense": ". . . coming from the ranks of the workers themselves during their own battles, they too will become, as they grow more popular, pages of American class struggle history."

Mike Gold placed Negro spirituals in the proletarian tradition, commenting that "their religious past becomes transmuted into a Communist present." Another writer praised folk material as "wholly class conscious." Yet another advocate of proletarian music suggested, while rejecting Wobbly parodies, that folk music exhibited a "spirit of resentment toward oppression or vigorous resistance to it. . . ." The folk song was also described as "ingenuous and infectious." These sporadic statements were primarily reflective of specific campaigns, such as Harlan, in which Stalinist writers saw folk songs as indicative of class consciousness. Once the organizing campaign was over, the songs were quickly forgotten. Only in the late 1930s would these ballads be revived as significant ongoing propaganda tools.

While most Stalinists only flirted with the notion of folk-styled revolutionary music, three writers in the early 1930s did present cogent arguments which would eventually lead to the adoption of folk music as a cry for justice. Lahn Adohmyan, one of the more radical members of the Degeyter Club, presented an argument which would be re-echoed in the late 1930s. In suggesting songs for workers' choruses, he wrote in the *Daily Worker:*

> In this country we have a virtually untapped source of folk songs which could be arranged, both for the "club" as well as advanced chorus. Negro songs of protest, work songs, railroad songs, cowboy and hill songs. These would be a colorful addition to our repertoire. Such an approach would carry us a long way toward rooting our work in the tradition of American music, it would give the lie to those who insist that our music is nothing but an importation from the outside . . . the workers audience will declare: This is our music.

In his search for a "Communist Joe Hill" Mike Gold added a qualified endorsement of folk music when he stated in his column, "The nearest things we've had to Joe Hill's kind of folk balladry had been from such southern mountaineer Communists as Aunt Molly Jackson and the martyred textile weaver Ella May Wiggins. Detroit has also contributed a popular ballad 'The Soupline Song' with words by Maurice Sugar." On another occasion Aunt Molly was described as a proletarian voice: "This fine militant mountain woman with her courageous laughter and deep proletarian love . . . she ought to be sent around the country to sing her ballads."

In November, 1935, at the beginning of the Popular Front era of mass organization building, Gold introduced Ray and Lita Auville to the readers of the *Daily Worker*. The Auvilles were natives of West Virginia and had defected from the Socialist party to join the Communists. Gold pictured them as a "revolutionary couple who write their own words and music, then, with a guitar sing to working class audiences . . . like Joe Hill. . . ." The Auvilles put out a collection of eight songs published by the literary John Reed Clubs. This collection included songs like "The Ghost of the Depression," "Painting the Old Town Red," "Mighty Fine Country," "Not Blue Any More," and "I'm a Civilized Man":

> *I'm a civilized man, I'm a Red,*
> *I have advanced thought in my head,*
> *I'd rather by far enlightened be*
> *Than own all the land, the sky and the sea.*
> *I care not for gold any more*
> *When others around are poor;*
> *Of me can be said,*
> *Old traditions are dead,*
> *I'm a civilized man, I'm a Red.*

As this lyric indicates, the Auvilles were closer to the formalism of the Composers' Collective than to the more simplistic folk style of either Ealla May Wiggins or Aunt Molly Jackson. Mike Gold's endorsement of the couple, however, was to be seen as a rejection of the WML position.

At this time many Stalinists still saw proletarian music as most properly in the province of the workers' choruses. In a John Reed Clubs Symposium, reported in the *Daily Worker*, Henry Cowell argued that "it is necessary to write with the simplicity of the folk style in order to create music that workers can understand *but* . . . technical innovations must be steadily and slowly introduced into workers music so that the workers appreciate it [more sophisticated music]." Carl Sand, a driving force in the WML and a *Daily Worker* columnist, supported this view, rejecting the efforts of the Auvilles as "a hybrid mixture of jazz and balladry." The Cowell-Sand position was not accepted, since on January 2, 1936, the *Daily Worker* published Ray Auville's "Rugged, Rugged Individualism," including guitar chords, next to a bitter attack upon the Workers Music League. Mike Gold raged that the Music League was guilty of "sectarianism" in dismissing the Auvilles. Americans were singing semijazz and songs concocted by Tin

Pan Alley while the WML was attempting to lead them into Schoenberg and Stravinsky. For Gold this situation was a "desertion of the masses." He sardonically asked in his *Daily Worker* article which appeared the same day:

> . . . would you judge workers' correspondence by the standard of James Joyce or Walter Pater? No, a folk art rarely comes from the studios; it makes its own style, and has its own inner laws of growth. It may shock you, but I think the Composers' Collective has something to learn from Ray and Lita Auville . . . they write catchy tunes that any American worker can sing and like, and the words of their songs make the revolution as intimate and simple as "Old Black Joe." Is this so little?

Gold's article was a milestone in that it altered the quest for proletarian music. The attempt to create music for the masses by the tenets of European standards began to disintegrate. Shortly after the Auville controversy the WML and the Composers' Collective were disbanded. The Auvilles' songbook was displayed in Communist bookstores in New York and elsewhere. The American Music League (AML) was constituted in place of the WML as a broadly based Popular Front music organization. One of the tenets of the AML was to "collect, study and popularize American folk music and its traditions."

This discussion of the so-called chorus movement illustrates the isolating role of utopian consciousness in the Communist subculture of New York City. The Composers' Collective desired working-class music, yet its model was from across the seas. The tenet expressed by Sand and others, that music must be created for the masses, took one element from *What Is to Be Done?* That is, the workers were not capable of creating their own revolutionary consciousness. Ideology also turned the Music League away from other sources of songs and pointed it toward the work of Hans Eisler. It required the advent of the Popular Front period, as voiced by Gold, to alter this consciousness of proletarian art. This change of propaganda vehicles turned the Stalinists to yet another musical form not known by the urban proletariat.

In the course of the trial-and-error movement toward the proletarian renaissance of folk music, several songwriters outside New

York, such as Maurice Sugar and Mike Quin, were writing revolutionary songs in the native idiom. Sugar came the closest to using the folk genre, while West Coast writer Mike Quin used predominantly popular songs.

Sugar, a Detroit ILD attorney during the thirties, was the unchallenged bard of "workers' songbooks." As Joe Hill's work dominated the pocket-sized hymnals, Sugar's work dominated the Communist songbooks. In *America Sings,* for example, five of the attorney's songs appear. Sugar wrote the lyrics of the best-known depression ditty, "The Soup Song," following a "speaking engagement at a 'Lodge' provided by the city of Detroit for homeless destitute men. . . ." This song was picked by the Unemployed Councils and the CPUSA and distributed nationally in the *Red Song Book.* In 1932 Sugar went to Geneva to the World Congress against War and to Tiflis in the Soviet Union as a fraternal delegate to the International Congress of Revolutionary Writers, as a representative of the John Reed Clubs. Upon his return Sugar, while on a national tour for the Friends of the Soviet Union, found that "the song was known and sung almost everywhere I went." "The Soup Song," put to the tune of "My Bonnie Lies over the Ocean," was the anthem of the depression for the American Left, since it captured much of the ethos of those turbulent years.

While this song was directed at the depression, a majority of Sugar's compositions were aimed at organizing the automobile workers. For this purpose he wrote such songs as "We Are the Guys," "I Belong to the Company Union," "You Can't Make a Living," "Be a Man," "Old Hank Ford," and "Sit-Down." "Be a Man" and "We Are the Guys" as well as "Sit-Down" were strike-oriented songs to be sung "on the line. "Be a Man," according to Sugar, was directed at "those workers who displayed some hesitancy in joining or staying in the strike movement."

The most widely sung of Sugar's tactical songs was "Sit-Down," written during the avalanche of sit-down strikes in the early months of 1937. The sit-down was originally a Wobbly technique used as early as 1906 in the General Electric strike in Schenectady. The rationale behind it was that "gun thugs" and police officers would be less likely to attack strikers if company property would be in jeopardy. The technique was highly effective. According to Sugar, " 'Sit-Down' was sung by the strikers in their meeting halls, and in the plant while the strike was in progress. In the plants, singing was part of the organized recreation of the workers, and they frequently improvised musical bands

[who] went . . . sled-length for folk songs . . . lots of hillbilly stuff . . . and lots of parodies . . . they went for 'Sit-Down' in a big way." Sugar's songs were generally based on familiar tunes, regardless of their genre or origin. During a civil rights case in the early 1930s, while defending a Negro, James Victory, Sugar used a spiritual and adapted it to the case. In "Song for Scottsboro Boys" he utilized another style. In some instances other musical genres were used for revolutionary songs. In sum, while Sugar was aware of the folk idiom, he rarely used it for propaganda purposes.

On the West Coast propaganda songs continued the familiarity pattern of the Industrial Workers of the World. For example, the Communist party newspaper, the *Western Worker,* stressed revolutionary lyrics put to standard tunes. One reason for this phenomenon appears to be the Wobbly influence upon western radicalism. The Pacific Northwest and areas farther south in California had been major locations of IWW organizational drives. Malvina Reynolds, for one, stated that Wobbly tactics and songs were transmitted by former members in the western states. Several Communist ditties support this hypothesis. "Someday We'll Pay Our Debts" by Mike Quin, the most prolific of the left-wing West Coast songwriters, was put to the tune of a Wobbly favorite. Quin, who is incorrectly considered by some to be the discoverer of Woody Guthrie, published a number of proletarian songs in his *Western Worker* column and later in the *People's World.* In 1933 in his "Seeing Red" column he presented "March, Worker and Soldier." Three years later, to commemorate May Day, Quin published a number of songs in his column, all put to popular tunes. "There's a Way, Working Man" was joined to the tune of "Dixie" and "Battle Hymn of Labor" revolutionized "John Brown's Body." The following month Quin wrote a piece on political tactics entitled "She'll Be Selling *Western Workers,*" altering "She'll Be Coming 'Round the Mountain," and another song denouncing the bosses, based on a Wobbly standard, "Tramp, Tramp, Tramp." The following lyrics convey the tone of most of Quin's compositions:

> *Bills, bills, bills are piling high, boys,*
> *Cheer up comrades there is hope,*
> *And someday we'll pay our debts,*
> *With our worker Soviets,*
> *We will give the boss what's coming to him then.*
>
> ("Someday We'll Pay Our Debts")

Mike Quin and family

Courtesy of *People's World*

In succeeding years Quin wrote sociopolitical verses to "Auld Lang Syne," "Home Sweet Home," and "Nancy Lee" to glorify the newly established *People's World* newspaper:

> *The* People's World *the people's voice shall be,*
> *A sheet that speaks for you and me.*
> *The* People's World *the people's voice shall be,*
> *The* People's World *their voice shall be.*

("The People's Voice")

Quin's compositions greatly reflected the material used on the West Coast by the Communist party in the years prior to 1939. During this decade folk songs generally were ignored by the West Coast party press. A few songs from musical shows and strike situations were published in the *Western Worker*. In December, 1934, the *Worker* reported that individuals confined under the Sacramento criminal syndicalism law sang the "Internationale" while in prison. Several months later the same newspaper printed the lyrics to Franklin Neuman's "The March of the Liberals," suggesting it be used as a composition for a musical show. One of the radicals convicted in Sacramento of criminal syndicalism wrote a propaganda song, "His Majesty, the Capitalist," added in Wobbly fashion to "When the Roll Is Called Up Yonder." Another piece which appeared in the western version of the *Worker* was "Bill Green's Song," sung to the familiar tune of "The Man on the Flying Trapeze." In all, very few songs appeared in West Coast party publications and those that did bore little resemblance to folk music. For example, in 1938 no propaganda songs were to be found in the pages of the *Western Worker*. Little if any mention was made of folk material prior to the initiation of the "Woody Sez" column in the May 12, 1939, issue of *People's World*.

The only radical concerned with folk music during this era, it appears, was Redfern Mason, the 1935 United Labor party's candidate for mayor in San Francisco. As a child Mason had heard English workers in Wales singing propaganda songs during a strike. In a 1935 article in the *Western Worker*, Mason described these ballads as having "an angry grandeur" and as functionally aiding the workers in winning strikes. Four years later in a *People's World* article Mason reiterated the value of folk music in respect to nationality groups.

In San Francisco the Young Communist League, in a similar vein, used songs printed in *People's World* like "Battle Hymn of Labor," "We Ain't Gonna Slave No More," "People's Song," and the Wobbly parody of "Casey Jones." One YCL tune was based on the standard "Hinky Dinky Parlez Vous," changed to "Brother It's the YCL":

> *Who's the bunch that's always there,*   YCL
> *Leading young folks everywhere?*   YCL
> *Who says "Young folks let's unite*
> *To make a world that's gay and bright"?*
> BROTHER IT'S THE YCL.

> *Who fights for the right to learn,*   YCL
> *For the right a wage to earn?*   YCL
> *Who says "Youth will die no more*
> *For profits in a bosses war"?*
> BROTHER IT'S THE YCL.

> *Who fights for a land that's free,*   YCL
> *A future with security?*   YCL
> *Who wants life that's filled with joy,*
> *Happiness for girl and boy?*
> BROTHER IT'S THE YCL.

YCLers also included popular lyrics from the hit parade of the day such as "You're a Sweetheart" and "Bei mir bist du schön." Several years later the traditional labor hymns "Solidarity Forever" and "Hold the Fort" became favorites. The radical movements in the western states prior to the introduction of Woody Guthrie and the Almanac Singers, who toured the area in 1941, generally did not employ the folk idiom as an opinion-formulating device.

Americanization and Folk Consciousness

In conjunction with the Popular Front era American Communists tried to nationalize their image and organization to a point many observers found to be ludicrous. Critical observers have cited the celebration of Jefferson's birthday and other insignificant historical events as proof that the Communists could never be "just folks." The so-called "Americanization" program at times did resemble the super-patriotism associated with the nationalist Right. Nevertheless, Americanization was not just a policy or a political program but, rather, was the basis for an entire subculture and intellectual ethos. Howe and Coser report that "the Popular Front was not merely a political tactic, it was also, and in the United States even more importantly, a *kind of culture* [with] application to almost any intellectual area."

It is in the context of this culture that the quest for proletarian music turned to native American forms. Richard Wright, recalling his experiences in the Communist party, said, "They don't know how to appeal to people yet" and "They had a program, an ideal, but they had not yet found a language." A correspondent wrote to the *Daily Worker* in 1932, "We are faced with a problem of vocabulary . . . without any explanation . . . [it] drives the uninitiated worker further away from us, rather than drawing him closer to the Party and its struggles." To combat the party's isolation in America and international fascism, the Comintern ordered the American version of the *Front Populaire*. Stalinism became "20th Century Americanism." "The Star-Spangled Banner" replaced the "Internationale" as the opening selection in workers' music books and at rallies. "The Song of Freedom" was published in the *Daily Worker* to mark Independence Day in 1939, paralleling the May Day practice. Musically, Americanization, which would eventually contribute to folk consciousness, was a sporadic and often haphazard process.

In 1936 Sidney Streat articulated the need for native choruses while rejecting foreign material. The following week Hans Eisler noted the rise of the New Singers as the first English-speaking chorus which was comparable to the European units. Several months later the New Singers appeared at the American Music League Festival, hailed by a *Daily Worker* reviewer as marking "the first practical step toward a people's music in America." An examination of the festival groups, however, does not totally substantiate this appraisal, since a majority of participants carried on the tradition of Europe—the Freiheit Mandolin Band, Italian and German workers' clubs, and the Ukrainian Workers. The significance of this review is that while the party desired Americanization of its music, its ability to do so was hampered by its composition and outlook. The influence of Eisler was still strong. For example, the first Stalinist-sponsored records were made by the New Singers for the Timely Recording Company in 1935. Their selections included the European standards "In Praise of Learning," "United Front," "Rise Up," and the "Internationale." The one American selection was "The Soup Song." At a concert, "America in Song," four years later the group presented Civil War and American Revolutionary ballads as well as stylized versions of "John Henry," "Sistern and Brethren," and "Lamentation over Boston." In the following years such choruses as the Lan Adomian New Singers adopted American material while maintaining the same "procult" structure. In the process of adopting American material, folk music became increasingly "in" among New York Communists.

The Americanization program brought about a misty type of folk consciousness where many forms of music became folk. Folk songs as defined in the Stalinist literature encompassed a wide range of musical forms from popular songs to, ironically, Wobbly ditties. One evidence of this confusion is found in the Frederick Adams *Daily Worker* review of *Songs of the People* (published in 1937), which the author characterized as "Folk Songs of the People." Adams began by debunking the notion that there was no music indigenous to the American people and that foreign music was superior: ". . . music is an artificial . . . element in our national culture, and we have to make the best of it. Such is the currently accepted idea of our best known musicians and most learned music critics." Adams criticized this view as class-bound and oblivious to the work songs of the country: "America has a musical life of its own, but a life that nobody ever thought it worthwhile to talk about or write down. This life does not concern our music critics nor those who sit on the Board of the Metropolitan or the Philharmonic . . . this real American music may be dangerous to these gentlemen." *Songs of the People* was, of course, the answer: "This new song book marks a definite step in advance of all previously published collections of workers' songs in that a majority . . . are American songs . . . which are known to the workers and sung by them throughout the country."

Adams's evaluation of *Songs of the People* illustrates the development of awareness of the "folk" in Stalinist circles. Yet few folklorists or anthropologists would judge the material in this "workers' " collection as indigenous to the folk. Twelve of the pieces included were foreign in origin. Four of this international group were Russian and five, including "The Peat Bog Soldiers," came from Germany. The remaining songs were American, reversing the dominant European orientation of previous anthologies like the *Red Song Book*. Six of the native selections were penned by Maurice Sugar, four came from the Wobbly songbag, and five emanated from the Workers Music League. The rest came from a multitude of idioms, including the theatrical stage and southern labor unions. One piece was Earl Robinson's "Death House Blues." While the actual folk basis of many of the tunes in *Songs of the People* is debatable, the songbook does typify the Americanization of Communist musical fare. After 1938 party campaign songs were to follow in the tradition of Jefferson, Clay, Polk, and well-known American political figures. Other selections to be used were put to "Casey Jones" and "They Go Wild Simply Wild over Me," both Wobbly standards:

> *They go wild simply wild over you,*
> *I mean the Republican Reactionary crew.*
> *When election time is right,*
> *They will promise you the sky,*
> *They are wild, simply wild over you.*

In contrast, the official Communist party campaign song of 1932, "Vote Red," was composed by the Workers Music League in the European style. One verse is illustrative of the structure:

> *The Communist Party will be our guide*
> *'Gainst the wars of the ruling classes.*
> *The Soviet Union we'll always defend,*
> *We'll protect the Chinese masses.*

On another occasion "The Ballad of an Evil Old Man" was hailed by William Wolff as a "new American folksong" and Maurice Sugar was cited as a "folk composer" by another Stalinist writer. As the "guardians of American traditions" the Communists frequently gave so-called agitprop pieces a historical basis or social origin which in fact was questionable. Nevertheless, this practice did further the accessibility of more genuine forms of folk material. In the latter part of 1935 the Music League announced plans for the publication of a new workers' songbook and proposed forty-eight possible songs. Of the suggested pieces, nearly a third were either Wobbly or folk pieces, including Garland's "Harry Simms." Increasingly, as Americanization became entrenched in party circles, folk music was enshrined. Forrest Mackay, describing the plight of the Chicano in the *Daily Worker,* wrote that "folk song . . . belongs to the common people, it has become the best chronicle of life and death in the desert. . . ." Samuel Chavkin, in discussing the Lawrence Gellert collection of Negro protest songs, characterized them in a *Worker* piece as embodying "the living voice of the otherwise inarticulate resentment against injustice, a part of the unrest that is stirring the South."

Other reviewers and writers pointed to the music of the South as indicative of a growing class consciousness and reprinted lyrics of altered spirituals like "Joshua Fought the Battle of Jericho":

> *Black and white together we'll win the vote,* (3)
> *The Communist Party will lead the fight.* (3)

The *People's World* described folk music on one occasion as "the songs of people, of farmers, of workers, of laborers, and they come from the directed contact with their work, whatever it is. . . ." Lawrence Emery, in discussing a band of calypso singers in the *Sunday Worker,* saw songs of this type as "folk expressions of our time." The topical Yiddish songs were equally portrayed as folk music. Songs based on familiarity themes and such tunes as "Take Me Out to the Ball Game," "Polly Wolly Doodle," and "Tavern in the Town" were labeled folk songs, since in the words of Brent Schumacher, in a *People's World* article, "American folk music is rich with contributions made by workers in the field, women in their work, men on the picket lines, workers who wanted to express in song things which they felt deeply." Folk music became people's or workers' music and vice versa, the latter most often being the case. William Wolff, in describing an unknown singer, Jilson Setters, summed up this transition in *People's World:* "He has probably never heard of Marx or Lenin, but there can be no doubt where his roots lay, as he sings."

A corollary to this elevation of folk music was its incorporation into the columns of *Worker* critics. Such writers as Bill Wolff and Sue Barry began to take serious issue with music not grounded in simplistic native material. Wolff argued that Soviet composers were using folk material and that Americans should do likewise. Barry singled out pianist Ray Green and lauded him for not exhibiting any of the characteristics of "your traditional long-haired, high hat artist." Instead, she went on, Green used "folk music" generated by the workers, which stirred people to "thought and action." Another writer praised Elie Siegmeister for his transition to folk material and to the music of the people. Finally, one critic, hailing the folk style employed by the Almanac Singers, decried the use of other, superficial versions lacking validity: "The problem of 'validity' in singing has long faced the vocal artist. I heard Paul Robeson sing trash in . . . 'John Henry' [which] failed. . . . When technique is lacking and/or when the premise is unsound or false, failure is inevitable."

The criterion for excellence of songs steadily became more native, socially conscious, and linked to American tradition. Despite the misinterpretation in party circles of what was folk, Americanization did in fact create a nebulous audience and appreciative critics for the transplants from Harlan County and elsewhere. Although party members felt they had found the musical roots of America, the folk music of the industrial 1930s was not the music of the American people. For example, Richard Wright had to introduce Leadbelly as a "people's artist" to *Daily Worker* readers. Leadbelly at that time was unknown to urban dwellers.

"Viva la Quince Brigada"

The most significant single event in the Red decade for the partisans was the Spanish Civil War. For historians this civil conflict is a space in time; for those involved in it, the war was a holy crusade. Outraged by the Fascist threat to the Spanish government, thousands of volunteers from the world over answered the cry of the Republican government for assistance. Latter-day "Lafayettes" crossed the Pyrenees, with great difficulty, to form the International Brigades. These "freedom fighters" included in their ranks adventurers, careerists, romantics, escapists, and true believers of many ideological shadings. Some of these men did not remain at the fronts of Jarma or Aragon for long, many died, a few deserted. Politically, the majority were Marxists of various factions and fads, primarily Stalinists. Others were socialists, democrats, and humanitarians who viewed Spain as the first international extension of German-Italian fascism. Along with fifty-seven other nations the United States supplied nearly 3,000 volunteers who made up the Lincoln Battalion of the International Brigade. Of the original number, only half returned to recall the heroics and betrayals of the holy war against Franco.

The emotional intensity of this two-year campaign or crusade for both the combatants and their supporters is difficult to document. Suffice it to say, the singing of a Civil War song still brings tears to the eyes of many who participated in the glories and agonies of the time: ". . . there is no one who can hear these . . . songs, and know all the background of them, who can fail to be genuinely inspired and lifted. . . ." William Z. Foster characterized the war as "the most glorious event in the entire life of the Communist Party."

For the American Left the war assumed the status of a *cause célèbre*. The CPUSA and the Young Communist League, according to Foster, organized volunteers, raised funds, gathered medical and other supplies, and staged rallies opposing the Roosevelt embargo. It was during this period that the songs from the olive orchards and the battlefields of Spain became very popular in left-wing circles. Lawrence Lipton, in discussing the period, stated in *The Holy Barbarians* that "army songs of the Spanish Civil War, brought back by young veterans of the Lincoln Brigade, were sung. . . . Anyone who could sing 'The Four Insurgent Generals' in Spanish was sure to be the life of the party." Rolfe, in *The Lincoln Battalion,* notes that Spanish tunes were merged with words of many languages; traditional Iberian songs were altered to recall the plights and few glories of the Loyalists and their foreign comrades. "Tit-Willow" became "Oop au aud oop au ay arro," "Red River Valley" emerged as "Jarma Valley," and "Viva la Quince Brigada" or "Ay Manuela" was taken from a dated Spanish folk ballad. These and many other songs saturated rallies and street-corner meetings in New York and elsewhere. Singers were employed by many organizations, such as the Spanish Refugee Appeal, Young Communist League, American Youth for Democracy, sections of the CIO, and others, to commemorate the events in Spain. One unit, calling themselves the No Pasaran Group, appeared for many weeks in New York's Union Square singing songs and performing sketches. Several years after the termination of the conflict several albums appeared containing Loyalist songs. In June, 1938, during an air raid on Barcelona, Ernest Busch, a German tenor, recorded the collection *Six Songs for Democracy,* which received wide circulation in left-wing circles (vol. 1 of Songs of the Spanish Civil War, Folkways Records, FH 5436, Notes). In the United States the songs were recorded and eventually presented over WQXR by an inspired Paul Robeson who continued singing "Peat Bog Soldiers" after the recording had ended. Erich Weinert described the purpose of this album in the notes: "We trust that they [songs] will again awaken, in the outside world, some of this fighting spirit, this fire, out of which they were born." Another album, *Songs of the Lincoln Battalion,* appeared in 1943, recorded by former Almanac Singers and a chorus of battalion veterans.

Despite the opinions of some overly romantic observers, the Spanish Civil War did not create the folk consciousness of the Communists. The Spanish Civil War did not begin the hootenanny or introduce folk music to American Stalinists. Songs from Spain did, nevertheless, further solidify the folk song in party circles. More important, the war in Spain legitimized the anti-Fascist movement, making access to the public somewhat easier. During this time some singers were attracted into front groups revolving around the Loyalist cause.

The well-known folk entrepreneur, Burl Ives, later to write the autobiographical *Wayfaring Stranger,* posed this question in the latter part of the thirties: "Was there no person in this representative conglomerate of people from all over the world and all parts of the United States who would understand my songs?" The answer to this rhetorical query was the Stalinist movement in New York City. Ives, for example, came across Will Geer, who introduced the balladeer into the "What's On" scene. Geer took Ives to a party and introduced him as "the best ballad singer in these here parts." The result of this affair, according to Ives, was that he became involved in the ferment of the Spanish campaign. The "Wayfaring Stranger" saw the Loyalist cause as encompassing freedom, democratic ideals, and common standards; the civil war was a "moral fight" of which he became a part. Ives recalled:

> The performers I met at Will Geer's believed as I did, but were doing something about it. They thought of the actor as having a

twofold job. I learned from them that the first job of the performer is to entertain people. . . . Secondly, an actor with ideals has a way to support what he believes in. He is asked to appear at benefits that help. . . . The Spanish Republican Government was on the list of causes to be helped.

My first opportunity came when a lady at the party asked if I would be willing to sing some ballads at a party to raise money for the Abraham Lincoln Brigade. I said, "Certainly. Where?"

At this fund-raising party Ives found his first enthusiastic audience. He commented, "Why did this particular audience understand me? It occurred to me that people so concerned about other human beings must be men of good will who would understand my simple songs about people." After this initial appearance Ives did benefits for many causes and groups, including the Theatre Arts Committee (TAC). Ives, along with a blues singer and Will Geer, entertained for a TAC dance which was an artistic flop. However, his performance did merit a mention in Mike Gold's *Daily Worker* column: "Geer . . . made up proletarian ballads and sings them in his raucous but curiously effective voice. His red-head friend Berle, was in the party, a man with a guitar. Berle was a revelation to me. He knows hundreds of ballads, has a fine voice, and is a guitarist in the grand flamenco style. . . . This man was a veritable treasury of the people's art." Such performers as Leadbelly and Josh White found a similar audience in the Stalinist subculture.

The significance of the Spanish Civil War in the sphere of folk consciousness was that it made party policy palatable to some singers who would later play important roles in using folk song as a weapon. A secondary effect was that folk song was further enshrined in the Communist orbit. In keeping with previous Communist practices, the songs of Spain were unknown to most urbanites, especially those outside New York City.

Another event frequently credited with aiding the emergence of folk consciousness is the advent of the CIO. The romanticization and mythology of labor lore has generally presented a picture of a so-called singing labor movement, comprised of characters from a Hugo Gellert sketch or Mike Gold short story bellowing songs which decry the abuses and sufferings of their socioeconomic or class position. As one observer and participant of labor song organizing has correctly suggested, a great deal of this stereotype falls into the area of mythology and wishful thinking. One member of the Almanac Singers, referring to the UAW, said, ". . . we were lucky if they knew two labor songs." An ILGWU official in San Francisco debunked the Almanacs, saying, "What do we need these hillbillies for? We have work to do." The songs that unionists did sing in strikes were situational, based on familiar tunes, and quickly forgotten. Published songs now identified with unionists often emanated from the pens of radicals and revolutionaries. Some of the best-known labor songs of the 1930s—"Old Hank Ford," "We Are the Guys," and "Sit-Down"—were written by Marxist labor attorney Maurice Sugar. As Page Stegner implies, many labor songs stemmed from the "poets who sided with the people" rather than from the workers themselves. The allies of the labor movement in the "Red decade" were Socialists, Trotskyists, and Stalinists, all Marxists who, as labor historian Sidney Lens observes in *Radicalism in America,* "passed out leaflets, held organizing meetings, led strikes with a zeal no one else could muster. They were willing to make *personal sacrifices in a way that the staid leadership of labor was not.*" He goes on to say that industrial unionism would not have had so great a resurgence without the aid of Communists and other radicals. Musically, the role of the radicals was equally significant. The Almanac Singers and Woody Guthrie, for example, addressed a good portion of their songs of persuasion to unionists. Timely Records in 1937 issued such picket-line songs as "Solidarity," "On the Picket Line," "Join the Union," and "Write Me Out My Union Card," which were played and sung at demonstrations. Despite the song-writing role of the Communists, most observers of this period have chosen to credit the labor movement with developing the song of persuasion. Nat Hentoff, for one, writing for *Pageant,* saw Woody as "singing for labor unions and writing wryly proselytizing union songs."

In 1965 Irwin Silber, in *The American Folk Scene,* described the events of the 1930s in the following terms: "In the depression years, textile workers in the South and garment workers in the North put their protest into song. The line of continuity embraced Woody Guthrie, the Almanac Singers, and the CIO organizing drives of the late 1930's." Following Guthrie's death in the fall of 1967, Silber altered this evaluation in several articles (see his "Fan the Flames" in *Sing Out*). Regardless of Guthrie's participation in union organizing, he was not an extoller of the labor movement but, rather, of the working class (see chapter 7). When he spoke of "one big union," it was more of a reference to the International than to the Lewis-led movement. Recalling his organizing, Woody wrote, in *American Folksong,* "I sung for cotton pickers and cotton strikers and migratory workers, packers . . . and all sorts of other country and city workers. . . . I heard William Z. Foster, Mother Bloor, Gurley Flynn. . . . I heard most all of them and played my songs on their platforms."

Such Communist publications as the *Daily Worker* frequently cited the need for labor songs and skits. Labor songbooks and occasional pieces from the picket lines were hailed as important contributions. One *People's World* writer lauded the pickets at the Western Union offices as follows: "They sing their picket songs. Songs which they have written themselves and sing to some of their favorite tunes, and to the finks in the office the snatches of songs that filter through the clatter of the machines must not be too encouraging. They are fighting songs, marching songs. They are the kind of songs that people sing when they are marching into battle—a battle that they are determined to win." Picket-line songs, however, were generally based on popular tunes and did not reflect any folk consciousness, although some Stalinist writers saw them as folk songs. Furthermore, these improvisations rarely outlived a specific strike. One Communist proponent saw folk music as the solution to the need for labor propaganda songs. Wolff, in his *People's World* article, reported a number of southern-based songs, such as "There Are Strange Things Happening in This Land" by John Handcox and "The Song of the Evicted Tenant," to his urban readers. In Zilphia Horton's collection, *Labor Songs,* and in a *People's World* article, "Labor Collects Its Songs in Two Anthologies," he advocated the use of the Horton collection for the Textile Workers Union by quoting John L. Lewis's introduction to the work: "A singing army is a winning army, and a singing labor movement cannot be defeated. When hundreds of men and women in a labor union sing together their individual longing for dignity and freedom are bound into an irrepressible force." In a subsequent article in the *Daily Worker* the same writer suggested that folk tunes were indices of the tenets of Marx and Lenin and should be used for new union songs. This argument in part would later be quoted by Woody Guthrie, the Almanac Singers, and other participants in the proletarian revival.

The fact that radicals saw folk material as ideal for the labor movement was more an ideological stance than a pragmatic one. The songs of the picket line, so quickly forgotten, were generally based on familiar tunes. As such, extrapolation of southern folk ballads to northern picket lines frequently conflicted with the workers' musical tastes. *Pins and Needles,* produced by the ILGWU and the Labor Stage, accomplished more than all of Will Geer's "raggedy-assed" folk singers in the thirties. The musical succeeded in finding that broad audience that the Communist party and its associated leagues were seeking in vain for during the entire decade of the thirties. The play was produced for over a thousand performances in New York and made one road trip. The musical material for the production was written by Harold Rome and the sketches were by Joseph Schrank and Arthur Arent. The players were union members granted leave by their garment industry employers. The dominant theme of the play was the working-class character of the show itself and the importance of social awareness. Originally, Communist reviewers were very impressed with this labor revue. Mike Gold wrote "Hats Off to the ILGWU for Pins and Needles." Such songs as "Why Sing of Stars Above," "What Good Is Love," and "Sing Me a Song with Social Significance" set the theme of art as a weapon. The last number decried "love and pie in the sky" as opposed to socialist realism:

> *Sing me a song with social significance,*
> *Or you can sing till you're blue.*
> *Let meaning shine from every line,*
> *Or I won't love you.*

The production contained seventeen to nineteen songs which frequently changed to correspond with changing social issues and topics. One theme remained constant—the role of the union and industrial organizing. Such songs as "One Big Union for Two" are illustrative:

> *When we have signed up and made the grade,*
> *We'll add a member—union made—*
> *Who looks like me and like you*
> *In one big union for two.*

The overall ideological tone of this musical revue was its social reformism, as seen in its satire and comedy. As Himelstein has observed, the revue did attack war, fascism, and censorship. It did not, however, present ideological solutions or reflect the policies of many of the New York left-wing movements. For example, the revue attacked the Stalin-Hitler pact, something the Almanac Singers would never do. The prime import of this play is that it did reach relatively large audiences, a feat most folk entrepreneurs did not accomplish until the late fifties. The major reason appears to be that *Pins and Needles* was in a medium familiar and acceptable to a broad range of people. The music was patterned on the Broadway show tunes of Irving Berlin rather than on the esoteric refrains of Ella May Wiggins or Aunt Molly Jackson.

This brief discussion of labor songs in the 1930s suggests that many union songs were written for workers by radicals. The few spontaneous songs that did emerge from urban strike situations were of short duration and put to popular tunes. Despite these social facts Stalinists were convinced that folk material was, in fact, the music of the industrial proletariat. The major use of the song of persuasion took place not in the labor movement but during the period called the proletarian renaissance of the late 1930s and early 1940s.

The Proletarian Renaissance

The proletarian renaissance (1939–1942) was a sort of folk music revival in miniature. It represented a subculture and a style of life which fitted into the working-class ethos of the Communist party. The renaissance was a manifestation of all the elements of folk consciousness—field contacts, ideology, tactics, and personnel. During this time folk music became what one listened to at informal gatherings and social affairs given by radicals. Folk entrepreneurs were featured performers at benefits for migratory workers, refugees of the Spanish conflict, and fund-raising drives for militant unions. The *Daily Worker* conscientiously reported all appearances of folk entrepreneurs in the radio and "What's On" sections of the paper. Woodrow Wilson Guthrie, known simply as "Woody," idealized the renaissance.

Woody was hailed as the personification of the renaissance because he was like a proletarian revolutionary from the pages of a Steinbeck novel. Art Shields described him as possessing "the wit of Will Rogers with the Philosophy of a Rebel." The philosophy was Marx's, the style Guthrie's. Guthrie's philosophy customarily has been portrayed as that of a labor movement radical. This characterization, as we have seen, is a romanticized one. Eulogizing Guthrie, Irwin Silber wrote in the *National Guardian,* "He believed in the power of the working class to set the world right and to bring into being a socialist structure which would allow a man to be a real man. . . ." On several occasions, in *Sing Out,* Guthrie described himself as the "most radical, most militant," and "most topical" of folk entrepreneurs. In an article entitled "My Constitution and Me," in the *Sunday Worker,* Woody said, "The best thing that I did in 1936 was to sign up with the Communist Party and start turning the open pages of some thicker books. I bought and gave away about a dozen of these little blue USSR Constitution books since 1936." While Guthrie's statement is historically inaccurate about time, place, and membership, it reflects the posture he presented to left-wingers.

Along with three members of the Garland clan, Jim Garland, Molly Jackson, and Sarah Ogan, the Dustbowl Balladeer provided a model and an impetus for the sectarian revival, as well as fitting the American image of the Communist party. Woody, however popular, was not the only prototype available to radicals. The transplanted members of the Garland clan were living examples of politically directed songsters from the rural South. Sarah Ogan, for example, was the sister of Jim Garland and the half-sister of Aunt Molly. Although she was not active in the NMU or other radical organizations in Kentucky, she did assimilate the tenets of radicalism from her husband, Andrew, and brother Jim. In 1935 the Ogan family migrated to New York City. Here Sarah associated with many other singers of radical material and learned the compositions of Leadbelly, Woody Guthrie, and Earl Robinson. She participated in the early left-wing hootenannies in New York City. She also composed a number of radical and polemical songs which were popular in Communist circles, such as "Down on the Picket Line," "I Hate the Capitalist System," and "I'm Going to Organize." The presence of these songsters influenced a number of intellectuals. Gordon Friesen, in paying tribute to Molly Jackson in the *Daily Worker,* stated, "There had arisen among college people and certain artists and writers, a movement to find and utilize 'folk' songs and stories as a new source of creative work. When Aunt Molly sang her genuine folk ballads they heard the real living song."

Another source of "real living song" was the folklore projects of the Works Progress Administration (WPA), especially the work of the Lomaxes. The WPA in the late thirties exhibited a number of folkloristic interests, many of which fed into the radical subculture of New York City. Some of these undertakings were the Folklore Studies of the Federal Writers' Project under B. A. Botkin; the Index of American Design of the Federal Art Project; the folk music recordings and social music activities of the Federal Music Project, directed by Charles

Woody Guthrie

Seeger; the Folksong and Folklore Department of the National Service Bureau of the Federal Theater Project; and the Lomax-directed Folk Music Archives of the Library of Congress. These projects both injected new material into the radical milieu and recorded a number of proletarian singers as folk artists. Alan Lomax recorded the works of Aunt Molly Jackson, Sarah Ogan, Jim Garland, and Woody Guthrie. Mary Elizabeth Barnacle also collected for the Library of Congress, using Garland and Ogan as informants.

Alan Lomax expanded the repertoire of several songsters, Burl Ives and Leadbelly in particular. His scripts from the "Back Where I Came From" radio program presented social commentary and traditional songs as well as providing occasional employment for the Almanac Singers, Woody Guthrie, Leadbelly, Burl Ives, and others.

The federal studies were complementary to the expansion of the folk ethos in New York. Some of the tenets of nativism found in the pages of the *Worker* were exhibited in the governmental collections of folk music. Gene Bluestein, for example, sees the ideological assumptions of the Lomaxes as based upon the works of Walt Whitman and Ralph Waldo Emerson. This observer argues in "The Lomaxes' New Canon of American Folksong," in the *Texas Quarterly*, that "democratic nativism" was the ideological underpinning of the research conducted by the Lomax family for the Library of Congress in the 1930s: "Whitman had complained about America's dependence on the Old World for its cultural resources. . . . In the vernacular speech of laborers, railroad men, miners, drovers, or boatman he [Whitman] found more poetry than in the books of all 'American' humorists." During the Popular Front period Mike Gold wrote, "Sing sing O new pioneers with Father Walt." In 1938 Earl Robinson composed "Ballad for Americans," a favorite in Stalinist circles, as a "Whitman cantata." For the next year this selection appeared as the featured work in the WPA Federal Theater production *Sing for Your Supper*, a portrayal of working-class conditions in America. He also put Carl Sandburg's "The People, Yes" into musical form.

In many respects Robinson was the ideal type of the intellectuals involved in the proletarian renaissance of the 1930s. He was a classically trained musician who, according to Anita Tilkin in the *Daily Worker*, left the University of Washington "looking for something like the left movement and a chance to write music that says something." This sentiment led him into composers' groups and the Workers Laboratory Theater. While in the agitprop company Robinson wrote a number of songs for the San Francisco waterfront strike. He frequently contributed to workers' songbooks, one of which, *America Sings,* he edited under the name of "Robert Earl." Robinson, like Siegmeister and others, participated in the quest for classically based proletarian music, eventually becoming an ardent proponent of "folk song" as the people's music. He argued that abstract music, such as that of the Workers Music League, was no longer possible to write. In 1938 he stressed the need for his comrades to affiliate themselves with the labor movement and to write in a genre intelligible to the workers. In discussing the need for labor songs in the folk genre, Robinson frequently was vague about what he meant. On one occasion he described jazz as "the folk music of the city." At other times he regarded IWW parodies as folk songs. His composition "Joe Hill," based on the Alfred Hayes poem, was seen as a folk song or labor song. In yet another interview, with Anita Tilkin, he advocated the use of folk music in the style of Carl Sandburg and Maurice Sugar: "The first thing to do is to push the folk song of the American people and the songs that we have in the progressive movement—to make certain that these songs are *taken up,* that they do not degenerate in the commercialism of present-day life." Robinson's view was representative of folk consciousness in that he was aware of the genre and its origins, yet there was a good deal of confusion in his mind about what constituted folk music per se. Yet folk music for him was still the music of the people and the ideal propaganda tool. These conclusions had little basis in fact.

Another leading spokesman of the folk agitprop school was actor-singer Will Geer, a graduate of the University of Chicago who had attended Columbia and Oxford as a graduate student. Geer's primary historical contribution to the proletarian renaissance was his ability to recruit "raggedy-assed" singers into the so-called radical scene of New York City. In addition to this function, Geer, like the transplanted Garlands, did much to advance folk music as revolutionary propaganda. Geer began his songwriting career in California with such pieces as "The Ballad of Wives and Widows of Presidents and Dictators," "The Song of the Blue Eagle," and "The Ballad of a Mine Hand." Leaving California to appear in such Broadway plays as *Let Freedom Ring* and *Grapes of Wrath,* he continued to use the folk and popular genres for political organizing. In 1935 he taught the striking weavers at Paterson the technique of "ballet"-making. Several years later Geer toured with Tony Kraber, presenting three one-act plays, interspersed with songs, for the Loyalists. In 1939 he returned to Los Angeles to appear in a

Earl Robinson

Lorentz movie and introduced such songs as "The Chamberlain Crawl," "Representative Martin Dies," and "It Can't Happen Here." It was during this stay in Los Angeles that he was introduced to Woody Guthrie by *People's World* columnist Ed Robbin. After his movie assignment Geer returned to New York to appear in *Grapes of Wrath* and influenced Guthrie to join him.

The impact of Robinson and Geer upon the renaissance is illustrated by a number of their productions involving the folk genre. They presented *Cavalcade of American Song*, a program featuring a myriad of American folk singers and folk entrepreneurs. Composed and staffed by performers with many different traditions and approaches, the show may be considered representative of the entire range of what is popularly called folk music. Performers W. C. Handy, the alleged author of "Saint Louis Blues," Josh White, and Leadbelly represented the Negro tradition. Aunt Molly Jackson presented a mixture of traditional southern white ballads and propaganda songs from the Harlan County coal mining campaigns. The Almanac Singers sang organizational and rhetorical ballads from the trade union movement and those dealing with the events of the day. Burl Ives and Tony Kraber manifested the stylistic approach for which Ives subsequently became renowned. Kraber sang his cowboy ditties like "Blood on the Saddle." Also on the bill was the formalistic American People's Chorus, directed by Robinson. In later years Robinson collaborated with Lewis Allen on *The House I Live In* and with Woody Guthrie in staging *It's All Yours*,

Leadbelly

which was presented in 1942. The latter was described as a musical or "a new revue featuring songs for the firing line," that is, songs for the war effort. Performers included the Almanacs, Richard Dyer-Bennett, Leadbelly, and other so-called celebrities in the folk music field.

Nativism, coupled with Marxism and Leninism, was the credo of the folk renaissance. Earl Robinson, a young minstrel in overalls, went around the country singing his compositions. Dropouts from Harvard imitated Leadbelly and Aunt Molly and other genuine articles by dressing in working-class garb and strumming banjoes and guitars. In-ness was hearing "Ballads for Americans" as sung by Paul Robeson on the airwaves. Magically, genuine folk singers became people's troubadours and urban intellectual folk singers became people's artists. In short, anyone reflecting Americanism in a socially significant manner became a spokesman of the people in the revolutionary circles of New York City. The first year of the proletarian renaissance was marked by a series of concerts, skits, benefits, and appearances of folk entrepreneurs or people's artists. The remainder of this miniature revival was to be dominated by the brief existence of the Almanac Singers and by left-wing hootenannies.

On March 13, 1940, Will Geer organized a benefit for rural migrants featuring a host of folk entrepreneurs, including Molly Jackson, Leadbelly, Bess and Alan Lomax, Burl Ives, Woody Guthrie, and a newcomer, Pete Seeger, who described his performance as a "real bust." The concert, according to a review by Woody in *People's World*,

was a success: "We showed 'em where singing started. We showed 'em
how come songs come to be. And we showed 'em something different.
We didn't have no fancy costumes, nor pretty legs, but we showed 'em
old ragged overalls, and cheaper cotton dresses . . . shows [folk
music] can be useful." In a later interview Alan Lomax saw that evening as the beginning of the folk song revival in America. This benefit
was the precursor of many others held for a multitude of causes—the
labor movement, veterans of the Lincoln Battalion, Southern New
Theatre School, Commonwealth College, and Stalinist publications.
One evening was dedicated to Aunt Molly Jackson. One of these ballad
evenings, held on Armistice Day eve, was billed by the *Sunday Worker*
as a "folk expression of anti-war feeling voiced in the songs of the
American people." The reviewer promised the unveiling of an au-
thentic antiwar folk song telling the story of a Negro worker who did
not want to go to war. Similarly, other gatherings were staged for
sharecroppers and the *New Masses*. The latter was a Robinson-Guthrie
revue, *It's All Yours,* and included many of the luminaries of the
renaissance. The social action orientation of these benefits pointed to
a political role for the ballad singer, that of the people's artist.

Elizabeth Gurley Flynn, while the "Rebel Girl" of the Industrial
Workers of the World, wrote of an imprisoned Joe Hill, "He has
crystallised the organization's spirit into imperishable forms, *songs of
the people—folk songs.*" Flynn's statement was unconsciously prophetic,
since it captured the entire ethos of the proletarian renaissance and
later People's Songs and People's Artists. Mike Quin, in praising a
radio appearance by Woody Guthrie, delineated the notion of a
people's artist: "Sing it Woody, sing it! Karl Marx wrote it, and
Lincoln said it, and Lenin did it." One such artist defined this trend as
a rejection of foreign and classic influences in music as elevating "a
worker serving the working class." The title "people's artist" would for
nearly two decades predominate in the performance of folk music in the
urban milieu and provide role expectations for the isolated folk
entrepreneur.

The social trends described in the last two chapters validated
Flynn's statement, "songs of the people—folk songs," and Larkin's pre-
diction that ballads would become *the* musical fare. Ballads did become
the music of the Stalinist orbit. Ten years from the time Ella May
Wiggins stood on a flatbed truck in Gastonia, the Stalinists found their
"Communist Joe Hill" in an Okie balladeer, Woody Guthrie, and in
the Almanac Singers.

The development of folk consciousness in party circles was fundamentally the idealization of one musical model. The European Eislerian chorus movement was replaced by rural songs of the "people." This change, as we have seen, was predicated upon the elements of folk consciousness, ideology, tactics, and the transfer of technique. The Popular Front period redirected the musical attention of the Communist party. Nearly any musical piece which echoed some American tradition became proletarian. The nativistic ethic found in Gold, Steinbeck, and the work of the Lomaxes further enhanced the prestige of ballads. One CPUSA publication labeled balladeers as "Grapes of Wrath Folks"; singers became spokesmen for the "people," a label which was legally incorporated following World War II.

The Communists' rejection of European propaganda songs in favor of "people's songs" was merely a changeover from one esoteric form to another. They, of course, were unaware of this fallacious action. Aunt Molly Jackson's songs were no better known by industrial workers than Eisler's works. Folk music, while American, was as foreign to those the Stalinists wished to mobilize as were the overly intellectual products of the music leagues. While change in musical forms took place, the isolation of the party remained virtually the same, especially with the signing of the Stalin-Hitler pact.

4

The Almanac
Singers

The formation of the Almanac Singers marked the first organizational attempt to put folk consciousness into practice. The Almanacs
both represented themselves as, and were lauded by their supporters as,
the culmination of the so-called folk tradition or folk memory of the
people. On one occasion an Almanac expressed this ethos: ". . . we got
our stuff from the people themselves, that's where the best music and
poetry can be found." Furthermore, they described their material as
being written "every day in places like the Ford picket line—the Har-
vester strike—Harlan County and other similar historical scenes." For
the political cosmopolitan the Almanacs epitomized proletarian culture.
They were great favorites in New York radical circles. Stalinist reviewers described them as musical illiterates who mirrored the music
of the people. A *Daily Worker* writer pictured the Almanacs as singing
"with a spontaneity of feeling that is so often lacking in concert artists.
They attended no music school to learn their songs. They did not sit
down in New York and memorize the words and music that they sing.
Rather they went to the four corners of the country talking and working with the people that sing these songs."

Such characterizations of the Almanac Singers continued the
ideological posture enunciated by Earl Robinson and others in the
1930s, namely, that picket-line songs were *ipso facto* folk songs. Perhaps
the Almanacs were stylistically closer to the folk genre than their urban
predecessors, but they were in no sense folk. Nor were they untrained
country musicians or transmitters of folk music. Many of the Almanac

Singers had some university or academic training. Pete Seeger was the son of one of the most prominent ethnomusicologists in the United States. His mother was a concert violinist. Bess Lomax, of course, was the daughter of a distinguished folklorist and the sister of yet another. Other members of the group were such trained writers as Allen Sloane, Millard Lampell, and Lee Hays. The projection of the noble savage image upon the Almanacs was more a reflection of the folk consciousness of the period than of reality.

The image of the Almanacs as transmitters of working-class culture from the four corners of the country was also more a product of ideology than of fact. Most of the original Almanac songs were written in New York City. After June, 1942, some were created in the Detroit office of the Almanacs. The remaining songs came from workers' songbooks or from members of the group, primarily Lee Hays and Woody Guthrie. What the Almanacs were projecting was proletarian or people's culture rather than the actual music of urban working-class people. The labor songs that Almanacs sang and recorded were either written by the group or came from radical southern social movements and were virtually unknown to northern workers, at least until the Singers introduced them. Once again the general public was rarely affected by these "people's artists." Only the displaced Okies in the automobile plants of Detroit could appreciate Carter-family runs in their music.

The Almanacs' infrequent coverage in the non-Communist press was generally negative. At times the singers were portrayed as fifth columnists supporting Moscow. *Time,* even when in accord with the Almanacs' isolationist position, branded the folk singers as an "anonymous Manhattan Communist ensemble." Through folk song the Almanac Singers attempted to aid the Stalinist cause and communicate their world view to the urban proletariat. The history of the Almanac Singers well illustrates the pitfalls of radical consciousness and utopian ideology.

The evolution of the Almanac Singers began in the milieu of revolutionaries, garrets, and pretenders of Greenwich Village. In December, 1940, a Harvard dropout named Pete Seeger joined with former Commonwealth College organizer Lee Hays for an appearance at the Jade Mountain Restaurant for the paltry sum of $2.50. From this inconspicuous beginning the duo would expand in size and write approximately 200 songs on a plethora of subjects, most of which mirrored the political concerns of the Communist movement in America. One or two esoteric songs of the group praised party leaders, but most addressed

Pete Seeger

Courtesy of Manuel Greenhill
Folklore Productions

the structural issues of trade unionism, political machinations in Europe, and the economy. "The Greatest of Them All" was a rare folk-styled poem to Earl Browder:

> *Away out west in Kansas—the center of our land,*
> *The heart of great America, where John Brown made his stand,*
> *Let's tip our hat to Kansas, where prairie breezes call,*
> *For she gave birth to Browder—the greatest of them all. . . .*

But their songs more commonly discussed war and peace and the union movement. The singularity of purpose reflected by the group was an interesting one, considering the diversity of personnel.

Pete Seeger typified the working-class intellectual in the leftist movement. The Great Depression had a tremendous emotional impact upon Seeger. He became aware of social injustice at a very early age. Through his father, then active in the Workers Music League, Pete assimilated the "art is a weapon" ethos. Also by way of his father, Pete was introduced to the folk genre at the Asheville Folk Festival in 1935. At this convocation the young Seeger was converted. Later he recalled, "It was love at first sight." Seeger enrolled in Harvard but left in his sophomore year to get out of the world of books and the "scholargok" of Pitirim A. Sorokin. By the summer of 1939 he was touring the countryside with three other politically committed young people in a 1929 Oldsmobile; they called themselves the Vagabond Puppeteers. Pete's primary function on this tour was to play the banjo and sing. Many of the songs he sang were adaptations of such Populist ballads as "The Farmer Is the Man." The songs, of course, were changed to fit the plight of dairy farmers, the group the Puppeteers were trying to organize. On a Canadian Broadcasting Company program in November, 1967, Seeger discussed his view of art at that time: "When I was an artist I joined Young American Artists and listened to the famous painter Rockwell Kent give a speech saying artists should join the fight against fascism. So it seemed to me natural that music should be a part of this."

In March, 1940, while appearing at a benefit in New York City for migratory workers, Pete met Woody Guthrie. Alan Lomax, for one, has characterized this meeting as the beginning of the "renaissance of American folk song." While this assertion is historically questionable, it is indicative of the importance of the two singers in the milieu of folk consciousness. Following this meeting the two men hitchhiked across the country appearing before assorted trade unions and political action groups. It was during this tour that the concept of the hootenanny was developed.

Upon his return to New York Seeger made the acquaintance of other performers interested in folk material and social change. One of these performers was former labor college instructor and singer Lee Hays. Hays, as noted, came from rural Arkansas, an environment very dissimilar to Seeger's cultured academic New England world. Besides being a labor organizer, Hays was an occasional contributor to the *New Masses,* frequently writing on the value of song as a political weapon. During the formative stages of the Almanacs much of their repertoire, it appears, reflected Hays's southern experiences. For example, he penned "The Ballad of Bob Wood," an Oklahoma Communist who was being tried for syndicalism; the song was one of the first performed by the Singers.

Another member of the original Almanacs was Millard Lampell, a University of West Virginia graduate. Lampell came into the group through the efforts of his roommate Lee Hays. Lampell was predominantly a fiction writer and essayist who had accepted the agitprop position advocated by Mike Gold. Consequently, he was closely attuned to Robinson's stance that music, too, must be a weapon in the class struggle. As a writer Lampell contributed many of the lyrics to the Almanacs' topical and protest songs, such as "The Strange Death of John Doe," "The Ballad of Harry Bridges," and "Talking Union." Upon leaving the Almanacs in the spring of 1942, Lampell collaborated with Earl Robinson in writing a musical tribute to Lincoln, *Lonesome Train.** Like Seeger, Lampell was a working-class intellectual creating proletarian culture for the masses. These three men were the original Almanac Singers.

The first appearance of the Almanac Singers took place at the 1941 National Youth Congress, held in Washington, D.C. According to a partially inaccurate account in the *Daily Worker,* it was at these meetings that "four young men" merged "their talents and energy to form a group since famous as the Almanac Singers." Actually, only three singers performed. The fourth member alluded to was Peter Hawes; he actually joined the trio several months later. What really happened was that Seeger, using the name "Bowers," was invited to the

* This tribute has been under attack by rightists despite its orientation. See William M. Dobriner, *Class in Suburbia* (Englewood Cliffs, N.J.: Prentice-Hall, 1963), p. 114.

meeting to perform. Hays and Lampell accompanied him and joined Seeger in entertaining the assembly. Following this initial appearance the Almanacs began to add various people who literally drifted in and out of the group. In June, 1941, Woody Guthrie was added to the roster and remained in the fold for nearly a year. Besides the afore-mentioned singers there were also eight or more persons who comprised a peripheral second team, which interchanged with the founders and frequently was to be heard on Almanac recordings. Some of the mem-bers of the support team were Pete Hawes and his brother Butch, Gordon Friesen, Agnes "Sis" Cunningham, Arthur Stern, Josh White, Cisco Houston, Brownie McGhee, Sonny Terry, Bess Lomax, and some-time group director Earl Robinson, who took charge of recording ses-sions.

The structure of the folk-singing cultural unit was perhaps best described by Pete Seeger when he termed it an "amorphous group—someone would leave and someone else would join up." The function of the group was Brechtian in that the message was all-important, not the cast or the players. Consequently, the group interchanged per-formers and tried other agitprop devices to communicate its ideological position. For example, shortly after their inception the Almanac Singers and Players presented a short-lived—two performances—labor revue, *Signs of the Times*. This revue primarily employed a vaudeville format, featuring Carol Channing, to dramatize social conditions under capitalism. Seeger, Lampell, and Hays sang folk-styled protest songs in the production.

As the group increased in size, several teams of Almanacs began to appear simultaneously before different audiences. In August, 1941, the *Daily Worker* reported that "at one time in New York three Almanac groups sang at different meetings on the same night." The following year the Almanac Singers had a Detroit branch appearing for the UAW locals at the Ford, Plymouth, Vickers, and Dodge plants. The Michigan group was staffed by Bess Lomax, Butch Hawes, Charley Polachek, and Arthur Stern. Concurrently in New York a skeletal group of Almanacs were appearing sporadically. It is almost impossible to speak of one specific unit of Almanac Singers. Instability and dual appearances reflected the Almanacs' ideological orientation in that personal aggrandizement of group members was kept to a minimum. The collective was to be dominant whenever possible. Individual credits for specific songs were excluded for what Lee Hays has called the "anonymity movement." This practice allowed Woody Guthrie to

The Almanac Singers. Left to right: Woody Guthrie, Millard Lampell, Bess Lomax Hawes, Pete Seeger, Arthur Stern, Agnes "Sis" Cunningham.

claim authorship later for many Almanac songs which were in fact group efforts, such as "Round and Round Hitler's Grave." In part this collective posture underlined the disdain of the group for Tin Pan Alley material and performances where hit songs and star performers predominated. New York audiences were frequently disappointed by the absence of "Pete Bowers" at an Almanac performance. Pete was a great favorite in the Stalinist orbit of New York. Despite the lures of personal glorification, getting the message across and obtaining opportunities to state their political solutions transcended other considerations, as the choice of name indicates.

The Almanacs derived their name from the second most influential book in pre-industrial America, *The Farmer's Almanac*. The name "Almanac Singers" was suggested by a phrase included in a letter written to Pete Seeger from California. Lee Hays recalled, in *People's Songs Bulletin:* "The name was picked out of a stray phrase in a letter from Woody Guthrie, who was writing reams of avuncular advice from the West Coast, and it was a good name which meant whatever anybody thought it meant." Millard Lampell stressed the ideological aspect, in an interview shortly after the formation of the group, by pointing out that the title was chosen on the ground that people in the past had formulated their actions and attitudes on the basis of material contained in the *Daily* or *Farmer's Almanac*. A fellow Almanac elaborated the purpose of the group: ". . . if you want to know what's good for the itch, or unemployment, or Fascism, you have to look in your Almanac. And that's what Almanac stands for."

As the choice of name suggests, the singing group's main function was to create a specific political consciousness. During the nonintervention period the Almanacs defined their goal as being "to write new songs of your own and parodies and poetry, and sing them so loudly that all the warmakers and native fascists and enemies of peace will hear you and tremble in their counting houses . . . remember that a singing army is a winning army." Stalinist reviewers correctly described the cultural unit as functioning to give voice to the grievances of workers; the *Daily Worker* declared: "Whenever men and women gather to protest or voice their struggles—The Almanac Singers have given them a way of doing it that is vital and effective." In an emotional outburst Theodore Dreiser glorified the Almanacs as the engine for a Communist revolution, exclaiming, ". . . if we had six teams like these boys we could save America."

As with all world changers of the time, the Almanacs addressed many of their early efforts to the trade union movement. Most of the best-remembered Almanac songs were directed at unionists. Six months after the inception of the unit they went on a cross-country tour singing for thousands of union members and radicals, telling them to "take it easy, but take it." They appeared before the transport workers in Madison Square Garden in New York City, for the longshoremen in San Francisco, and before other workers and union gatherings. During the summer tour the Almanac Singers traveled 10,000 miles and supposedly reached a million persons, a highly doubtful figure given by Lillian Lowenfels in the *Daily Worker*. This tour, designed to increase labor militancy and class consciousness, illustrated some of the dilemmas of being labor propagandists while not being trade unionists. In San Francisco one longshoremen's union official asked, "What do we need these hillbillies for? We have work to do." At many other union meetings workers did not know the songs the Almanacs characterized as being written every day on picket lines. According to one former member, some unionists resented the hyper-proletarian manner and dress of several of the Almanacs. The Almanacs may have traveled 10,000 miles to radicalize unionists, but their effectiveness as propagandists was limited.

The Almanacs' primary contribution to the labor movement was *Talking Union* (Keynote 304), a collection of six songs, including "Which Side Are You On," "Roll the Union On," "Talking Union," "Union Maid," and "Get Thee behind Me, Satan." Several of these songs were imports from the organizational drives of the South. The rest were written by Hays, Lampell, Seeger, and Guthrie. Guthrie wrote "Union Maid" in March, 1940, while visiting Bob Wood in Oklahoma. Lampell reportedly added the last verse in New York. This album was blared from many sound trucks on picket lines in Detroit and elsewhere. The songs from *Talking Union,* although receiving some attention in trade unions, and even in *Time,* were better known in bohemian and leftist circles than in the ranks of labor.

The Almanac Singers' style of life reflected what Michael Harrington has called "the intellectual poor," that is, a chosen poverty revolving around politics and bohemianism. Originally, Hays, Seeger, and Lampell lived in a Greenwich Village loft appropriately called Almanac Loft. It was here that some of the better Almanac songs, found in *Talking Union* and the *John Doe* album, were written. Following the summer tour the three founders rented a three-story building in the Village. The house was also named after the group. Almanac House was to serve both as a residence and as a creative center for "people's artists," particularly those working in the folk genre. Here the first hootenannies were held. A hootenanny may be defined as a gathering of folk musicians and fans in which a person who is in charge selects certain people to play or sing. The term was coined at a Democratic fund-raising social event held in Seattle in 1940, where Pete Seeger and Woody Guthrie picked it up. At this political rally metal chips labeled "one hoot" were used as currency to purchase food and drinks.

Performers at the early New York "hoots," which charged an admission price of 35 cents, included Seeger, Guthrie, Sarah Ogan, Jim Garland, Aunt Molly Jackson, Bess and Alan Lomax, Tony Kraber, Josh White, Leadbelly, Sonny Terry, Burl Ives, and other members of the Almanacs. These performances comprised the chief source of income for the residents of Almanac House. Many of the artists supplemented the meager proceeds from such basement gatherings by appearing at other meetings, rallies, and what bookings were available. One writer stated, however, that "bookings there were, but the pay was meager." Brownie McGhee told this author, "The best we could get was five dollars a night." The monetary plight of the Almanac Singers stemmed in part from two factors: the defined purpose of the group, which was to communicate ideology, and the lack of interest in their music outside left-wing circles. Elaborating on the second point, Pete Seeger has observed in *Sing Out,* that ". . . except for a few unions, there never was as much singing as some people now suppose. From listening to the *Talking Union* record and reading a couple of novels about the labor struggles of the 30's, one might jump to the conclusion that the United States was full of class-conscious harmonizing in those days. 'Taint true." Ironically, Seeger would be one of those who jumped to conclusions after the war, viewing the trade union movement as a ready vehicle of change and an audience for songs of persuasion.

The description of the socioeconomic status of the Almanac Singers and their cohorts suggests the beginning of the dichotomy of the urban folk music movement. On the one hand, we have those performers who were ideologically isolated from the rest of society. On the other hand, we have those who were becoming integrated into the mainstream of American show business. In more simplified language performers were gradually dividing into those directed toward the political and those oriented toward the commercial. Burl Ives began his slow drift out of the isolated community of the Stalinist Left and got a number of bit parts in New York plays. He progressed to feature roles, climaxed by a singing part in *The Boys from Syracuse,* a highly successful production. He then graduated to the nationally broadcast "Wayfaring Stranger" show on NBC. The program became popular, slowly expanding the audience for folk material to those outside the Left. In contrast, the Almanac Singers were physically struggling to survive in pursuit of their activities; the group grossed $18 to $20 per night and divided it among six to eight individuals.

Audiences for commercial artists like Ives grew while the ideologues continued their "hard travelin'." This condition was a product more of ideological choice than of design. The blacklist had not yet been applied to folk entrepreneurs. To illustrate, Woody could have been as commercially successful as Ives. While on KFVD in Los Angeles Guthrie was the most popular personality on the air. In 1940 he obtained a role on the "Model Tobacco" program for $200 per week; but after a dispute about the type of song he could or could not sing, Woody quit. His withdrawal of services was also due to the producers' insistence that he cease writing for the *Daily Worker.* In contrast to his colleagues Woody occasionally did take jobs that contradicted his principles. However, as he told one Almanac, ". . . he was not a very good Stalinist," a sentiment the party seemed to share. These compromise jobs usually were of short duration. The Almanacs rarely had any such lapses; they did not take employment which conflicted with their value system.

Brand, White, Ives, and Ramsey explain the beginning cleavage in terms of the dupe hypothesis. They suggest that numerous folk entrepreneurs associated with and performed for the Communist party and other groups because these fronts were the only ones interested in their type of music at the time. They argue that the Stalinists provided audiences and employment for folk singers. When other opportunities appeared, these artists turned to more respectable audiences and other media of communication. Burl Ives, Leadbelly, and others are the cases most frequently cited to support this hypothesis. There is some merit in this view. Certainly, radicals were the dominant audience for folk entrepreneurs in the 1930s and 1940s. Nevertheless, to employ such a view as a sweeping generalization, as some writers and political skin-savers have done, is to ignore many historical facts, for example, the participation of several affluent songsters in People's Songs Inc. Here such performers as Tom Glazer and Burl Ives put on two hats, one for their radio audiences and another for People's Songs. More significantly, a number of folk entrepreneurs, particularly the Almanacs, were dedicated to a radical cause and shunned economic rewards in the capitalistic sense. The degree of radical consciousness of the Almanac Singers is best evidenced by their relationship to the stormy events in Europe in 1940 and 1941.

In the opening months of 1939 the American Communist party, along with all leftist groups, opposed fascism throughout the globe. Earl Browder and other party functionaries gave countless speeches denouncing the totalitarian threat from Fascist Italy, Spain, and Nazi Germany. Any suggestion of a Nazi-Soviet rapprochement was dismissed as reactionary thinking. In August, 1939, the von Ribbentrop–Molotov nonaggression pact was signed. This unexpected international realignment prompted the antiwar phase of the CPUSA. In view of the pact, the Soviet government maneuvered to keep the United States out of the troubled European arena. American Stalinists parroted this wish with such slogans as "The Yanks Are Not Comin'" and "Keep America out of the War." The *Daily Worker* serialized Dalton Trumbo's antiwar novel *Johnny Got His Gun*. In the Stalinist press a constant deluge of antiwar propaganda appeared, centering upon numerous "peace" committees that were being formed. American Peace Mobilization (APM) was the major party front. In this effort APM, like most fronts, was a "paper organization." Nevertheless, it was effective in publicizing its cause with such attention-getting devices as a perpetual peace vigil in front of the White House, which Woody Guthrie glorified in his song "Why Do You Stand There in the Rain?":

> *It was raining awful hard on the old Capital yard,*
> *When the young folks gathered at the White House gate.*
> *And the President shook his head and to these young folks said,*
> *"Tell me, why do you stand there in the rain?"*
>
> *"Tell me, why do you stand there in the rain?"* (2)
> *These are strange carryings on on the White House Capital lawn.*
> *Tell me, why do you stand there in the rain?*

The Almanacs actively supported the nonintervention campaign of the Communist party and its front, the APM. They wrote a songbook for APM and recorded a strongly worded antiwar album, *Songs for John Doe*. The contents of the album contained the seeds of controversy, typified by "The Ballad of October 16," described by Howe and Coser as the "ditty that was popular among the Party faithful during the years [*sic*] of the pact." Many of the sentiments expressed in the songs were stated in such a way that little room for retraction was possible. Moreover, these lyrics opened the possibility of hostile responses from pressure groups which could regard the material as insulting and inflammatory. On the other hand, sentiments verbalized in the *John Doe* album were not dissimilar to the violent anti-Roosevelt statements expressed by the political Right, such as the America First Committee.

Selected excerpts from "October 16" appeared on the front pages of several New York dailies when the group was under attack. Another selection receiving wide press coverage was "The Washington Breakdown." Two verses from this song are illustrative:

> *J. P. Morgan is big and plump,*
> *84 inches around the rump,*
> *Around the rump, around the rump,*
> *84 inches around the rump.*

> *Wendell Willkie and Franklin D.,*
> *Seems to me they both agree,*
> *They both agree on killing me.*

Songs for John Doe was issued in the spring of 1941 and contained three ten-inch, 78 rpm records. Selections included "The Strange Death of John Doe," "Washington Breakdown," "C for Conscription," "The Ballad of October 16," "Plow Under," and "Billy Boy." The basic theme of the songs, exhibiting little subtlety, was that the United States should remain out of the European conflict. The songs were topical, not such traditional peace songs as "Down by the Riverside." They were all originals composed by the Almanacs, dealing with such events of the period as the conscription bill and the role of the president. One example, not included in the album, was "Franklin, Oh Franklin":

> *Franklin, Oh Franklin, we don't want to go to war.*
> *Franklin, Oh Franklin, we don't want to go to war.*
> *We want to stay at home.*

> *Franklin, Oh Franklin, sent Harry over the sea.*
> *Franklin, Oh Franklin, sent Harry over the sea.*
> *But Franklin, you can't send me.*

Franklin, Oh Franklin, we once heard you say.
Franklin, Oh Franklin, we once heard you say.
Ill-housed, ill-clothed, ill-fed.

Franklin, Oh Franklin, you rode the New Deal train.
Franklin, Oh Franklin, you rode the New Deal train.
But you've come to the end of the line.

On October 16, 1940, 16,500,000 men between the ages of twenty-one and thirty-five were registered according to the provisions of the Selective Service Training Act, the first peacetime military conscription in the nation's history. Congress passed this act in preparation for possible intervention abroad. The Almanacs composed several tunes to commemorate and protest the "god-damned bill." One of these was "The Ballad of October 16," put to the tune of "Jesse James":

It was on a Saturday night and the moon was shining bright,
They passed the Conscription bill.
And the people they did say for many miles away,
T'was the president and his boys on Capital Hill.

CHORUS:

Oh Franklin Roosevelt told the people how he felt,
We damned near believed what he said.
He said "I hate war and so does Eleanor but
We won't be safe till everybody's dead."

When my poor mother died, I was sitting by her side,
Promising to war I'd never go.
Now I'm wearing khaki jeans and eating army beans,
And I'm told that J. P. Morgan loves me so.

(CHORUS)

I have wandered over this land a roamin' workingman,
No clothes to wear and not much food to eat.
Now the government foots the bill, gives clothes, and feeds
Me swill, and gets me shot and put underground six feet.

(CHORUS)

The song "Billy Boy" is a traditional ballad which many writers have used to impart many ideas, both political and commercial. The Almanac Singers employed it as an antiwar song. Of this version, Henry Davis writes, in the *New Masses*, ". . . one voice invites the other to go to war using such old lures as silver medals, seeing the world, and uniforms girls will fall for. Modern American Billy, however, is a wise boy. He answers back that no desire does he feel to defend Republic Steel." One verse, as sung by Mill Lampell and Josh White, contained the following lyrics:

> *Don't you want to see the world,*
> *   Billy Boy, Billy Boy?*
> *Don't you want to see the world,*
> *   Charmin' Billy?*
> *It wouldn't be much thrill*
> *To die for Dupont in Brazil,*
> *He is a young boy and cannot leave his mother.*

Other writers have used "Billy Boy" to advantage since the above arrangement of this tune.

Another song included in the album was "Plow Under" by Allen Sloane. Based on a traditional folk music artifact, it stresses the use of militarism as a means of economic recovery. One section of the song expresses the idea in this manner:

> *They said our system wouldn't work,*
> *Until we killed the surplus off,*
> *So now they look at us and say . . .*
>
> *Plow the fourth one under, plow under,*
> *Plow under, plow under,*
> *Plow under every fourth American boy.*

The limited number of reviews the album received, mostly in the Communist press, were highly favorable. Typical of these articles was one Stalinist's comment that not enough such songs were released. This writer went on to suggest the need for another such album: ". . . for the second edition the Almanac Singers can fit in a gem like their famous 'Get out and Stay out of War.'" *Time*'s music critic was not nearly so enthusiastic: "Professionally performed with new words to old folk tunes, *John Doe*'s singing scrupulously echoed the mendacious Moscow tune: Franklin Roosevelt is leading an unwilling people into a J. P. Morgan war. . . . Honest U.S. isolationists last week got some help from recorded music that they would rather *not* have received." The same week of the *Time* review *New Masses* offered *Songs for John Doe* at half price with a subscription. Any hope for a second edition of the album at half price disappeared on June 22, 1941, with the German invasion of Russia.

The anti-intervention posture of the group can also be found in the labor songs recorded by the Almanacs prior to Operation Barbarossa. These songs urged organization of the workers and, if needed, walkouts and strikes. "Talking Union" is a projection of this theme in song. The piece was composed in 1941 in New York and advocated action despite the bosses' patriotic ploys:

> *They'll raid your meetings, they'll hit you on the head,*
> *They'll call everyone of you a damned red, unpatriotic,*
> *. . . Japanese spies . . . sabotaging national defense . . .*
> *Take it easy, but take it. . . .*

During this period the CPUSA persisted in its idealized hopes for a labor movement. In fact, as some observers have noted, the party increased and intensified its campaigns in the labor front during the pact interlude. One hypothesis is that the Communists further encouraged militant labor activity in the hope that an intensification of industrial discord would keep to a minimum level the support given the English by the American lend-lease program. One member of the Almanacs, Woody Guthrie, devoted much space to this subject in the *Daily Worker*. According to several members of the Almanac Singers, the invasion of the Soviet Union was very traumatic for the group, still on its summer tour. The Nazi invasion cut the Almanacs' repertoire in half. Antiwar songs were no longer appropriate now that German tanks thundered on Russian soil. There was even some talk of disbanding the unit after the completion of the tour. The first war song was Woody Guthrie's "Reuben James," written in November, 1941. This was the only Almanac song prior to the bombing of Pearl Harbor which deviated from their total silence on the European theater. Similarly, many union songs from June 23 to December 7 were not particularly useful, since strikes would only harm the U.S. effort to aid the Allies. As of this writing the Almanacs' use of labor songs from

July through December is very unclear. Following the bombing of Pearl Harbor and the outbreak of World War II, the Almanacs, however slowly, began to write prowar songs urging the workers to produce at greater rates. The Almanacs' songs began to exhibit a militant patriotism previously absent from their work.

One of the first prowar songs, written by Pete Seeger in February, 1942, was a talking blues entitled "Dear Mister President." In part the lyrics apologized for the sentiments expressed in the *John Doe* album and urged that domestic conflict cease until the War against Fascism was won:

> *Now I hate Hitler and I can tell you why,*
> *He caused lots of good folks to suffer and die.*
> *He's got a way of shoving folks around,*
> *I figure it's time we slapped him down,*
> *Give him a dose of his own medicine . . .*
> *Lead poisoning.*

> *Now Mister President, we haven't always agreed in*
>   *the past I know,*
> *But that ain't all important, now,*
> *What is important is what we got to do,*
> *We got to lick Mr. Hitler, and until we do,*
> *Other things can wait,*
> *In other words, first we got a skunk to skin.*

> *War means overtime and higher prices,*
> *But we're all willing to make sacrifices,*
> *Hell I'd even stop fighting with my mother-in-law,*
> *We need her too, to win the war—old battle axe.*

> *Now Mr. President, you're commander-in-chief,*
>   *of our armed forces, ships and the planes,*
> *And the tanks and horses.*
> *Guess you know best just where I can fight,*
> *All I want is to be situated right . . .*
> *To do the most damage.*

> *So what I want is for you to give me a gun,*
> *And we can hurry up and get the job done.*

The Almanacs wrote a few other war songs—"Countersigns," for example—during the spring of 1942, but they, like most of the Communist movement, did little in the way of writing war songs. Not until nearly a year after the invasion of the Soviet Union did the Communist press take up the issue of war songs.

Samuel Sillen, art and music critic for the *New Masses,* published an appeal for war songs, "Battle in Search of a Hymn," reminiscent of Mike Gold's quest for "people's music." Sillen posed the question, "Why don't we have a good war song?" In very familiar terms he went on to outline the criteria for the type of song needed: "We want songs not corn. Songs that make us burn and hate against the Fascist enemy. Songs that make us cheer the heroism of our armed forces. Songs of dignity and hope and courage. Fighting songs that rouse and rally. Songs that celebrate our great fighting allies." Sillen predictably documented the use of song in the American Revolution and the Civil War. At this point he reintroduced a timeworn theme: "The people are sick and tired of jerks and jeeps and oceanic caresses. Tin Pan Alley: business as usual with a few war angles tossed in." Another writer complained that Earl Robinson's songs were not being published because the music industry "is afraid there's no money in really good war songs." What were needed, argued Sillen, were songs that had the "will to victory in them, the life of the people in them" and "which quickened the heartbeat of the nation."

The July 7 issue of *New Masses* brought several replies to the Sillen exhortation. The first was from Elie Siegmeister, who agreed and added, "We don't need one good war song, we need ten, fifty, a hundred. We need songs for the tankmen and songs for the air corps; songs for the women's army and for the maritime workers, songs about heroes. . . ." Siegmeister offered to compose one such song a week if his schedule permitted. The second response came from Earl Robinson, who stated that the material being recorded by Tin Pan Alley was inferior. For Robinson this type of music did not meet the needs of the people in relation to the war effort. The composer pointed with hope to the work being done by folk entrepreneurs: "Outstanding examples of good war songs which hit the nail on the head are those of the Almanac Singers." He suggested that their songs were not of interest to the music monopolists, better known as Tin Pan Alley. He went on to say, "Our great folk singers of the South and West also are composing songs like Leadbelly's 'Tear Hitler Down' among others." On July 10 the *Daily Worker* published three war songs by the Almanacs,

"The OCD Song," "Gerald K. Bound to Lose the Day," and "Open Up the Western Front." The latter song was described as being written on June 20, 1942, and as being inspired by "the good news that Mr. Molotov and Mr. Churchill were in Washington discussing the opening of a second front." Once again the themes of the 1930s reappear: popular culture is not people's culture and the interests of the Soviet Union come first.

Following the surprise attack upon Pearl Harbor most American propaganda songs were put to such popular idioms as big band swing, sentimental ballads, and, for the rural folk, country and western music. The popular idiom was exemplified by the Andrews Sisters, who belted out "Don't Sit under the Apple Tree" and "Any Bonds Today," which urged citizens to "buy a share of freedom." The country and western field abounded with propaganda songs—"I Spoke to Jefferson at Guadalcanal," "Remember Pearl Harbor," and "Have to Slap That Dirty Little Jap." Hank Snow recorded several maudlin selections such as "There's a Star Spangled Banner Waving Somewhere" and "Mother I Thank You for the Bible You Gave." The first song dealt with the attempts of a cripple to join the war effort. Bob Wills recorded Red Foley's composition "Smoke on the Water," which advocated making Japan into a graveyard on the glorious day of victory. While these songs, especially today, may be considered camp, they were manifestations of the mass culture of the war years. In spite of Sillen's ideologically colored approach to the subject, war songs of any genre were apt to be well received in light of the international crisis. This benefited the Almanac Singers, at least temporarily.

After Pearl Harbor the party called for "Everything for National Unity." Earl Browder promised unconditional support for the war effort. During this United Front period the stock of the Almanac Singers began to rise, however briefly. Woody Guthrie's fictional description of a stormy night in *Bound for Glory* reflects this public acceptance. He described soldiers and sailors gathered around a platform in a bar requesting Woody and Cisco Houston to sing topical war songs, to which the military men responded favorably. The "we" feeling engendered created a greater sense of national solidarity against a common enemy, and a person's ideological set became considerably less important. The Almanacs benefited from this, since they found a larger group of persons accepting their anti-Fascist songs. Some were even willing to hire them.

Norman Corwin of the Columbia Broadcasting System employed the group and other performers on nationwide broadcasts dealing with the war effort. Corwin is frequently described as being the vital force in radio during the forties. He produced many successful radio programs for CBS as well as other networks. During the war's early months he organized such programs as "Labor for Victory," "Green Valley, U.S.A.," and others, employing folk entrepreneurs and folk material very effectively. Corwin used Woody Guthrie and his material to pacify anti-union midwesterners' objections to "Labor for Victory." Woody appeared and sang a number of selections, including "The Farm-Labor Train." George Garrett, in a *New Masses* article, reports that "letters the next week from the farm belt apologised for the former antagonisms." Corwin presented other programs which stressed the need for Negro-white unity, such as a sketch dealing with the folk hero John Henry, the legendary steel driver, starring Paul Robeson. Earl Robinson and poet Langston Hughes wrote a new song specifically for the program titled "We'll Hammer It Out Together." On the last program of the CBS War in Europe series "Round and Round Hitler's Grave" was played. Exposure of the group via radio was massive in terms of audience size, but such engagements were few and infrequent. The Almanac Singers also sang for the Allied Armies overseas, including those on the front lines, over shortwave radio, administered by the Office of War Information (OWI). In addition, several members of the Almanac Singers found time to record an album of songs of the Lincoln Battalion.

Increasing public exposure of the group outside their usually limited audiences, composed generally of unionists, intellectuals, foreign-language groups, bohemians, and leftists, provided new opportunities for the performers. Pete Seeger recalled in *Mainstream,* ". . . once in a while we'd get a radio job. It was as the result of one of these radio jobs ["We, the People"] that an agent working for the William Morris Agency got interested in us." This interest culminated in a successful audition for the group and agreement by the agency to represent them. Gordon Friesen writes in *Broadside* that after years of struggling and hard work the Singers in 1942 were "signed by the William Morris agency for a nationwide tour; signed by Decca Records to record their songs; booked into the Rainbow Room at Rockefeller Center; and hired by a radio network to do a daily show consisting of topical songs they were to write on the happenings of each day."

This description of the success ethos as applied to the Almanac Singers is an interesting but optimistically exaggerated account. An agent from the Morris agency did arrange an audition for the performers at the Rainbow Room. Within the group there was conflict over the advisability of performing in such an environment as a plush nightclub situated in no less than Rockefeller Center. But they nervously agreed. They sang "Round and Round Hitler's Grave," which was greeted very favorably by the management. The next selection was the satirical song "New York City," in which the conflict within the group manifested itself. In the middle of the song Lampell, followed by Woody Guthrie, began improvising verses, one of which attacked the founder of the center, archcapitalist John D. Rockefeller. The management still regarded this as part of the comedy act. After the audition the nightclub operator expressed some interest in hiring the group. He insisted, however, that they wear "Li'l Abner" costumes. "We didn't take too kindly to that suggestion," said one member of the Almanacs afterward. As a consequence the Rainbow Room job did not materialize. This incident reinforced the Almanacs' view that commercial entertainment was not for them and further illustrates their non-show biz orientation, since an acceptance by the Rainbow Room would have tremendously boosted the Almanacs along the road to economic success.

In 1942 under the direction of Earl Robinson the Almanac Singers recorded the album *Dear Mr. President,* advertised as "war songs for Americans." The title of the collection was based on the talking blues piece written by Pete Seeger urging national unity behind the president. The album contained five other songs: "Round and Round Hitler's Grave," "Deliver the Goods," "Belt Line Girl," "Side by Side," and "Reuben James." The basic theme of the album, as one member recalled, was that the people were not going to "let a monster like Hitler get away with his crimes against humanity." Most of the songs were written in the spring of 1942 when Bob Miller published the compositions in sheet-music form. The best known, of course, is "Reuben James," written primarily by Woody and edited by his colleagues. During the war Pete Seeger's production number "Round and Round Hitler's Grave" received the most exposure. One observer has stated that the Columbia Broadcasting System opened and closed the war with the Almanac Singers' rendition of the song. CBS featured it on a program at the time of the U.S. intervention in Europe and on the hour-and-a-half V-E day program. The lyrics were put to music by Woody Guthrie and Millard Lampell to the traditional square-dance tune "Old Joe Clark":

> *Mussolini won't last long,*
> *Tell you the reason why,*
> *We're agonna salt his beef,*
> *And hang it up to dry.*

CHORUS:

> *Hey, round and round Hitler's grave,*
> *Round and round we'll go,*
> *Gonna lay that poor boy down,*
> *He won't get up no more.*

> *Mister Hitler's traveling mighty fast,*
> *But he's on a single track,*
> *He started down that Moscow road,*
> *But now he's coming back.*

The Almanac Singers in New York wrote a number of other songs which fit this pattern, describing the role of the working man and his union in promoting the war effort. Woody Guthrie described these songs: "We made up songs against Hitler and Fascism, homemade and imported. We sang songs about our Allies and made up songs to pay honor and tribute to the story of the trade union workers around the world." Woody, in collaboration with the Almanacs and alone, composed a large number of these songs—"Biggest Thing Man Has Ever Done," "Talking Merchant Marine," "Talking Sailor," "Taking It Easy," and many others. "Taking It Easy," although a patriotic ballad, was objected to by the Office of Civil Defense because it suggested that bomb shelters were an ideal place to make love. The government bureau also objected to the lack of urgency implied by the title. While "Reuben James" and "Hitler's Grave" were the best war songs produced in New York, the Detroit branch of the Almanacs contributed several excellent ones. Most popular was "The UAW-CIO Song" by Butch Hawes. This song reportedly was sung at 125 rallies in the Motor City by a depleted Almanac trio of Sis Cunningham, Charles Polachek, and Arthur Stern. Several verses of the piece are illustrative:

I was standing down on Gratiot Street one day,
When I thought I overheard a soldier say,
"Every tank in my camp carries the UAW stamp,
And I'm UAW, too, I'm proud to say."

CHORUS:

It's the UAW-CIO that makes the Army roll and go,
Turning out the jeeps and tanks, and airplanes every day;
It's the UAW-CIO that makes the Army roll and go,
Puts wheels on the USA.

Most of the Almanacs' songs were of this type, although occasionally a song like "Western Front" was performed. The opening of a second front, of course, primarily benefited the Soviet Union. Both the United States and the United Kingdom opposed Stalin's plan.

The changeover in the attitude of the Almanac Singers toward the war is an excellent illustration of the isolation of utopian ideology. The Almanacs supported nonintervention and the Stalin-Hitler pact until the invasion of the Soviet Union. After June 22, 1941, the singing unit became pro-intervention. This attitudinal change was not reflected in American public opinion. Indeed, prowar sentiment in America hardly changed at all after the invasion of Russia.

The amorphous aggregate of folk consciousness began to disintegrate in the spring of 1942. One member of the group had been expelled for disruptionist tendencies the previous December, and Millard Lampell and Woody Guthrie had drifted away by the summer of 1942. Guthrie became part of a short-lived group, the Headline Singers, with Leadbelly, Sonny Terry, and Brownie McGhee. (In a *Daily Worker* interview Sonny Terry and Brownie McGhee stated that the name of the group was Streamline Singers rather than Headline Singers.) The Almanacs were also cut off from any further advances in the popular media by articles published in New York newspapers. In February, 1942, the *New York Post* devoted a column to the politics of the Almanac Singers and the *World Telegram* followed the lead of its afternoon competition. These papers took the position of Harvard professor Carl Friedrich, whose article in the *Atlantic Monthly* argued that the Almanacs frequently reflected the Moscow line rather than

American folk song.* The accusers argued that the Almanacs had compiled a book of songs for the American Peace Mobilization which contained antiwar ballads attacking the personalities of government leaders. The songbook's foreword was described as urging that it be used
so that ". . . warmakers and native fascists and enemies of peace will
hear you and tremble." Furthermore, the Almanacs had performed at
countless rallies, singing peace and antiwar songs. The essence of the
argument presented by Friedrich, and subsequently by segments of the
New York press, was that the group was a disloyal, Moscow-oriented
fifth column; the *New York Times Herald* declared: ". . . these lads
and lassies who, before Russia went to war against Germany, had nothing but the ugliest things to say about FDR, the Congress and other
things American."

The February attacks by the New York papers were based on the
group's participation in a war morale program. These accounts strongly
objected to the appearance of the Almanacs on the same program with
a message from President Roosevelt, in light of "The Ballad of October
16." One Almanac described the effect of this press coverage: "We were
red-baited in one of the New York papers—the *World Telegram*, I
think—and the agent quit trying to get us any work." Any possibility of
a recording contract was nullified by this newspaper report. As one
participant later stated, ". . . it was the beginning of the end." Another, referring to the Rainbow Room, added, "Well, you don't have
to worry anymore about wearing those gunny sacks." But the New
York papers, which resumed their attack in January, 1943, did not
bring about the demise of the Almanacs. As a functioning unit the
New York Almanacs ceased to exist after the summer of 1942. In June
Arthur Stern took Bess Lomax, Butch Hawes, and Charley Polachek
to Detroit, where they began another branch of the Almanac Singers.
Sis Cunningham stayed in New York to mind affairs, answering correspondence and performing other clerical duties. In the fall of the
same year Sis appeared with Sonny Terry and Brownie McGhee, or

* A different interpretation appeared in *Broadside,* a publication
which specializes in topical songs. Gordon Friesen argued that the Almanacs'
position shift was in keeping with the trend of American public opinion: "As
the Fascist menace further advanced millions of Americans changed their
minds about war participation." This incorrect interpretation appears to be
another example of the historical confusion surrounding the Almanac
Singers.

with Woody and Cisco Houston, as the "Almanacs." According to one folklorist, ". . . this hardly was the old Almanac group, and bookings were infrequent." In December, 1942, Sis Cunningham and her husband, Gordon Friesen, moved to Detroit. Bess Lomax and Butch Hawes returned to Gotham and were married but never performed again as Almanacs.

Despite these facts, in January, 1943, another front-page article appeared which criticized the Singers for their songs of the nonintervention period. One tabloid reiterated that the Singers had gone from peace singers (a reference to *John Doe*) to "war minstrels." The article demanded to know why the Office of War Information had employed or was employing such subversive characters. The following day several other New York dailies, including the august *New York Times,* carried similar articles. The *Times* reported, "The Almanac Singers are no longer thumping out their alleged folk songs for the short wave propaganda system." Press accounts went on to criticize as militantly prolabor the songs performed by the group on OWI programs. Replying to press criticism, the Office of War Information claimed that the agency had made a mistake in hiring the Almanacs. The articles did not name the songs the singers performed over government channels except in the vaguest terms. "One of these songs," noted the *Times,* "dealt with the CIO victory over Henry Ford, and the other with the American Federation of Labor (AFL) in terms reported to be uncomplimentary."

The primary objection to Almanac performances, so far as reports indicate, was that the group was not going along with the drive for national unity, which stressed the cessation of conflict between labor and management. The Communist issue was not paramount, although the *Times Herald* did not neglect to mention this association. According to one former member, the disintegration of the Almanacs was not caused by these articles. Following the attack on Pearl Harbor the need for manpower affected all sectors of American life, including the new folk community. In 1942 and 1943 the Almanacs lost many members to the war effort.

From then on the members of the group went their separate ways. Pete Seeger was drafted into the Army. He is reported to have entertained the troops with numerous Army songs he learned in the area as well as with the traditional and political material he performed as a civilian. Lee Hays was involved in war relief work on the East Coast. Woody Guthrie and Cisco Houston shipped out to sea in the

Merchant Marines, where Woody served as a mess hand for eleven months until he was drafted into the Army toward the end of the war. During this period Guthrie composed a number of songs, including "Talking Merchant Marine" and "Talking Sailor," as well as others which were not recorded and subsequently lost. Mill Lampell went to work for the radio script-writing firm of Hyman Brown. Allen Sloane became a staff writer for *Parade* magazine, and Arthur Stern began teaching a class in art history. Other members of the group also performed in various capacities in aid of the Allied war effort. In short, the war dissipated the previous manpower of the singing aggregate to the point that it ceased to exist as a group. Hence, their demise was caused by the lack of personnel.

The Almanac Singers reflected the events of the "Red decade" and the first formalization of folk consciousness. Bob Claiborne in "Folk Music of the United States" described the group:

> In 1940 all these influences were gathered together by the Almanac Singers. In and around this remarkable group were Lee Hays, once a Sharecroppers Union organizer; Woody Guthrie, folk poet of the "dustbowl" migrants; "Aunt Molly" Jackson, poetess laureate of the Kentucky miners; Elizabeth and Alan Lomax; . . . and more sophisticated musicians and writers like Pete Seeger, Millard Lampell and Earl Robinson. All had in common an active interest in folk music and its inherent democratic values.

One may argue with the above statement and cite other variables, political and ideological, as providing the social glue that kept the group together and Almanac House functioning. On the other hand, the Almanacs were the end product of the rural organizational campaigns and the intellectual political concerns of the 1930s. The function of the group was propaganda, which was not limited to ideology but also had a musical dimension. About propaganda, they advised political songsters to "say the truth as simply as you can and repeat it as many times as it has to be repeated"; and "they're just conversations that you can say over and over without getting tired of it—'til you hammer some single lesson home." The popularization of the folk genre was also important: "We think this is the first time there has ever been an organized attempt of this kind actually to sing the folk songs of America." This function, synthesizing means and ends, limited the ability of the group to a mere reaffirmation of existing ideology. The product of the Almanacs appealed primarily to those in sympathy with the content of their songs and to those who saw folk music as the people's music. *New Masses* reviewer Thomas McGrath saw the Almanacs as "timely and topical and an aid in the class struggle." A short-time associate of the group described them in the following manner: "They were to have a kind of belt-line mechanism—a kind of cultural arm of the party, where the total party function is to associate with labor and protest various things. . . ."

The Almanacs' ability to communicate with those outside the Stalinist sphere was hampered by their musical style as well as by the content. Their messages, as the attacks by the New York press suggest, offended the uncommitted who heard them. Such Stalinists as Theodore Dreiser, however, "could laugh until tears came" at *Songs for John Doe,* especially "The Ballad of October 16." Like the Communist party, the Almanacs rarely could reach the very people they desired to because of the masses' lack of folk consciousness.

An assessment of the Almanac Singers presents difficulties. The major difficulty lies in the selection of a standard of judgment. Are they to be viewed within the framework of their music and their performing abilities or within the framework of their political commitment? Are both variables in operation simultaneously? The Almanac Singers were a direct reflection of the radicalism present in the United States at the time of the group's existence. The Almanacs experienced the style of life of the political radical. Forgoing many possible economic rewards, they were capable of striving for goals they considered to be of greater value. The Rainbow Room incident and its aftermath is an example of this. The style of life begun in part by the American Left, and participated in by the Almanacs, has created an ethos and lore which persist to this day on the east side of New York City as well as in Berkeley, California. This style carries on the way of life of the Left coupled with the bohemian subculture which preceded the isolated community of the Left.

The firing of the Almanacs by the OWI, and the manner in which it was done, might in more stable times be considered a rash action based upon political expediency rather than reason. The group had demonstrated an ability to communicate with certain segments of people where other media were ineffective. Despite this ability one government spokesman is quoted as saying, ". . . they'll jolly well stay canned." The OWI's action was only a prelude to a far more extensive practice with regard to folk entrepreneurs in the private sector of the entertainment business, the blacklist.

The ideology found in the songs of the Almanacs reflected the dominant social concerns of American Stalinists. However, the question about the number of Almanacs who were actually members of the CPUSA has never been satisfactorily answered. Allen Sloane, an associate of the Almanacs, in testifying before the House Un-American Activities Committee, presented the following view during a hearing:

MR. TAVENNER: Do you know of any Communist Party member who collaborated with the Almanac Singers in the composition of their material?

MR. SLOANE: I must say, since I have sworn to tell the truth as I know it, that I do not of my own knowledge know that these people who were Almanac Singers were actually Communist Party members, save myself and young Lampell, and we both used to sing here and there with them . . . if asked to definitely state yes or no if asked if I know they were Communist Party members, *I could not do so.*

Another member stated that there were Communists in the group but the musical goals of the Singers transcended the partisanship of ideology. In discussing the Almanacs, the fact that some of them signed a party card is less important than their commitment to radical consciousness, which cannot be overlooked in their musical material. This ideological commitment, mirroring that of the Stalinists, is the key to understanding the historical role of the Almanacs.

The lack of success of the Almanac Singers can be attributed to a number of factors—the type of material they utilized, the Red baiting of the New York press, the decreasing number of members because of the war effort, and the marginal interest in folk material at the time. The audience for their music, as compared to other forms of art, was not large enough to support various types of folk music entertainers. Only the auto workers can be cited as exceptions to this rule. Certainly the Communist sectarians were not affluent members of society. Other members of the folk music public, such as intellectuals, were not numerous enough to economically support the folk entrepreneurs. The dominant reason for the group's lack of success was their isolation from the values and attitudes of mass man. The Almanacs performed songs which were artistically unassailable but which did not, until the attack on Pearl Harbor, reflect the political goals and ideological values of that nebulous mass commonly referred to as the people. It is significant that only after the war did the popularity of the entertainers briefly transcend their ideological environment.

The contribution of the Almanac Singers to the recent folk music revival is not insignificant. The group provided a form or structure for presenting folk music, i.e., trios, quartets, etc. The Almanacs also furthered the practice of singing propaganda songs in the urban society, and they furnished a training ground for the majority of folk entrepreneurs who performed during the forties and fifties.

5

People's Songs Inc.
and
People's Artists Inc.

"The worst was over," observed one of the founders of People's Songs Inc.; "the future was filled with infinite possibilities and the common man was to be once again enthroned." Following World War II the Communist interest in folk material was revived with a vigor and enthusiasm not seen since the formative days of the Almanac Singers. Folk-styled protest songs once again became an integral part of party life. Guitars and banjoes appeared at nearly every rally and rent party. "The Party member that did not appreciate Pete Seeger," notes David Shannon in *The Decline of American Communism*, "was an independent soul indeed." Hootenannies were reintroduced with many of the familiar names appearing. Veterans of the Almanac House days were joined by Fred Hellerman, Irwin Silber, Betty Sanders, Ernie Lieberman, and others. All helped to rekindle the hopes and dreams of the 1930s by joining together in an organization called People's Songs Inc. (PSI).

During its brief life People's Songs attempted to mobilize trade unionists with song, taught classes on the art of writing "people's songs," and participated in the stormy presidential campaign of Henry Wallace. The efforts of PSI ended in bankruptcy in 1949. People's Artists Inc. (PAI) endeavored to carry on the work of the Almanacs and PSI during the McCarthy era, but they fared no better than their predecessors in mobilizing the urban masses around "progressive" causes or, indeed, folk music. Both "people's" organizations traveled down the same esoteric trail blazed by the Almanac Singers.

99

People's Songs Inc.

On January 2, 1946, A. Olds wrote to the *Daily Worker* urging the resurrection of the Almanac Singers. In the same edition Mike Gold joined in, once again issuing a call for labor songs. This time the "Change the World" columnist held up the Almanacs as a prototype for cultural workers. Gold's quest for a "Communist Joe Hill," it appears, was over. On January 31 People's Songs Inc. was officially incorporated in New York City. The organization described itself as a membership corporation with the goal and purpose of stimulating and developing an understanding and appreciation of worthy American music, songs, and cultural and civic traditions, and of carrying on these objectives in a nonpartisan way. The board of directors and the sponsors were of note, including some of the outstanding musicians and artists in the United States, both in folk music and in other forms of artistic expression. The actual birthdate of the organization was December 31, 1945, one month prior to incorporation, when Pete Seeger collected $155 at a meeting. The meeting was of "30 miscellaneous folk singers, leaders of chorus', union education leaders, and stray interested persons." With the donated money, twenty members, the newly acquired mimeograph equipment contributed by Oscar Brand, which he had purchased while in the Army editing a newspaper for psychiatric patients, and a great number of high hopes and expectations, PSI was founded.

Mike Gold was one of the first to take note of the embryonic corporation. After attending one of the first postwar "hoots," the *Worker* columnist compared the performers—Lee Hays, Pete Seeger, Woody Guthrie, and Eleanor Smith—to Djamboul, the Soviet folk minstrel from Tadzhikistan. In glowing terminology Gold outlined the value of People's Songs Inc. for "America's proletarian future":

> . . . I repeat this "plug" for People's Songs, Inc. not for any advertising reasons, but to hold them up as an example for some of our baffled intellectuals who are now reviving the old, stale problem as to where the line comes between art and politics. The Djambouls never met such a problem. A people's artist sings about the life and deeds and joys and sorrows of the people. If that is politics so much the better. They want to be of service to their people. It is as simple as a song by Lee Hays . . . or the great Djamboul.

People's Songs Inc.'s service to the people was to be in the realm of political and musical education. In this sense PSI was a continuation and expansion of the folk consciousness of the prewar years. As a Communist writer suggested, "They're determined to help organize America against fascism, finishing up the job that wasn't done in the war itself." There were, nevertheless, several structural differences. The Almanac Singers specialized in being stage performers, bringing their songs to trade union and workers' organizations. PSI, as Lee Hays indicates, was to write songs *for* the unions and other groups. "The Almanacs was strictly a performing group and we're [PSI] a songwriting group now, performing on the side." As did the Almanacs, PSI stressed the role of cultural worker rather than individual stature or performing ability. Mike Gold's description of Pete Seeger is illustrative: "He is one of the best banjoists in America—could easily star in any big-name musical outfit, but has his heart set . . . on inspiring his people with freedom's great songs."

One deviation from the anonymity ethos pioneered by the Almanacs was that *People's Songs Bulletin* did give individual credit to songwriters. As in the prewar years, PSI attempted to address its educational efforts to the trade union movement. But the receptivity of friendly unionists to people's songsters had changed. With the advent of the Cold War, utopian consciousness became a political liability. Even the handful of previously friendly organizations turned their backs on "progressives," including songsters. Moreover, the lyrical content of many a PSI product came to be regarded as suspect, making it impossible for folk entrepreneurs to continue on as they had hoped to do.

Perhaps the most significant difference between the Almanac Singers and People's Songs Inc. was their relationship to the Stalinist movement. The Almanacs were intrinsically tied to the party, while PSI was more independent of the Communist movement. In many ways PSI fit the criterion of a political front. That is, it reflected party policy but appeared to operate outside the Stalinist sphere. Some of the members did not hold party cards or, indeed, accept the Marxian view of reality.

The organization's primary base of support was in the postwar Communist orbit. Artists from the group taught classes at Jefferson School. People's Songs contributed songs to their sporadic and short-lived *Daily Worker* column "Timely Tunes." One year a May Day hootenanny was staged to celebrate the international workers' holiday.

Oscar Brand, Fred Hellerman, Sis Cunningham, and other People's Songsters provided the background music for a film based on the May Day parade of 1947. The organization added music and song to many other Communist functions.

The first issue of *People's Songs Bulletin* carried a preamble outlining the goals of the organization:

> The people are on the march and must have songs to sing. Now, in 1946, the truth must *reassert* itself in many singing voices.

> There are thousands of unions, people's organizations, singers and choruses who would gladly use more songs. There are many song writers, amateur and professional, who are writing these songs.

> It is clear that there must be an organization to make and send songs of labor and the American people throughout the land.

Pete Seeger elaborated the propaganda function of People's Songs Inc. to Woody Guthrie as Guthrie reported in the *Sunday Worker:* "To organize all of us that write songs for the labor movement, to put all our collections of songs into one big cabinet, and to send any union local any kind of song, any kind of historical material about any thing they might need, to shoot it out poco pronto, in today out tonight." The political purpose of People's Songs Inc. was to aid labor in its historical mission of class struggle. This would be achieved by providing songs and, if desired, entertainers for the rallies and meetings of the various union and labor-oriented organizations. In order to accomplish their goals, People's Songsters began a number of projects to collect old songs and to write new ones.

PSI assembled a vast library of topical and political songs, ranging from old Wobbly parodies to rousing songs of historical value, from both inside and outside the United States. According to one correspondent, PSI had "a library of 20,000 songs, many unavailable elsewhere." It was one of the largest collections of its kind outside the confines of the Library of Congress and the British Museum. Several noted folklorists such as Alan Lomax and B. A. Botkin were active supporters; therefore the methodology of folklore was not foreign to the group. John Greenway, later to become an eminent folklorist, based a large part of his doctoral thesis on the material contained in the People's Songs library. This folkloristic aspect of PSI has led some contemporary observers, particularly of a liberal political persuasion, to characterize the organization as "basically a folk music club furthering interest in folk music." Folklore scholarship was only incidental to PSI's prime function, that of propagandizing. Pete Seeger, the driving force of the organization, noted that the name of the unit was chosen "to distinguish it from scholarly folklore societies." While the library served a somewhat academic function in that it compiled a vast number of songs, it was put together to aid the people on the march.

To increase the number of protest songs available to unions, People's Songs undertook another educational project, that of teaching classes on the use of music for political action. One of the first such classes was held at the Jefferson School in New York City under the direction of PSI librarian Waldemar Hille. Hille explained the course as operating "to raise the whole level of songbook making, and the whole level of the use of songs as a weapon." Alan Lomax, Lee Hays, Bernie Asbel, Felix Landau, Pete Seeger, and others were scheduled to lecture on the tradition of protest in folk song, the use of music at mass meetings, etc. Once again people's songs were to be written *for* the people. Courses also were given in Boston, Washington, Chicago, and elsewhere to teach and demonstrate the political power of song.

Issues of *People's Songs Bulletin* nearly always exhorted readers to write and send in songs for many campaigns and causes, such as those sponsored by the CIO Political Action Committee (PAC) and allied labor groups. The following excerpt from the May, 1946, issue of the *Bulletin* is a typical urgent appeal: "There is a job for every singer member in putting across election songs, regardless of what his particular talent and interest is. At this moment, the emergency need is for new songs—peppy, singable tunes, and a lot of them for use at meetings, on sound trucks, and for radio shows." The songs written and collected during the first year of PSI's existence were sung at all kinds of labor disputes, union rites, and in the political campaigns of PAC-supported candidates. During this first year members of the organization appeared at many trade union rallies in Paterson, Portsmouth, Pittsburgh, Chicago, and many other large metropolitan areas. Pete Seeger performed for the CIO leadership at the annual convention of the industrial union.

Fortune, a promanagement magazine, even took note of PSI as a potential antibusiness threat. The publication reported that "if the tune is catching it may do more to persuade the public than an armful of press releases." There is little evidence to support this claim. The article continued to disconcert its corporate readership by announcing that People's Songs promised "to deliver red hot up to the minute campaign songs, along with instructions on how to achieve maximum moral and propaganda effect." Lee Hays is quoted by the *Fortune* writer as saying that People's Songs was basically an indication of the involvement of intellectuals in the labor struggle.*

Felix Landau, the executive secretary of PSI, in his first annual report noted the successes of the organization. He pointed to the expansion of the *Bulletin* from a mimeographed six-page magazine to one photo-printed with twelve pages. He went on to say that People's Songs had 2,000 subscribers living in thirty-eight of the forty-eight states. He concluded on a highly optimistic note: "That just about winds up the resume of last years activities. Plans for 1947 include doubling the subscribing membership, publishing songbooks, and issuing records on a People's Songs label, the promotion of people's songs and singers; in short, using every musical means available to bring the democratic message to the American People."

Both Landau's and *Fortune*'s assessment of People's Songs Inc. proved excessive in evaluating the organization's strength and its relationship to the trade unions. Objectively, PSI was in no way comparable to the high-powered public relations agencies of corporate management. On the other hand, People's Songs' interpretation of "self" was equally optimistic, as Woody Guthrie indicated in the *Sunday Worker:*

> The bosses and the monopoly folks own their leather lined offices, pay clerks, pay experts, pay detectives, pay thugs, pay artists to perform their complacent crap, pay investigators to try to keep our [Communist] stuff beat down, and the only earthly way we can buck against all of this pressure is to get all together into one big songwriters and songsingers union, and we will call our union by the name of People's Songs. And if we all stick together, all hell and melted teargasses can't stop us, nor atoms hold us back.

After 1946 PSI's relationship with the trade union movement would begin to sour, thus changing the political goals of the organization.

---

* Entitled "Roll the Union On," it is this article that began the myth of the term "hootenanny." Guthrie claimed that the word was derived from a "legendary queen whose lusty voice stirred the lumberjacks."

As the unions grew increasingly anti-Communist, PSI began to drift into the security of the Stalinist orbit.

In their first year of existence People's Songsters divided their time between the politicization of trade unionists and the popularization of what they considered folk music. This last activity, despite the claims of partisans, took place once again predominantly within the Communist party orbit of New York City. Here popular music was still being rejected on the ground of its contamination by the poisons of capitalism. Pete Seeger no doubt received a favorable response to his *New Masses* article which argued that the "heavy hand of the entertainment monopoly" prevented people's music from reaching the public. Seeger cited a number of folk singers, such as Josh White, who deserved a chance to be heard. As was the case with the Almanac Singers, PSI members hoped to make folk music popular.

Mike Gold repeatedly hailed this effort of People's Songs: ". . . one of the best organizations that is building working class culture in the USA. I mean People's Songs, which is doing much fine work in the field of popular songs." Gold, long an advocate of proletarian culture, saw People's Songs as the vehicle which would fill the air with a "good spirit" and "proletarian satire." Pete Seeger echoed this theme. People's Songs was to expose and make popular folk music in the mass society. Seeger's hypothesis was that popular music was an inferior product. Folk music, according to the banjo picker, was a far superior art form: "I knew it was about time for people to realize how much better folk music was than the stuff they were getting on the radio." Beginning with this assumption from the old Almanac days, Seeger viewed unions as the vehicle which would achieve a transition in popular musical taste.

The purpose of People's Songs was in part to create a singing labor movement. The singing movement would in turn serve as a catalyst for a national folk song revival. Some historical precedent could perhaps be cited as justification for this position. Seeger noted, for example, the Scottish and Czechoslovakian folk revivals, which were coupled with nationalist movements in these countries. The primary goal of People's Songs was a desire to get labor singing and, as they grew in political power and influence, to affect the musical tastes of all America. Seeger, in presenting his argument for the popularization of folk music, acknowledged the isolation of the Almanacs and the esoteric nature of folk material in the urban environment. If the Almanacs had been successful in their mission, it would not have been necessary to expose people to folk material. If folk music was in fact people's music, the need for popularization would not be present. Indeed, another reason for the establishment of People's Songs was to provide an outlet for folk entrepreneurs and their musical products.

The hootenanny proved to be the major vehicle for the dissemination of folk music. The "hoot" was also one of *the* social events in Communist party circles, especially in New York. The first People's Songs hootenanny was held at a private home, with an attendance of about eighty persons. The second was held in an apartment in New York, and a total of 112 supporters attended. The third such performance reached an audience of 300. The audience increase continued when the next affair was held at a high school; the response of the spectators was enthusiastic. One observer wrote, "Everybody stood up because they couldn't sit still." Despite the steady increase reported here, audiences were still very small when compared to other fields of entertainment. Nonetheless, the postwar hoots were considerably larger than those of the Almanac days. Now these musical gatherings were held at such places as guild halls and the clubhouses of fraternal organizations. People's Songs sponsored a series of folk-jazz programs called "The Midnight Special" at New York's Town Hall. PSI also presented other hoots to celebrate various holidays, political events, and personalities. As Irwin Silber's excellent characterization of the hootenanny indicates, it was fundamentally self-supportive and stressed social commitment. The ingredients of a hootenanny, according to Silber, are:

1. Audience participation. Hootenanny audiences come expecting to sing as much as possible. . . .

2. Topicality. Hootenannies have always served as the basis for musical comments on the events of the world. In general, these comments have reflected a "left-of-liberal" political outlook characterized by belief in and support for the trade union movement, world peace and co-existence with the Russians, and an antagonism to such representative political symbols as Senators Bilbo, Taft, and McCarthy.

3. Variety of form. Hootenannies, while based on the folk song tradition, have always included many forms of theatrical and musical expression.

4. New performers. Hootenannies have always featured new and young artists. Many a hootenanny performer has never

appeared before an audience larger than 250 people or so prior to getting up before the microphone.

  5. The audience. The most important quality about hootenannies has been the fact that its audience is composed predominantly of young people—teenagers and college students—who have found that a hootenanny communicates *music, ideas, and a sense of the real America to them.**

As trade union audiences increasingly eluded People's Songsters, the hoot became the most important enterprise of the organization. Moreover, PSI began to play a greater role in party affairs. People's Songs Inc. provided singers for CP rallies. The cultural unit contributed a column to the *Daily Worker* titled "Timely Tunes." Some of the songs which appeared in this column included Woody Guthrie's "Union Maid," Earl Robinson's "May Day Song," Lewis Allen's "No Jim Crow," and "China Must Be Free." One May Day the unit staged a hoot honoring the annual parade in New York City. By the end of 1947 PSI was almost totally dependent upon the sectarian milieu of the CP. Several prominent names by now had drifted out of the organization, including Woody Guthrie, who decided to give up singing to devote his time to writing the novel *Study Butte*.† The overall membership of the group had not expanded as hoped and money was becoming even scarcer. Only the emergence of the Progressive party campaign postponed the inevitable collapse of the group.

People's Songs' major exposure outside the Stalinist milieu was in the Progressive party campaign of 1948. The opening of the Progressive party convention caused many observers to speculate on the absence of the traditional brass band. The appearance of Pete Seeger and other People's Songs partisans provided an explanation. Curtis D. MacDougall writes in *Gideon's Army*, "[Seeger] ended the speculation of reporters as to why the traditional convention band was missing. If there was anything distinctive—and there was—about the New Party

* See Irwin Silber, *Hootenanny at Carnegie Hall,* Folkways Records, FN 2512 (Notes). This record is an excellent example of the way hootenannies are received. One album of a McCarthy-period hoot is available: *Hootenanny Tonight,* Folkways Records, FN 2511.

† It would appear that at about this time Guthrie was not getting along well with the party and its publications. Several of his articles were rejected. A Guthrie piece, "A Minstrel in Tobacco Land," in the *Sunday Worker,* was roundly criticized by John Tisa, in a *Sunday Worker* article, "Unionist Condemns Guthrie's Article." Tisa labeled Guthrie a "prima donna."

convention, it was its music, sung to the accompaniment of banjos and guitars. It was truly a singing convention and the music was folk music." Other students of the Progressive party and the election drive of 1948 have commented on the so-called "folksyness" of the campaign, especially the role played by vice-presidential candidate Glen Taylor. Karl M. Schmidt, in *Henry A. Wallace: Quixotic Crusade*, suggests that folk music was an integral part of the campaign and describes the manifestation of folk consciousness: ". . . rallies and meetings invariably opened with a period of audience participation in both folk and campaign songs. 'The Same Old Merry-Go-Round' and 'Everyone Wants Wallace' were sung coast to coast in third party circles with 'several hundred thousand' song sheets reported sold. . . . Wallace-Taylor rallies always featured the rich baritone voice of Paul Robeson or the banjo and the ballads of young Pete Seeger."

While political parties in America have historically used songs, these ditties generally originated in the popular idiom. "Oh Dolly," "Happy Days Are Here Again," and other presidential ditties have been coupled with such well-known favorites as "The Sidewalks of New York," "Oh Susannah," and "Sweet Betsy from Pike." The use of folk-based material by the Progressives was an innovation paralleling the use of "Harry Simms" by the Communist party in the early 1930s. Thus Wallace's use of songs of persuasion based on folk-styled material was a manifestation of folk consciousness. As one historian, MacDougall, in his *Gideon's Army*, was to comment,

> In no sense of the word could this be considered folk music. It did not grow out of the experiences of the group that was singing it, in relation to the political situation of the time, as had been true of political songs in the 19th century and earlier. In modern times, the Spanish Loyalists and the early CIO pioneers developed some folk music and used it effectively. . . . Some of the best musical brains in New York helped to make that [folklore] of the Progressives professional in quality. . . .

The "best musical brains" in New York were gathered in the People's Songs offices. The organization, like much of the politically oriented Left, supported the Progressive party. People's Songs Inc. volunteered its services, solicited songs from its nationwide membership, and provided artists who appeared at the Philadelphia convention and throughout the unsuccessful presidential campaign of Henry Wallace. Reportedly, People's Songs Inc. received $4,000 for their efforts. This

Henry A. Wallace and Pete Seeger

contribution, it appears, kept a financially shaky PSI functioning a while longer. Pete Seeger, for one, traveled from coast to coast with the presidential candidate and sang folk and topical songs like "Passing Through"; afterward the former vice-president would speak on the issues of the day.

People's Songs composed new lyrics, edited song sheets, and made records, despite a musicians' union recording ban. These "folk-conscious" pieces were put to the music of traditional hymns and songs such as "Great Day," "Jacob's Ladder," "I've Got Sixpence," and the timeworn "Battle Hymn of the Republic," which became "The Battle Hymn of '48." Several verses of the last song are illustrative:

> *From the village, from the city,*
> *   All the nation's voice has roared;*
> *Down the rivers, 'cross the prairies,*
> *   Like a torrent it has poured!*
> *We will march like Gideon's Army,*
> *   We will fight with Gideon's sword,*
> *For the People's March is on!*
>
> *Glory, glory, hallelujah,*
> *Glory, glory, hallelujah,*
> *Glory, glory, hallelujah,*
> *For the People's March is on!*

In November, 1948, the so-called "quixotic crusade" failed to muster even its predicted 5 percent of the vote; PSI had not restored folk music to a position of national importance.

Several months later, on its third anniversary, *People's Songs Bulletin* announced,

> Volume 4, number 1, is the final issue. The national office has been forced to close its doors for lack of funds.
>
> The staff has been instructed to meet all outstanding financial obligations to the best of its ability and to take legal steps necessary to end the functioning of the national organization.
>
> People's Songs was started on a shoestring, and it was a miracle that so much was accomplished on so little. But while many members made loans and gifts and staff members went for weeks without salaries, sooner or later printers and other commercial concerns had to be paid. . . . The American people, along with the people of the rest of the world, have a fight on their hands for peace, democracy and security, and the members of People's Songs, we know will be in the thick of this fight.

The demise of PSI was ostensibly caused by a lack of funds. As one member recalled, "We couldn't raise the (for us) huge sum of $3000 to pay printers and landlords. But the singers and songs carried on." As one knowledgeable observer has noted, PSI would probably have folded much earlier had it not been for the financial support the organization received from Wallace's campaign chest.

People's Artists Inc.

The campaign to popularize people's songs and proletarian ideology was carried on by People's Artists Inc. (PAI). Founded in 1946, this organization was begun by progressive entertainers to accomplish three goals: having professionals manage the less expert; raising the economic return for those involved in cultural work; and, finally, efficiently servicing labor unions, political action groups, and fraternal organizations. In its first three years of existence People's Artists was fundamentally an agitprop booking office handling many kinds of performers, as opposed to PSI, which emphasized the song of persuasion. People's Artists continued and expanded upon the New York hoot, already an institution in left-wing circles.

Another step in the campaign was the revival of the *Bulletin* in a new form, *Sing Out!* The name of the magazine was borrowed by Irwin Silber from a line in "The Hammer Song." Part of the credo of the publication and of People's Artists Inc. was, as described in the first issue:

> We propose to devote ourselves to the creation, growth and distribution of something new, yet not so new, since its beginnings have been visible, or rather audible, for some years now. We call it "People's Music." What is this "People's Music"? In the first place, like all folk music, it has to do with the hopes and fears and lives of common people—of the great majority. In the second place, like that other music . . . it will grow on the base of folk music. We propose that these two hitherto divergent lines of music shall now join in common people and that is what we will call "People's Music." No form—folk song, concert song, dance, symphony, jazz—is alien to it. By one thing above all else will we judge: How well does it serve the common cause of humanity?

Robert Wolfe was the original editor, soon to be replaced by Irwin Silber. Early contributors included Paul Robeson, Howard Fast, Walter Lowenfels, Alan Lomax, Earl Robinson, Waldemar Hille, and Pete Seeger. The magazine's circulation of 500 subscribers was far below that of *People's Songs Bulletin,* and hootenannies once again served to pay impatient printers and the maintenance costs of an East 14th Street loft. While PAI exhibited the same radical consciousness as its predecessors, its difficulties were heightened by the political climate of the time. Many adherents were driven underground by the Smith Act trials and such congressional investigators as Wood and McCarran. Agents from the Federal Bureau of Investigation frequently kept the headquarters of People's Artists under surveillance. Several folk entrepreneurs were asked to become undercover agents for the FBI. An editorial in *Sing Out!* stated, "Now cultural workers are faced with making a choice. They can try to get so small and insignificant that the red-baiters will not see them. For that approach, we have only one question—'How small can you get?' "

In the McCarthy period People's Artists Inc. was even more segregated from the masses than its predecessors. As Josh Dunson, in *Freedom in the Air*, has observed of the 1950s, ". . . the Left [CPUSA] was already being seriously isolated and weakened by McCarthyism and McCarranism, by the hysteria accompanying the Korean War, and to a certain extent by the *tactics of the movement itself*." Hoots, for example, stressed topical songs, particularly Almanac Singers' compositions and songs of the Spanish Civil War, in an era when even liberalism was suspect: ". . . the same sectarian tendencies that plagued the Left movement in the 1950's also influenced *Sing Out!* Early *Sing Outs!* were filled with predominantly topical material of variable quality on the issues of the day: the Santiago Continental Congress of Culture, the Progressive Party campaign of 1952, and the Trenton Six . . . the orientation was one sided because it favored such songs, as well as Spanish Civil War and union songs, over anything else."

Dunson's analysis of People's Artists and *Sing Out!* only partially suggests the isolating trends in the early years. It was almost as if PAI were attempting to return to the days of the Workers Music League and the Eislerian model. The third issue of *Sing Out!* began a lengthy series of monthly columns by Ralph Ditchik, who was teaching a class and workshop at the Metropolitan Music School for trade union, community, and youth organizations. The articles were designed to promote the formation and functioning of choruses; their slogan was "Sing, Perform, Organize." Many Russian, Korean, and Chinese folk songs appeared in the pages of *Sing Out!* Songs reminiscent of Popular Front days commemorated the American Revolution. "The Dying Sergeant" was introduced as follows, placing it in the framework of the Korean conflict: "This ballad was supposedly written by a mortally wounded British soldier during the American Revolution. Of course, it might also be a clever piece of 'American propaganda.' In any event, try it for Washington's birthday and similar patriotic celebrations. Depending on your introduction it could be a mighty topical number."

At the end of its first year of operation *Sing Out!* restated its aims and goals: "We have felt that the true flowering of a people's culture can only come as it reflects and reinforces the desires and struggles of the people. . . . Songs are an expression of the deepest feelings of people. Our magazine should have that quality, and with your help it will." This expression of public acceptance was in vain, since the publication continued to become more musically esoteric and more politically sectarian. Articles appeared praising the Unity Chorus, the St. Louis Neighborhood Folk Chorus, directed by Hille, the Washington Peace Chorus, and the Minnesota-based North Star Singers. Other features also harkened back to the early 1930s. Irwin Silber in "Racism, Chauvinism Keynote US Music" argued against white supremacy in the music industry and raised a question about the efficacy of whites singing Negro material. This position was used to attack the Weavers, who were perceived as being guilty of "white chauvinism." On another occasion the editor of *Sing Out!* denounced Tin Pan Alley for alleged song piracy of a "growing Negro people's cultural movement." The concerns of *Sing Out!* continued to reflect the growing sectarianism of PAI.

With congressional committees moving closer to People's Artists, loyalty and anti–House Un-American Activities Committee (HUAC) sentiments became dominant. Oscar Brand, Burl Ives, Josh White, and others were called stool pigeons and sellouts. One editorial stated, "Josh White didn't get small enough for them [HUAC] until he publically repudiated every decent thing he had ever stood for. Tom Glazer has a sweet smell about him these days because he is busy writing paeans to MacArthur. . . . Didn't you forget Benedict Arnold, Tom?" Editorially, *Sing Out!* railed against congressional summonses and the government's indictment of such Communist party leaders as cultural work director Victor Jerome. In an open letter to readers in June, 1952, People's Artists tacitly admitted its isolation: "For many years People's Artists has been trying to make its work felt outside of New York City. The need to reach the millions of peace-loving Americans throughout the country with our songs is a most urgent one." As a remedy to this isolation the organization requested loans of from $10 to $50 to produce a number of records on the Hootenanny label. Almost as an aside *Sing Out!* announced that it would cease publication for a two-month period.

The magazine resumed in September with a ringing endorsement of Hallinan and Bass, the Progressive party candidates for president and vice-president. As in 1948, PAI provided the entertainment for yet another quixotic crusade. For several months readers were urged to contribute time, money, and songs to the Progressive party. Following the predicted overwhelming defeat of Hallinan at the polls, *Sing Out!* returned to such sectarian issues as the World Youth Festival in Romania, Hungarian youth choirs, criticisms of the Weavers for an "absence of folksongs of social protest," male supremacy and the folk song, and finally the *cause célèbre* of the Left—the defense of alleged atom spies Ethel and Julius Rosenberg. Interspersed with those esoteric accounts were the always-present appeals for money to continue publication. Despite these economic difficulties People's Artists did manage to publish the second people's songbook, *Lift Every Voice,* edited by Silber. Stalinist reviewers hailed the work and the songs as being "of the common people of all lands who are contributing all their strength to humanity's finest cause, peace." Given the constant pleas for support in *Sing Out!* in the fall of 1954, it appeared that few if any of the common people were listening to or singing with People's Artists. Owing to lack of funds the magazine was cut back to the *People's Artists Quarterly.* The solicitations for funds multiplied; congressional subpoenas were handed to a growing number of People's Artists; and the peak circulation enjoyed by *People's Songs Bulletin,* only 2,000 readers, was still not reached.

In 1956 the Communist movement was shattered by Khrushchev's secret speech exposing Stalin. Within the party the Gates-Foster debate arose. Foster, who supported Moscow as the leader of international communism, was victorious, but the victory was a shallow one. Gates and his supporters fled the movement, leaving little hope for reconstruction. The speech and the Hungarian invasion did what the government had failed to do. These events objectively destroyed the American Communist party. On November 2, 1956, Pete Seeger mailed out a form letter announcing the termination of People's Artists Inc.:

> After many months of discussion, the Executive Board of People's Artists has reached a decision to dissolve our organization.
>
> As you can imagine, this was not easy to decide. However, we came to the conclusion that the important function originally served by People's Artists since its inception in 1949 could best be carried forward in new ways. It is a tribute to the groundbreaking work of People's Artists, and its predecessor, People's Songs, that there are today many groups and individuals carrying forward the job of promoting and popularizing folk music.
>
> Our magazine SING OUT! will continue to be published in an expanded form. We plan to use all the resources of People's Artists in a concentrated effort to improve and expand the magazine. . . .

We do face a serious problem, however. At the present time, People's Artists has a number of outstanding financial obligations. These debts total approximately $3,000. Much of it is in the form of personal loans from devoted friends. We would like to pay as large a proportion of these debts as possible before closing for good. . . .

History had once again repeated itself. Like People's Songs Inc., the organization passed away owing $3,000. The one thing that can be stated in favor of People's Artists was that, despite harassment, it outlived both the Almanac Singers and People's Songs. Perhaps the best description of People's Artists was offered by *Daily Worker* writer Joseph Starobin in his characterization of a hootenanny staged in 1953: "It answered the deep need of our time [that] of solidarity."

PSI and PAI exhibited similar political and aesthetic goals. Both organizations failed in their missions, went into debt, and finally disbanded. In a ten-year span the original high hopes of the founders of PSI to create a "people's culture" evolved finally into a posture of self-maintenance or what Starobin tactfully called "solidarity." Overtly, the last major attempt at traditional agitprop had failed due to a lack of acceptance and backing. This scarcity of support, common to most politically militant organizations, apparently was caused by PSI's and PAI's ideology and the resultant social sanctions applied to them.

In July, 1947, Walter S. Steele appeared before HUAC and identified PSI as a Communist front. In the transcript Steele cited half a page of names of individuals in the organization. In a letter to the *Daily Worker* in May, 1948, Pete Seeger and Irwin Silber, officers of PSI, wondered if Congress "will be getting after us." Three weeks later the Quebec government seized and confiscated all copies of the *People's Song Book,* charging subversion. In 1949 the Tenney committee of the California state legislature published a report dealing with PSI:

People's Songs Inc. appears to be directly descended from the Almanac Singers, which prior to World War II published "songs for the workers" (workers as used by Reds is synonymous with Communists) .

People's Songs Inc. is now writing songs and plays, promoting choruses and schools for Communist fronts. Many of its songs have been adopted by left-wing CIO and AFL unions, the Communist Party and its units, American Youth for Democracy, Civil Rights Congress, the International Workers' Order, Congress of American Women, and the Southern Conference for Human Welfare, and other fronts.

The report cited numerous individuals and organizational activities, following the pattern established by the testimony of Walter Steele before the House Un-American Activities Committee. The Tenney committee concluded its description, finding that

> People's Songs is a vital Communist front in the conduct of the strategy and tactics of the Communist Anti-Imperialist War technique of the Seventh Period of Communist strategy in America, and one which has spawned a horde of lesser fronts in the fields of music, stage, entertainment, choral singing, folk dancing, recording, radio transcriptions and similar fields. . . .

> It especially is important to Communist proselytizing and propaganda work because of its emphasis on appeal to youth and because of its organization and technique to provide entertainment for organizations and groups as a smooth opening wedge for Marxist-Leninist-Stalinist propaganda.

Harvey Matusow in a series of headline-provoking HUAC appearances supported this allegation and indicated PSI, the Weavers, and People's Artists Inc. as Communists. His testimony was later retracted, as indicated in his book *False Witness*.

In August, 1949, Paul Robeson was scheduled to give an open-air concert with performers from People's Artists Inc. Pete Seeger was to be one of the featured performers on the program, along with Lee Hays and Woody Guthrie. The outdoor concert was to be for the benefit of the Civil Rights Congress. Members of the American Legion in the Peekskill area and their cohorts mobilized a parade in front of the stage area, blocked traffic, and harassed concert-goers. Howard Fast recalled in *Peekskill USA:* ". . . that whole great mob rolled down upon us, well over a thousand of them now, we began to sing, 'We Shall Not—we shall not be moved. . . .' Many, many times, for as long back as I can remember, I have heard people singing that old hymn, but I never heard it sung as it was sung that night, swelling out over the lunatic mob, over the road and over the hills, full of the deep rich voices of men who fought so well." Because of the riot the original concert was postponed. The commander of the Peekskill Post of the American Legion declared to the *New York Times,* "Our objective was to prevent the Paul Robeson concert and I think our objective was reached."

On the day following the disorder the Westchester Committee for Law and Order was formed and invited Robeson to return to Peekskill. Robeson responded by promising to return the following Sunday, September 4, with his supporters, including folk-singing members of People's Artists. The battle lines were drawn: the superpatriots of upper New York opposing the patrons who came to hear the concert as well as to do battle with the Legionnaires. Warren Moscow described the audience: "The crowd that came to hear Paul Robeson sing or at least make sure that he was allowed to sing was larger and tougher than the crowd that tried to stop him."

On the day of the open-air concert, Howard Fast wrote: ". . . singers and musicians from People's Artists had arrived a little earlier . . . Pete Seeger, Sylvia Kahn, and a number of others [Lee Hays, Woody Guthrie]. . . . They were thrilled by the occasion, the crowd, the sea of human beings. *When had there been a chance to sing to a mass of people as great as this?"* Seeger, Guthrie, and other partisans sang traditional and topical songs of a time, according to Fast, "when treason and hatred and tyranny were not the most admired virtues of America." Robeson followed with a medley of songs ranging from the Loyalist cause to civil rights in America. The mission of giving a Peekskill concert had been accomplished. However, following the musical affair an estimated 48 to 145 persons were hurt or injured as the buses returning to New York City were stoned by the Legionnaires and their supporters. The Robeson aggregation, although the victims of the attack, were criticized for their "we dare you" stance. Pro-Robeson people claimed inadequate police protection, pointing to the fact that the son of the Peekskill chief of police was one of the persons arrested by the New York State Police for overturning automobiles.

The Peekskill riots were of significance to all sectors of the polity. On the Left Schmidt relates that this outbreak was one factor which moved Henry Wallace to leave the Progressive party. For other segments of the body politic the Peekskill affair notified political writers and politicians that "Red baiting" and other actions against leftists were not unthinkable. Five months later the junior senator from Wis-

Paul Robeson at the Peekskill concert

consin began his campaign to "find Communists in high places." On the Right the outdoor conflicts can be interpreted as a public expression of the opening scenario for the McCarthy period. It was in this climate or *Zeitgeist* that People's Artists attempted to carry on.

The failures of PSI and PAI are attributable to a number of factors, all of which are associated with the radical or utopian consciousness of the two organizations. The particularistic belief system and value structure of both groups contributed directly to their downfall. PSI functioned on the assumptions of the 1930s with a theme of "let us continue." These assumptions nearly always conflicted with the common-sense world. People's Artists Inc., seeing a number of avenues of support disappearing, chose to look entirely inward, to the point of abandoning their original purpose while still advocating "progressive" ideology. The radical consciousness of PSI and PAI focused upon two general tenets: (1) a quasi-Marxist idealization of the American proletariat drawn from the 1930s and (2) a view of folk music as people's music and as a political weapon. These two tenets, it is suggested, caused social sanctions to be applied to the organizations and also accounted for their general lack of success.

PSI was founded to provide labor unions and other movements with propaganda songs. This was their first misinterpretation of the common-sense world. As early as 1946 the CIO passed the following resolution: "We the delegates . . . resent and reject efforts of the Communist Party, or other political parties and their adherents to interfere in the affairs of the CIO." Shortly after the passage of this resolution the labor organization began to clean house by expelling unions considered to be Communist-controlled. To avoid expulsion, several unions purged Communists, and several pro-Stalinists overnight became anti-Communist labor leaders. While Seeger and his fellow People's Songsters were eying labor as the major consumer of their songs of persuasion, unionists were already beginning to turn their backs on them. People's Songs' misinterpretation of the American trade union movement was not unique. They, like many other leftists, idealized the union movement as a vehicle for profound social change, when, in fact, it was interested in little more than bread and butter issues. Pete Seeger, in retrospect, has commented, "Most union leaders could not see any connection between music and porkchops. As the cold war deepened in '47 and '48 the split in the labor movement deepened. 'Which Side Are You On' was known in Greenwich Village but not in a single miner's union local."

Seeger's analysis points to yet another difficulty created by the radical consciousness of PSI and PAI, that of folk music as agitprop. Few people outside the organizational milieu of the American Left saw folk songs as proletarian in nature or as a cry for justice. The result of this was that PSI's total membership never exceeded 2,000 nation-wide. A majority of the membership was located in New York City, although Detroit and Los Angeles were also centers of some activity. Like the Almanacs, People's Songs as an organization was virtually un-heard of outside left-wing circles. Several members, such as Burl Ives, were famous but not as political propagandists. The only national exposure the organization received was during the Progressive party convention of 1948. The esoteric roots of PSI's and PAI's ideology in-vited the sanctions applied during the early Cold War years. Such legislative committees as HUAC and the Tenney committee cited PSI as a "Communist front group." These citations did in time hamper the access of the organization to those outside the radical milieu. The efforts of the two agitprop organizations were rejected on the basis not only of their politics but also of their idealization of folk music.

Folklorists generally denounced PSI. The following statement appearing in *Gifthorse* by D. K. Wilgus is illustrative:

> The inconsistencies and sophistries of the "democratic" interpre-tation, the substitution of politics for scholarship and well-meant sympathies for facts, should not lead one to conclude that folk-song is *undemocratic;* but one must recognize that it is *non-political* (in the sense that political considerations cannot rightly influence its definition or interpretation) , even though it may in some cases arise from politics or be used for political purposes. American folksong is not exclusively Republican, Socialist, Pro-hibitionist, Vegetarian, AFL, or CIO; it resists all exclusive labels.

On another occasion the same writer, in discussing PSI, stated, "It is rather unfortunate that some of the questionable activities of this group have been associated with a more serious consideration of the problem" of folk music. For Wilgus PSI's political activities harmed the cause of folk music rather than enhanced the study of the subject.

Other folklorists have objected to the cry for justice orientation and the idealization of the folk. Numerous articles, although not es-pecially directed at People's Songs, have supported this rejection. Richard Dorson, for one, has written in the *Journal of American Folk-*

lore: "By fakelore, I meant the long haired folksingers . . . the writers of invented tales about Paul Bunyan and pseudo heroes, and similar types who have identified folklore with the quaint, the cute, and the folksy. There is no connection whatever between the popularization of this fakelore and the serious cultural study of folklore." Others echoed these arguments, stating that folk singers could only reflect their own urban culture. Consequently, a significant portion of the folklore community was opposed to the relationship of PSI and PAI to folk music. Thus many of those interested in folk music—a natural base of support for PSI—violently opposed the organization.

These factors, which brought about the demise of PSI and PAI, all involved the radical consciousness of the groups. The idealization of labor unions, folk songs, and political trends all reflected the utopian Marxist perspective. The exposition of views outside the common-sense world of the Cold War made social sanctions possible. The actions of legislative committees and several rightist organizations forced both financially ill-equipped groups to devote their limited resources to self-maintenance, leading to total isolation and political failure.

6

The Isolation
of Ideology
and Folk Music

The majority of folk performers and composers who began their careers in the thirties gave many of their performances under radical sponsorship. Burl Ives recalled before the Senate Internal Security Subcommittee, "As a matter of fact, my first audience as a singer was various unions and so-called progressive organizations. At this time I sang for various groups wherever I could get an audience, because nobody would listen to me before, and to have an audience to sing my songs to made me very happy." In a discussion of Leadbelly in *The Leadbelly Songbook,* Pete Seeger reaffirmed the Left's particular interest in folk singers: "We loved him, but I wish we hadn't been his only audience." The reason for this is relatively simple: it was the Stalinists and several Communist-oriented unions that were predominantly interested in folk music during this period. By interacting with Communists and fellow travelers, many of these performers joined their ranks. In this milieu the folk entrepreneur assimilated the values and style of life of the socially isolated New York left-wing scene.

The basic tenet of Karl Mannheim's sociology of knowledge is that ideology is a product of one's political opponent's social position. It is assumed that his viewpoint is false, in keeping with Marx's notion that ideologies not reflecting the profit relations of a social system do not reflect objective conditions. In *Ideology and Utopia: An Introduction to the Sociology of Knowledge,* Mannheim incorporates the notion of false consciousness into his definition of "particularistic ideology": "The particular conception of ideology is implied when the term denotes that we are sceptical of the ideas and representations advanced by our opponent. They are regarded as more or less conscious disguises of the real nature of a situation. . . . These distortions range all the way from conscious lies to half consciousness and unwitting disguises, from calculated attempts to dupe others to self deception." Inherent in this view is the idea that certain social positions give rise to a false consciousness which is political in nature. S. M. Lipset's conceptualization of the "politics of isolation" follows in the Mannheimian tradition. Lipset, in *Political Man: The Social Bases of Politics,* presents the hypothesis that groups with few ties to the social order are most prone to political extremism. William Kornhauser, in *The Politics of Mass Society,* has elaborated the politics of isolation to signify that those "who have the fewest opportunities to participate in the formal and informal life of the community have the weakest commitments to existing institutions." This conceptualization is predicated upon the structural location in society hypothesis, originally suggested by Mannheim but developed by Kerr and Siegel, in an essay in *Industrial Conflict,* to explain the degree of strike-proneness in industry. According to these observers, individuals in remote regions interact only with one another and have little contact with the outside world. Lipset argues that this special segregation allows for the development of ideology which conflicts with the dominant value system and is therefore apt to be politically radical. The syndicalist Industrial Workers of the World, for example, drew much of their support from rural hamlets and the mining and logging company towns of the Northwest.

Social and political isolation is not entirely a physical or geographical phenomenon; many urban groups are also detached from the general value system. As Bittner, Nahirny, and others have noted, social movements which are nonconformist in nature can also be perceived as apart from the common-sense world or total ideology. Daniel Bell, in analyzing the American Communist movement in a study in *Socialism in American Life,* suggested that Stalinists were "perpetual aliens living in hostile territory." The CPUSA was founded and originally supported primarily by immigrants who were socially isolated by both language and ethnicity. In time Stalinist tactics and policy shifts kept the movement from achieving political potency. Irving Howe in one characterization of the American Left appearing in *Dissent* suggests the isolation of political extremism in the New York City of the 1930s: "The Movement was my home and passion . . . while we thought of ourselves as exposed to the coldest winds of the coldest capitalist city . . .

we still lived in a somewhat sheltered world . . . because the Movement had a way of turning in upon itself, becoming detached and self-contained, and finding a security in that isolation, which all its speeches bemoaned."

Membership in the CPUSA, like Lipset's remote communities, involved being "immersed in a movement that permeated almost every aspect of life." An important aspect was the cultural one. Communists preferred Russian movies to the domestic product. People's songs and specific proletarian art forms transcended other styles of art and music. Magazines like the *New Masses, Mainstream,* and others were favored over the Luce publications and other capitalist slicks. Howe and Coser paint the style of life in the 1930s as follows:

> This was a style of life in which Bohemianism combined with quasi-military discipline; a righteous estrangement from the mores of American society with a grotesque mimicry of Bolshevik toughness; a furious effort to break past the barriers of hostility encountered by Communism at almost every point in American life with a solemn and consoling absorption in the rituals of the movement. Throughout these years the party remained a sect, that is, a compact assembly of the chosen, bound together by the faith that in their ideology alone resided Historical Truth; that all those who deviated from their path would soon be tumbling greedily into the arms of the Devil.

Adherents thus lived in an isolated culture with values, tastes, and an orientation in art and literature that differed significantly from mass culture.

Despite this objective fact of isolation Stalinists nearly always labeled their qualitatively esoteric artistic preferences people's art. During the reign of the Composers' Collective European and Soviet songs were considered to be the ditties of the American proletariat, despite the fact that most of them were not written in English. When the party's emphasis became nativistic, the Almanacs, unknown to those outside the left-wing orbit, became "spokesmen of the people." Folk entrepreneurs associated with the Communist party generally shared this radical consciousness. Folk material was seen by Communists as one possible vehicle through which the proletariat could be propagandized. However, folk music, while the genre of the folk, was not the music of the urban working class; they preferred the ditties of

Tin Pan Alley. Nevertheless, the Stalinists' particularistic view of the bourgeois control of the music industry made the use of popular offerings ideologically untenable. The result was that in maintaining ideological purity, the Stalinists refused to adopt the type of music that might have appealed to the urban worker. As Thelma McCormack suggests, in the *Canadian Journal of Economics and Political Science,* it is certain from the jukeboxes in remote hamlets and urban cafés that the enthusiasm of Communists to carry on the folk tradition was not shared by the working class. In an article in *Partisan Review,* André Malraux aptly summed up the essence of the Marxist view of the working class: "Thousands of human beings can be united by faith or by hope in the revolution, but (except in the language of the propagandists) *they are not then masses,* but peers; united often by action, always by what, in their own eyes, *counts more than themselves.*"

The Isolated Folk Entrepreneur

The advancement of the individual or his conversion to a specific group involves a learning process, or what Mannheim, in *Essays on the Sociology of Knowledge,* has termed the concept of fresh contacts. Upon entering a movement, the individual begins accepting its definitions and expectations. As Howard Becker suggests in *The Outsiders,* individuals entering a nonconformist or aberrant subgroup, whether of drug addicts or political radicals, exhibit a career pattern of learning the values and role expectations of the deviant group. A deviant group for Becker is any collectivity not conforming to the rules generally accepted by a majority of people in society.

An examination of the careers of isolated folk entrepreneurs suggests two idealized patterns. The first of these patterns is that of the working-class intellectual. Pete Seeger and other cosmopolitans typify this social role. As we have seen, Seeger came from the Harvard campus to take up the folk genre. In the process of doing this, he very consciously dissociated himself from the entrapments of academe, at one point changing his name to Bowers: "There I was trying my best to shed my Harvard upbringing, scorning to waste money on clothes other than blue jeans. . . . [Leadbelly] didn't need to affect that he was a workingman." The working-class intellectual can ideally be seen as an individual who for aesthetic and/or politico-ideological reasons rejects the urban mass culture to identify with the working class, the people, or the proletariat. Such performers as Earl Robinson and Mill Lampell, as well as Seeger, followed this path into the cult of the noble savage. This pattern was to repeat itself in the folk music clubs of the 1950s and in the coffeehouses of the 1960s, where cosmopolitan collegiates would emulate the dress and mannerisms of folk hero Woody Guthrie.

The other general category of isolated folk entrepreneurs is that of the cultural transplant—individuals who find themselves removed, temporarily or permanently, from their folk cultures of origin and who take up the radical ideology of their new milieu. Performers like Molly Jackson, Jim Garland, Sarah Ogan, Josh White, and Leadbelly are a few examples of this orientation. An illustrative joke in Communist circles during the late 1930s was "You bring the Negro, I'll bring the folk singer." As Lawrence Lipton has contended, a proletarian balladeer was sure to be the center of any social gathering. This type of social acceptance influenced a number of so-called traditional performers to sympathize with, if not accept, their new comrades. In discussing Leadbelly, Sven Eric Molin writes in the *Journal of American Folklore:* ". . . his native wit and his native ear always led him accurately to judge what his audience wanted." Professor Charles Seeger, in describing the New York left-wing music scene, in his essay in *Folklore and Society,* recalls,

> To my personal observation, it took Molly Jackson only a few months [sic] to convert herself, when expedient, from a traditional singer, who seemed never to have given any particular thought to whether anyone liked or disliked her singing, into a shrewd observer of audience reaction, fixing individual listeners one after another with her gaze, smiling ingratiatingly, gesturing, dramatizing her performance. Leadbelly was already an astute handler of the non-folk by the time I met him. Woody Guthrie was another case, almost swamping his native talent in Greenwich Villagese.

Pete Seeger wrote of Leadbelly, "Up north he met a new kind of white people, the enthusiastic young people in the progressive movement [sic] in New York City. . . ."

Many of the rural transplants adopted the values of the political milieu into which they were accepted. Greenway, in introducing the songs of Aunt Molly Jackson, noted that "when Aunt Molly was run out of Kentucky in 1931 she went to New York and learned from more sophisticated people the universality of the truths she had discovered in her own experiences, and these became the themes of her best songs." Refugees from Harlan County and elsewhere provided living models for working-class intellectuals to emulate. Woody Guthrie illustrates a number of aspects of the career pattern of the isolated folk entrepreneur. As one eulogizer, Greenway, wrote, in the *Journal of American Folklore,* "At the end of America's Red Decade he [Woody Guthrie] drifted into New York, drawn by that strange centripetal force that brought together such disparate rebels as Aunt Molly Jackson from the coal mines of Kentucky and Pete Seeger from the classrooms of Harvard. There they hammered folksongs into weapons of subversion."

Woody Guthrie, as most of his varied biographers suggest, was a unique individual. Nonetheless, he typified several "ideal" or recurrent patterns which are generally applicable to isolated folk entrepreneurs. Guthrie was both a cultural transplant and a working-class intellectual. Woody came from the oil fields of Oklahoma imbued with the bitterness of poverty and the Populist tradition of the area. Like many Oklahomans, he went to California, where he made the acquaintance of *People's World* columnist Ed Robbin, who in turn introduced him to actor-singer Will Geer. It was in Los Angeles that Woody became part of the Stalinist scene, although at the time he was more of a fellow traveling minstrel than a party member. On May 12, 1939, he began to write a column for the *People's World* entitled "Woody Sez."

Geer left Los Angeles that year to accept a leading role in the stage version of Steinbeck's *Grapes of Wrath.* At Geer's urging Woody came to New York, where he became an integral part of the proletarian revival. He continued his column for the *People's World* and contributed frequently to the *Daily Worker.* He resumed his cross-country hitchhiking tours, once with the youthful Pete Seeger, and also traveled with the Almanac Singers. Following the war, during which he served in the Merchant Marines, Guthrie participated in People's Songs Inc. until he decided to discontinue song writing in late 1947. By now Huntington's chorea, which would eventually kill him, was becoming apparent. Guthrie's physical deterioration was coupled with a number of bizarre and unfortunate incidents which put him in conflict with family, friends, and law enforcement agencies.

Guthrie, like Aunt Molly Jackson, Sarah Ogan, Jim Garland, Leadbelly, and many others, fled from the privations of rural America and from police confrontations. He found a highly receptive audience among Communists and radicals for his product, the protest song.

Woody, as legend and lore would suggest, was not an illiterate or semi-literate folk poet. As one member of the Almanac Singers stated, Guthrie was a well-read individual. On one occasion, when visiting Bess and Butch Hawes, he corrected the grammar in a paper Butch had written. His book *Bound for Glory* shows little of the folk grammar used in "Woody Sez." As Archie Green has noted, not one Guthrie propaganda song was found among the Okies and Arkies who fled the Dustbowl for California. His political material was well accepted, predominantly by urban radicals and Communists in New York and elsewhere. Guthrie's popularity in Communist circles was generally due to his emphasis upon the Marxian-Steinbeckian glorification of the working class of the time. His columns and many of his songs were marked by a sort of Will Rogers or hillbilly approach to Marxism. Excerpts from several "Woody Sez" columns will illustrate his style: "Until You Workin Folk All Get Together To Beat Wall Street, the Bean will be a subject of popularity." Or "History is a Blow by Blow write up of the Match Between the Money Folks and Workin Folks." In reference to the "Ham and Eggs" movement: "I am a workin on a plan called Bacon and Beans—which we foreclose on the banker, and give the property back to the widow." In terms of politics: "Which way to turn . . . just take the left hand turn in every road, go left and you'll be right, go right and you'll be wrong."

In left-wing jargon Woody was an opportunist, since he frequently used his popularity to further his own aims. An acquaintance of Guthrie's provides the following rhetorical example: "What about the Woody Guthrie that drifted into the office of the American League Against War and Fascism back in the late '30's, in Los Angeles, used up a month's supply of their mimeograph stencils running off a song-book to peddle, left the place looking like a lost cyclone hit it, and got out before the boss got back. . . ." On more than one occasion Guthrie was heard to muse that he wished he was more dedicated to the cause. Reportedly, he submitted membership applications to the Communist party on several occasions and was repeatedly refused. In a 1949 *Daily Worker* piece Guthrie claimed membership in the CPUSA since 1936, but this statement and other inaccuracies in the article suggest otherwise. Guthrie did follow the party line when it suited his personal philosophy, which had many similarities to Stalinist ideology but was a strangely unique hybrid of its own.

Guthrie's assimilation into the New York "hootenanny" scene was similar to that of most performers of the period. Will Geer introduced him to folklorist Alan Lomax. Woody played to the values of the Stalinists and militant trade union audiences, ideals which by and large he shared. He saw folk music as the people's music and art as a weapon against the Rich Folks and the monopoly of Tin Pan Alley.* In several ways Guthrie exemplified some of the career patterns of both types of isolated folk entrepreneurs. He was a rural migrant who directed his material to the "class struggle." He was an intellectual of sorts who divorced himself from the world of books, except perhaps his own. He accepted, when convenient, the values of the Left and used folk music as a weapon in the "Battle Between the Rich Folks and the Workin Folks."

The above discussion can be summarized in these terms: the Left, because of its ideology and other factors which produced a given value system, was socially and ideologically isolated from the values of the dominant society. Individuals coming into the isolated group assimilated the values of the group. The only study in the sociological literature dealing with the careers of folk singers was conducted in the early 1950s in San Francisco and Berkeley. In this work Arlene Kaplan defined folk singing as being juxtaposed to the values and homogenizing practices of mass society. She also found that folk singers were generally isolated and alienated from society and engaged in the symbolic protest of songs of persuasion. In the postwar period the non-political folk-styled song grew in public acceptance while the Communist movement was reduced to a political sect. The isolated folk entrepreneur, however, did not reject the song of persuasion even though some of his colleagues became successful by rejecting political folk consciousness. Those singers who did not were publicly labeled deviants and suffered a number of social sanctions.

The isolated folk entrepreneur of the 1930s and 1940s accepted the tenets of utopian ideology or radical consciousness. He saw his role as that of a world changer and his weapon was the song of persuasion. As we have repeatedly seen, the song of persuasion had little impact because most Americans were unaware of the folk-styled propaganda song. Nevertheless, the messages in the songs of Woody Guthrie or the Almanac Singers did not go unnoticed. Recall the attacks of the New York press on the Almanac Singers' *Songs for John Doe*. The New York

---

* Early in his career he was identified as a Communist before the Dies committee, and in a number of columns and articles Woody attacked the activities of HUAC. Therefore, he was a logical choice to be called before HUAC.

papers did not treat the Almanacs as spokesmen for the American people but, rather, as Moscow-oriented fifth columnists.

During Roosevelt's third term legislative committees of the American Congress began to see isolated folk entrepreneurs as political deviants. As early as 1941 the Dies committee "exposed" Woody Guthrie and Will Geer as Communists: ". . . Guthrie, a Communist, is a guitar-playing ballad-singing entertainer, brought to New York by Will Geer, also a Communist . . . during the past three or four years Woody Guthrie has become one of the outstanding entertainers in the Communist Party, Communist Party fronts and other left-wing organizations. . . ." Three years after this identification the same committee described the Almanac Singers as "Communist entertainers," despite the fact that they were no longer a functioning unit. These citations, while causing some comment in party circles, did little harm to those cited because Communist political activity had been suspended during the war effort. CBS radio continued to play "Round and Round Hitler's Grave."

The Cold War atmosphere in the United States lowered tolerance for divergent political ideologies, and the level of official leeway for dissenters sharply declined. One illustration is provided by Pete Seeger in *Sing Out!:* "The Cold War came along and American labor unions kicked out most of the militants and radicals, the very ones who had always been the enthusiastic singers and song writers." Following the Berlin blockade every aspect of the Stalinist movement became suspect. Folk entrepreneurs were not excepted: during July, 1947, Walter S. Steele appeared before the House Un-American Activities Committee and identified People's Songs Inc. as a "Communist front." Steele cited names, organizations, and the affiliations of these individuals and groups:

> So important have the songs produced by People's Songs Inc. become in Red ranks that the Communist school in Hollywood —People's Education Center, the (Communist) California Labor School in San Francisco . . . have inaugurated classes in the science of agitational song-writing. . . . A special song [by Leadbelly] was written for use at subscription gatherings for the *People's Daily World,* west coast Communist organ.

In his testimony Steele cited half a page of names of individuals in the People's Songs organization.

In 1949 the California Senate's Fact Finding Committee on Un-American Activities reported that the defunct Almanac Singers and People's Songs Inc. were affiliated with the Communist party and were dangerous to American youth. Harvey Matusow, a professional congressional witness, supported this allegation and indicted People's Songs, the Weavers, and People's Artists. Steele's testimony was the sweeping guilt by association type in that he did not directly accuse any specific member of the Almanacs or People's Songs of being associated with the Communist party. Matusow, however, was not so discreet: he rattled off names, dates, and places. The following is an excerpt from his testimony:

MR. TAVENNER: Now, in what manner did the Communist Party use its influence and control of People's Songs?

MR. MATUSOW: The officers whose names I have just read were all members of the Communist Party cell operations in People's Songs, and all officers, that is, full time employees, members of the permanent executive committee, were members of the Communist Party and were instructed to run the organization along party lines.

MR. TAVENNER: Can you give us the names of any other members of the Communist group . . . ?

MR. MATUSOW: Yes. . . .

The witness went on to describe the functions of People's Songs Inc., the manner in which they disbanded, although Matusow claimed they had just changed their name to avoid the committee, and other facts about their activities as he perceived them.

On June 22, 1950, a 213-page book entitled *Red Channels* was issued by the publishers of *Counterattack,* a magazine devoted to zealously "fighting Communism." This book listed the names of 151 entertainers and individuals in the entertainment media "with the alleged Communist-dominant organizations and causes to which they were 'reported as' belonging or having once belonged." The impact of this publication, as Merle Miller notes in *The Judges and the Judged,* was "both immediate and widespread." The basic function of the book was to provide a guide both for employers in the entertainment industry and for the cultural fundamentalists of the Right. Included in it were numerous folk entrepreneurs, for example, Burl Ives and Pete Seeger. Many folk entrepreneurs in the early fifties were affected by the blacklist thus created by the authors of *Red Channels*. For example, when the Weavers appeared in a bistro or theater, the management would receive a copy of *Red Channels* or several issues of *Counterattack* in which the quartet was cited, occasionally with the name of the Weavers, a folk-singing group led by a former Almanac, circled in red ink. At times this technique was successful. To avoid sanctions, as will be seen, several folk entrepreneurs listed in *Red Channels* went before Congress to clear themselves. In the summer of 1951 the Weavers, enjoying their new public acceptance, were signed to appear on a major television program hosted by Dave Garroway. The users of *Red Channels* tried to prevent this, and three days prior to the appearance of the Weavers it was announced that their booking had been canceled. *Counterattack,* although coming out several days after the announced dismissal, claimed explicit credit for the feat.

With increasing numbers of citations and anti-Communist attention given to folk entrepreneurs, it was only a question of time before the committee would call these performers. In the next decade, the fifties, the trek to Washington began. The folk entrepreneurs summoned appeared before two committees, the House Un-American Activities Committee and the Senate Internal Security Subcommittee, chaired by Senator Pat McCarran of Nevada.

The relationship of the House Un-American Activities Committee to the isolated folk entrepreneur and to the entire field of folk music has been one of open conflict. People's Songs Inc. and other groups of singers composed songs directly aimed at the committee, such as "Ballad for Un-American Blues" and "The Investigator's Song." The committee responded with a citation which was based on data from the Tenney committee in California and on previous congressional witnesses who had identified individual folk entrepreneurs and their organizations as Communists or fellow travelers. Not until the height of the McCarthy period did individuals in the folk scene begin to receive invitations to Washington to visit with Senator McCarran and/or the congressmen on the committee. *Sing Out!* responded predictably: "As this issue of *Sing Out!* goes to press, Betty Sanders and Irwin Silber [editor] . . . are preparing to go to Washington in response to subpoenas issued by the House Committee on Un-American Activities."

This was only the beginning. In later years many performers and others associated with the Almanac Singers and People's Songs Inc. would be called. The interaction between the isolated folk entrepreneur and Congress was one of open hostility and conflict. Political songsters adopted a basic "Thou Shalt Not Fink" ethos which strongly discouraged cooperating with the committee. Pete Seeger expressed this ethos to the committee in the following manner: "I am not going to answer any questions as to my associations, my philosophical or religious belief, or how I voted in any election or any of these private affairs. I think these are very improper questions for any American to be asked, especially under such compulsion as this." Betty Sanders and Irwin Silber in a song popular at New York "hoots" lambasted the investigators with "Talking Un-American Blues":

> *Now I like chicken and I like duck,*
> *And I don't object to making a buck;*
> *Well, I ain't got wings and I can't fly,*
> *But there's one bird that I won't buy—*
> *Stoolpigeon: I'm strictly in the market for doves of peace.*

Malvina Reynolds in a song dedicated to William Mandel commemorated the "Black Friday" HUAC riot in San Francisco:

> *Were there pigeons in the square,*
> *Billy Boy, Billy Boy,*
> *Were there pigeons in the square,*
> *Charming Billy,*
> *There were pigeons in the square*
> *And stool pigeons on the air,*
> *And they fouled up the City Hall rotunda.*

In brief, the individuals we have described as isolated folk entrepreneurs had little regard for HUAC, especially after many of their required appearances before the legislative branch of the American government in the fifties. Cooperation with the committee was not the thing to do.

An examination of the testimony of folk entrepreneurs indicates that a majority of those called before congressional investigating com-

Irwin Silber before the House Un-American Activities Committee

mittees did not cooperate. Most invoked the Fifth Amendment when questioned about their past and present organizational affiliations. One People's Songster, Bob Claiborne, did admit to having been a member of the Communist party but not for several years. Others who still held party cards or were at one time members remained silent or invoked constitutional amendments, as was their right. Of the uncooperatives appearing before congressional bodies, seven invoked the Fifth Amendment and two the First. The first folk entrepreneur to cite freedom of speech and association, Pete Seeger, appeared before the House Un-American Activities Committee in the late summer of 1955. Seeger refused to answer the questions put by committee counsel and the congressmen on the ground of impropriety. The cooperative witness from the ranks of isolated folk entrepreneurs was a rarity. The radical consciousness of these songsters opposed any *détente* with the committee; those who did cooperate were denounced as traitors.

In October, 1951, Oscar Brand, in part to maintain his "Folk Song Festival" program on the New York airwaves, made a public statement denouncing Communist influences in folk music and charging People's Songs Inc. with censoring his material. The following month *Sing Out!* ran an article entitled "Folk Singer Oscar Brand Joins Witch Hunt Hysteria." The article charged that Brand had joined the ranks of "ex-Communists" and had engaged in Red baiting. The censorship issue was brushed aside:

. . . we can only conclude that Oscar Brand is attacking those groups in the folk music field who have been most subject to red-baiting attacks in recent years, groups like People's Songs and People's Artists. Since Oscar was active with both of these groups it seems strange that there was never any mention of "influential censorship" of his song material at that time. . . . Perhaps the sound of those voices will remind you of a time when YOU were a people's singer, or if that memory is too bitter, an honest man.

In this editorial piece the style of public denunciation became clear. The folk entrepreneur who cooperated with HUAC was a sellout to both ideology and principle. A year after the Brand statement *Sing Out!* issued an editorial dealing with the testimony of Burl Ives before the "witch-hunting McCarran Committee": "Burl Ives is singing a different kind of song these days . . . [he] cooperated with the Committee by acting as informer on former friends and co-workers. The future of Burl Ives should be interesting. We've never seen anyone sing while crawling on his belly before. But maybe Burl Ives will be able to figure it out. It shouldn't be too hard. Nothing's too hard for a stool pigeon—except keeping his integrity."

The defiance of congressional investigators by isolated folk entrepreneurs underlined their basic estrangement from the dominant values of the society. During the 1950s noncooperation with HUAC or the Senate Internal Security Subcommittee was viewed as an admission of subversive and unpatriotic attitudes. Those invoking the First or Fifth Amendments of the Constitution were severely sanctioned. Employment opportunities were denied and lost and occasionally jail sentences were imposed. Despite these consequences the isolated folk entrepreneur, in keeping with his political beliefs, chose to defy his legislative questioners.

The uncooperative testimony of ideologically oriented folk entrepreneurs was based on a radical consciousness. Their stance was in line with the particularistic value system they adhered to, despite the fact that pleading the First or Fifth Amendment effectively barred them from any significant media exposure. Illustratively, Pete Seeger was barred from American television until the fall of 1967, when the Smothers Brothers had him on their ill-fated show. Despite these costs isolated folk entrepreneurs chose to remain loyal to the radical consciousness of the period.

The Weavers. Left to right: Erik Darling, Bernie Krause, Ronnie Gilbert, Fred Hellerman, Lee Hays, Pete Seeger, Frank Hamilton.

Courtesy of Vanguard Records

The Integrated Folk Entrepreneur

During the "Red decade" the primary patrons of folk-styled material in the urban enclave were Communists and their supporters in the trade union movement. After the war the popularity of the folk genre increased. This achievement is due, as Brand notes, to the "unorganized efforts of many individuals, groups, and political movements." The American public was at least aware of this form of music after the war and "familiarity is part of the key to popularity." One evidence of this increase in interest was found at municipally owned radio station WNYC, which offered the "Folk Song Festival" program after World War II. On this show Oscar Brand featured a group called the "no-name" quartet and offered a prize to anyone who could produce a name. The quartet later called itself the Weavers. Comprised of former People's Songsters, the Weavers were signed by Decca Records. So began a minor foray of the isolated folk entrepreneur into the commercial field. Pete Seeger explained this new posture for himself and his fellow Weavers in *Sing Out!:* "I started doing some hard rethinking about my own work. Here I'd been knocking myself all these years, congratulating myself on not 'going commercial' and the result was that I was not . . . much use to the Brooklyn ALP [American Labor party]. . . ."

The Weavers existed for a relatively brief period of time. Organized in 1949 after the demise of People's Songs Inc., they performed as a group until the end of 1952. During their original existence as a group they appeared on national radio and television programs and sang in leading nightclubs and theaters throughout the country. It has been estimated that "1952 sales of their recordings exceeded 4,000,000 copies." The Weavers were a commercial success after many years of isolation. This success, according to *Time,* "made them the most widely imitated group in the Business." During this period the individual folk entrepreneur (Belafonte, for example) also rose in popularity in the commercial field. What distinguished the Weavers and Belafonte from People's Songs Inc. and the Almanac Singers was the lack of ideological or political content in their music. The Weavers did record several songs of persuasion for the esoteric, protest-oriented Hootenanny label under the name of the lead singer, usually Pete Seeger. Their commercial Decca recordings were not at all ideological or, indeed, particularly folk. The brief success of the Weavers demonstrated that folk music, at least as arranged by Gordon Jenkins, could be popular in

Burl Ives

the mass media as long as radical consciousness was not expressed in the songs. "Hold the Line," a Weaver recording dealing with the Peekskill riots of 1949, was known only in Stalinist circles, whereas their "Goodnight Irene" and "So Long" received a great deal of public exposure. The world of Tin Pan Alley was a far cry from the Almanac days or the People's Songs Inc. milieu. One group of integrated folk entrepreneurs is quoted as saying, "When we fight . . . it's mostly about business—what to invest in."

During the late 1930s and the 1940s integrated folk entrepreneurs like John Jacob Niles occasionally appeared before radical groups. As noted, the American Left was basically the starting point of the urban folk music movement because the only audiences available during that period were generally part of this ideologically isolated community. In the early years the majority of artists who later claimed political innocence sang at rallies for the CIO and for a myriad of Popular Front causes. Appearances of such singers as Dyer-Bennett, Niles, Ives, and others were faithfully advertised in the *Daily Worker*. One of the most overt examples of this type of career pattern is that of Burl Ives.

Ives was not a stranger to the early hoots for Spanish refugees and the *New Masses*. Because of these appearances he received several favorable mentions in the Communist press as "an artist, a real singer of the people." Ives was at best a lukewarm fellow traveler and was never a vital part of the leftist movement in New York City. Woody Guthrie, never at a loss for words, referred to Ives as a "lace panties" singer, deriding his bourgeois orientation. According to Gordon Friesen, the Almanacs were even contemptuous of his singing style. They made up the following ditty about him expressing their attitude:

> *On top of old Smoky,*
> *All covered with snow,*
> *Burl Ives keeps on singing*
> *At forty below.*
>
> *His voice is so folky,*
> *With sobs and with tears,*
> *He's been cashing in on "Old Smoky"*
> *For the past fifteen years.*

Ives was a marginal man who operated in two cultures, that of the professional theater and that of the left-wing community. Originally, the professional theater was the dominant role for the "Wayfaring Stranger." He still occasionally participated in the proletarian renaissance, but he did not accept, in toto, the value structure or ethos. He has testified before Senate Internal Security Subcommittee, "I was asked to join them [the Almanac Singers] a long while ago, but I didn't for the reason that they wrote a song called 'I Hate War and So Does Eleanor' ["Ballad of October 16"] which was against the President and I thought this was in bad taste and didn't agree with it." During this time Ives's career as an actor began to rise. He received a small part in the successful play *The Boys from Syracuse,* which led to his employment in other big shows and eventually to his own radio program, "The Wayfaring Stranger." He was basically one of the first commercial folk entrepreneurs to emerge from the urban radical scene. This is not to convey the impression that, as some authors have suggested, the moment individuals are economically free of the Left, they completely dissociate themselves from the movement. For Ives this was not totally the case until 1950. Ives was one of the sponsors of People's Songs Inc., although he denied having participated in the organization. He also disavowed his support for Henry Wallace's presidential campaign.

During the McCarthy period and the investigations of the entertainment world, several right-wing publications, such as *Red Channels,* began to point to Ives as a subversive. To avoid the blacklist and to preserve his entertainment career, Ives went to the Federal Bureau of Investigation and subsequently appeared before the McCarran committee in the Senate. Ives pleaded the innocent dupe position, stating at one point that the use of his name by a number of Stalinist organizations was "unauthorized." Other evidence of his participation in the proletarian renaissance was treated in a similar manner or with the rationale that the "Wayfaring Stranger" did not know the political ethos involved in other events. The testimony that followed can best be characterized by the following statement: "I am very sorry that I have to bring up names in this manner, because I would like to be able to not mention names, but I can't. I will have to do it, because these people will have to do as I have done, and many others. They will have to make up their minds on this matter. So in my heart, I have to mention these names, although a couple of them are very good friends of mine."

Several other songsters, all associated with the mass media, either renounced the Stalinists in print or appeared voluntarily before congressional committees in closed or open session. Josh White, also in response to a *Red Channels* citation, argued that he had been fooled and misled by the Communists. He began his testimony by stating that an effective exposure of Communist activities in the theatrical and musical fields was long overdue. He continued to guardedly discuss his career as a singer and his participation in left-wing organizations. White stated in *Negro Digest* that many groups he supported were "phony false-faced political rackets, exploiting my eagerness to fight injustice." The blues singer concluded with a statement of allegiance to the American creed and a denunciation of the Communists because "they're my enemies."

These actions were a direct violation of the norms inherent in the isolated community of folk entrepreneurs. *Sing Out!* editorialized, "The well-known folk singer who once joined voices with good men and women in singing 'Solidarity Forever' has a different tune today. It might be called 'Ballad for Stool-pigeons' or the 'Strange Case of the Wayfaring Stranger.'" Ives, as this description indicates, was by this time considered a "fink" and a traitor to the group. First, his value system reflected the strong anticommunism of the time. Second, he turned his back on his friends still in the nonconformist subculture. Third, Ives performed most of his songs for nonpolitical or economic reasons. Finally, asking to testify and then informing on his past associates before a congressional committee totally barred the singer from the new folk community. Ironically, Ives and the others who had pioneered the way for a new ethos in folk music never really profited as would the Kingston Trio in the late 1950s, when the first fruits of their labor appeared in the form of the urban folk revival.

7

Folk Music and the Radical Right

The relationship of the radical Right to political folk singing has been a curious one, as ideologically colored as that to the Left. The radical Right is fundamentally a nativistic movement which stresses traditionalism and superpatriotism. Most studies of this political phenomenon characterize it as a regressive or resistance group formed to hinder progressive social change. Nevertheless, assertions that the Right desires only to go back in time do not refute the fact that their idealization of the past becomes part of their utopian blueprint for the future. Two students of political protest, David L. Westby and Richard G. Braungart, in a paper presented before the American Sociological Association 1967 meetings, have made several observations about "conservative mentality": "The direction or route of change, following general conservative theory, is a *return* to a former state of affairs idealized as a perfect or near perfect condition. . . . The conversion is a total one, involving a complete societal transformation and embracing all conservative principles. Piecemeal efforts and partial reforms are out." This world view closely parallels the millennarian aspects of American Marxist movements. The paramount difference between the Left and the Right, it would appear, is that the latter enjoys a certain respectability because it appeals to the symbolism and rhetoric of American political history.

In two penetrating studies of the roots of the American Right, appearing in the *Western Political Quarterly* and in *Annals,* Victor Ferkiss argues that it is an indigenous growth based on the Populist creed. He observes that opposition to Big Business and Government, nationalism, the conspiratorial view of government, and emphasis on the individual as citizen and entrepreneur are all tied to the agrarian protesters of the 1890s. These principles, however, have dissolved because "the Radical Right appropriated its demogogic nationalism and anti-communism and because its Populist-inspired economic panaceas lost their relevance and appeal as a result of changes in the conditions of American life." Since the advent of the Cold War the radical Right's prime ideological focus has been on the growth of collectivism and individual evil caused by what they consider to be international communism. For the radical Right folk singing has been but one indication of these machinations of the Communist conspiracy.

As we have seen, the Communist party and its supporters used folk material as "people's music" for nearly two decades. The influence of the party in this area was particularly strong in the 1930s and through the 1940s. By the time of the commercial folk music boom the notion that folk entrepreneurs were pawns of the Kremlin was difficult to support. Ironically, as Communist influence in this idiom waned, the attacks from the Right increased. In fact, the absorption of folk music into the mass culture intensified rightist claims of a Bolshevik plot. The attack against folk entrepreneurs as subversives began during the tenure of the Almanac Singers and increased after World War II. The ultimate outcome was the media blacklist and the summoning to Washington of a number of People's Songsters during the 1950s. Encounters between congressional investigators and some folk entrepreneurs would serve as justification for the accusations of the radical Right in the following decade.

In 1963, the peak year of the hootenanny craze, right-wing publications revived the argumentation of the McCarthy period. The first salvo occurred in the context of the Right's concern with elementary school textbooks. One objectionable text was the *Fireside Book of Folk Music,* which was receiving considerable use in the New York school system. The foray upon the text was couched in the rubric "songbooks can subvert." Edith Kermit Roosevelt condemned the *Fireside Book* in *Freedom Press* for including songs which glorified "the U.S.S.R., the Ukrainian communist guerrilla fighters and the Red Chinese Workers." The article also objected to the inclusion of "Hallelujah! I'm a Bum," "Careless Love," and "Every Night When the Sun Goes Down," described as being about illegitimacy. This volley against the *Fireside Book,* while a portent of things to come, was primarily in the context of much larger campaigns to change the schools themselves.

The actual assault upon the commercial folk song revival was launched by the Fire and Police Research Association of Los Angeles (Fi-Po) in August, 1963. In response to the scheduled appearance of Pete Seeger and the Freedom Singers in southern California, Fi-Po issued a manifesto:

> . . . it is becoming more and more evident that certain of the "hootenannies" and other similar youth gatherings and festivals, both in this country and in Europe, have been used to *brainwash and subvert,* in a seemingly innocuous but actually covert and deceptive manner, vast segments of young people's groups, and . . . there is much evidence indicating an accelerated drive in the folk music field is being made on or near the campuses of a number of high schools and colleges by certain individuals of questionable motivation, including members of the Communist conspiracy.

The Fi-Po resolution was the prototype of many to follow. It identified the folk music boom as part of a conspiracy to "enslave and capture youthful minds." This position, one traceable to Plato, is perhaps the foundation of the Right's attack upon folk song and later rock music.

As Winston White notes in his differentiation of right- and left-wing ideology in *Beyond Conformity,* the former view of the world revolves around the "rehabilitation of the individual." A recurrent theme in the literature of the Radical Right is that youth must be saved from their own weakness and from the temptations of evil placed before them. In keeping with this motif, much rightist literature has concentrated upon the demonology thesis, pointing to the susceptibility and gullibility of those exposed to folk music. For example, another section of the Fi-Po resolution reads, "The dialectics of the Communist movement have successfully used, and are now using, all modes and media of communication with young people, including the subtleties and verbal subterfuges of applied dialectics in both poems and songs. . . ."

The Fi-Po resolution generated a considerable tempest, since it was made at the peak of the hootenanny craze. Pete Seeger, at whom the document was primarily directed, held a press conference at the Ash Grove twelve hours after its issuance, calling it "ridiculous . . . the craziest kind of charge I ever heard in my life." Seeger, using his banjo to dramatize several of his answers, went on to reiterate his stance vis-à-vis HUAC and to argue that the Fi-Po statement was part of a John Birch Society plot. This assertion was not too far off the mark, since the Fi-Po organization has joined forces with the Birch Society on a number of occasions, most recently in opposing the candidacy of a black city councilman for the office of mayor of Los Angeles. During the press conference Seeger evaded most of the questions dealing with the alleged Communist influence in folk music. In microcosm this indirect exchange exemplifies the relationship of the radical Right to the folk music revival, as well as the response of People's Songsters to the Right. Both groups sensed a conspiracy being brewed by the other. Each side possessed some grains of truth in its arsenal but ignored many objective facts which might have contravened the major thesis being exhorted. Pete Seeger was surely not the apolitical innocent portrayed in his interview with the Los Angeles press. On the other hand, the Communist party's influence on American folk song in 1963 was infinitesimal, a fact underlined by the junior U.S. senator from New York.

Senator Kenneth Keating took note of the Fi-Po resolution, stating that while folk music did have its roots in social unrest, it was "thoroughly American in spirit." He went on to parody the charge of Communist domination and concluded that the resolution was "but another demonstration of the absurd lengths to which the amateur ferrets of the Radical Right will go in their quixotic sallies against the Communist menace." The House Un-American Activities Committee, to whom the Fi-Po resolution was addressed, duly acknowledged its arrival, thanked the association for its vigilance, and took no action. Gordon Browning, a director of the association, violently attacked Senator Keating for his stand: "To distort our position through verbal gymnastics and mock humor is not fair to hundreds of patriotic artists in this field." He went on to suggest that Keating was under pressure "from certain of the economic and professional areas of this media."

Lawrence Cott, writing in the *Freedom Press* the same month as the Browning rebuttal, presented a lengthy list of HUAC citations to establish Seeger's Communist affiliations. Several campaigns were undertaken on the basis of these charges to prevent Seeger's appearance in several communities. These campaigns were generally unsuccessful, but Seeger did lose a considerable amount of sleep because of the crank calls which plagued his concert tours.

A year after the Fi-Po resolution the John Birch Society alerted its members to the danger of "the Communist folk-song propaganda which has permeated our college campuses." Writing in *American Opinion,* Jere Real, who previously had exposed the arrest record of civil rights leader Bayard Rustin, outlined the congressional records of Pete Seeger and Woody Guthrie. Real's portrayal of Seeger was reprinted nearly verbatim from the Cott article. Having established that some performers were in the Communist orbit, the John Birch Society writer then accused Joan Baez and Bob Dylan of carrying on the Guthrie-Seeger tradition. As the Right was beginning to weave Baez and Dylan into the fabric of a Communist conspiracy, the latter was rapidly falling into disfavor with Old Leftists. In the fall of 1964, as will be seen, *Sing Out!* was generally critical of Dylan for what it called his lack of social concern. But its attacks did not dissuade the radical Right from its belief that folk music was controlled by the CPUSA.

Acting upon this viewpoint, individual members of the Right did occasionally affect the economics of the revival. One of the better-reported examples occurred in the nation's capital, where FBI agents were called in to examine several folk music books." A customer at Campbell's Music Company complained to the manager, who in turn summoned agents from the Federal Bureau of Investigation. The original objection, according to an employee of the store, was to Oak Publications' *We Shall Overcome,* a collection of civil rights songs. The FBI took away three unidentified Oak songbooks and a Pete Seeger guitar instruction album and book set. Several journalists were outraged by the incident, although nothing ever came of it.

In 1965 the Right mounted campaigns to ban a number of popular songs such as "The Eve of Destruction" and the recordings of the Beatles. The Christian Anti-Communist Crusade objected to "The Eve of Destruction" because, according to David A. Noebel's *Rhythm, Riots, and Revolution,* it was "obviously aimed at instilling fear in our teenagers as well as a sense of hopelessness. 'Thermonuclear holocaust,' 'the button,' 'the end of the world' and similar expressions are constantly being used to induce the American public to surrender to atheistic international Communism." This campaign was relatively successful because the American Broadcasting Company and many independent stations bowed to the demands of the Right and refused to air "Eve of Destruction." The Beatles, meanwhile, were another matter. Only stations with large fundamentalist audiences barred the Beatles in retaliation for John Lennon's famous utterance that the group was "more popular than Jesus now!"

Judy Collins

One right-wing group adopted the posture of "if you can't beat them—join them." Dr. Fred Schwarz, leader of the Christian Anti-Communist Crusade, hired a folk performer to sing anti-Communist ballads. Janet Greene, a former children's show hostess in Columbus, Ohio, was introduced as "a new and effective anti-Communist weapon [with] a clear message, a rich voice, wonderful music. Ideal for young people." Unlike her female counterparts—Baez, Collins, and Saint-Marie—Miss Green wore suits or formal dress to rallies. Her hair was short. Her songbag contained several original compositions such as "The Fascist Threat" and "Be Careful of the Commie Lies," put to the tune of "Jimmy Cracked Corn," popularized by Burl Ives. One stanza included ". . . communism is on the rise, and Satan has a new disguise." In another song a line read "I'm just a poor left-winger / Duped by a bearded singer." Ironically, the remainder of her repertoire consisted of old Trotskyist hymns and parodies like "The Old Bolshevik Song," obtained from some "anti-Communist college students in Indiana," according to Dr. Schwarz. At the time of this remark it seemed quite likely that the Marxist origin of "The Old Bolshevik Song" was unknown to either Dr. Schwarz or Miss Greene.

The Christian Anti-Communist Crusade was the only radical Right organization in the urban Northeast to make use of a folk entrepreneur. Southern-based organizations like the Ku Klux Klan and George Wallace's American Independent party used country and western performers to sing the praises of their causes. Marty Robbins, for one, occasionally campaigned with Governor Wallace and recorded such songs as "Ain't I Right" under the pseudonym of Johnny Freedom. Some of these recordings were to be found in John Birch Society bookstores outside the South, but their distribution was limited to those already committed and to occasional browsers.

The most prominent proponent of the Right's thesis of folk song *qua* subversive music was David A. Noebel. Noebel, a protégé of Billy James Hargis, first attracted national attention with his pamphlet *Communism, Hypnotism and the Beatles.* In this booklet Noebel contended that the Beatles were using Pavlovian techniques to prepare American adolescents for a Communist takeover. He cautioned, "Make sure your schools are not using these communist records. Cybernetic warfare is the ultimate weapon and we can't afford one nerve-jammed child! Throw your Beatle and rock and roll records in the city dump . . . let's make sure four mop-headed anti-Christ beatniks don't destroy our children's emotional and mental stability and ultimately destroy our nation. . . ." Following this success Noebel wrote a series of articles for the *Christian Crusader* indicting a host of school districts for their use of Young People's Records. He charged that Young People's Records was owned and distributed by the Communist party. In fact, the originators of the record company did have some left-wing connections, but the company had changed ownership in 1951. By 1965 there were no Communist influences in the record company. However, as in the case of the folk music revival, this change in status did not penetrate the ideological vision of the accusers. Noebel's tour de force was *Rhythm, Riots, and Revolution,* published in 1966. The 352-page book subsumed much of the author's previous work dealing with the corruptive influences of the Beatles and, of course, the *Fireside Book of Folk Music* and Young People's Records. The remainder of the book was a scathing denunciation of the "Communist use of folk and rock music."

Unlike the above accounts, Noebel's work was presented in quasi-historical fashion. He began by indicating that the choice of folk music as a Communist tool was made in the Kremlin: "The Proletarian Musicians Association, meeting in Moscow in 1929, made it explicitly clear that classical music was 'bourgeois' whereas folk music [was] a type of music usable for 'the ultimate victory of the proletariat builders of Communist society.' In 1945–46 the Red conspirators . . . formed a specific corporation dealing with folk music—People's Songs, Inc."

With this initial association apparently established, Noebel went on to cite the participants of People's Songs Inc. and their relationship to the commercial folk music revival. Using a plethora of congressional citations and quotes from *Sing Out!,* the writer made a relatively convincing case. Ironically, his thesis does not reflect the actual relationship of the American Communist party to folk music. For example, he argued that a 1929 edict from Moscow began the Stalinist use of this musical genre. As we have seen, folk music was not seriously considered a cry for justice until the late 1930s. Indeed, the Workers Music League was oriented toward the classics until 1936 and the advent of the hypernationalistic Popular Front era. As in the case of Young People's Records, Noebel took many other historical liberties. Illustratively, anyone cited or mentioned in congressional testimony was considered a Communist regardless of the date of the testimony. This problem is especially acute in the treatment of Pete Seeger, who warranted an entire chapter in the book. In the case of Pete Seeger and the Weavers the use of congressional citations created some factual difficulties. The basis of the identification of Seeger and the Weavers as Communists was Harvey Matusow's recanted testimony. Nearly all radical Right literature, including Noebel, relies upon this citation, despite the fact that Matusow was convicted of perjury for his congressional appearance. Inherent in this process is what historians call the standardization of error: *Red Channels* states that X is a Communist; *National Review, American Opinion,* and the *Christian Crusader* expose X years later, citing the *Channels* citation as evidence.

Noebel's lengthy documentation notwithstanding, *Rhythm, Riots, and Revolution* was only another form of political reaffirmation for believers, because by 1966 the folk song revival was popular music history. His chapter on Pete Seeger, however, would receive considerable use in years to come. For many folkniks Pete Seeger has come to symbolize the folk song. As one appreciative observer labeled him, Pete was "the tuning fork of America." For the radical Right Seeger was the standard-bearer of the Communist conspiracy. Pete had been an Almanac, an officer in People's Songs Inc., and a member of People's Artists. He defied HUAC and became a college circuit favorite. For the Right Seeger was visible and therefore easily attacked. The revival somewhat altered his role as a folk entrepreneur. Despite a media blacklist which still applied to Seeger, Columbia Records signed him to a recording contract. Shortly thereafter he made several appearances on the religious-oriented "Lamp unto My Feet," a CBS-TV program on in the wee hours of Sunday morning. This was Seeger's first network appearance since the caviar days of the Weavers. Although many expected the "Hootenanny" show of ABC to hire the banjo picker, they were to be disappointed. The National Educational Television network finally signed Seeger to do a series of programs, "The Rainbow Quest," which was syndicated to NET affiliates, many of which were owned and operated by universities and academically directed foundations. While "Rainbow Quest" was a breakthrough, it was still a considerable step away from prime-time, commercially sponsored, network television.

On September 12, 1967, after seventeen years of being blacklisted, Pete Seeger appeared on "The Smothers Brothers Comedy Hour." Tommy and Dick Smothers had begun their careers as the Homer and Jethro of folk music. They used folk songs to highlight their comedy routines and were fairly successful on the nightclub and college concert circuit. After one disastrous fling at a situation comedy series, the brothers were hired by CBS to host a summer replacement variety hour in the same time slot as the highly rated "Bonanza" series. To everyone's surprise, the Smothers Brothers program held its own in the ratings against re-runs of the Cartwright family. During the course of the summer series Tommy Smothers decided to invite Pete Seeger to appear on the program, much to the dismay of CBS executives. In what was later to become normative, Smothers and the CBS brass fought and finally compromised. Seeger could appear if his material was not objectionable. The announcement of Seeger's appearance generated a considerable letter-writing campaign, sponsored by the John Birch Society and many other right-wing groups. On this occasion it was to no avail. Seeger did appear on the variety show, but what many considered a victory against the last vestiges of McCarthyism quickly turned into a censorship fight, one of many revolving around the Smothers Brothers program. CBS, Seeger charged, would not allow the final verse of "Waist Deep in the Big Muddy" to be sung on the air. Consequently, the entire number was crapped. He complained that "it is wrong for anyone to censor what I consider my most important statement to date. It's as if the *New York Times* interviewed someone and then left out his most important statement."

"Big Muddy" is a song about a platoon of soldiers which blindly follows its commander into a river where many are drowned. Each verse concludes with the lines "We're waist deep in the Big Muddy and the big fool says to push on." In the fall of 1967 there was little doubt that the Big Muddy symbolized Viet Nam and the "big fool" was Lyndon Johnson. In 1968, with growing anti–Viet Nam war sentiment sweeping the nation, the Smothers Brothers invited Seeger back to the show. Besides such traditional songs as "Liza Jane" and "Living in the Country," this time Seeger did sing "Waist Deep in the Big Muddy" as the finale to a medley of antiwar songs. Pete Seeger's tenure on the blacklist, it appeared, was over. Since the Smothers Brothers show Seeger has appeared on several other prime-time variety programs, such as "Music Scene," where he sang another anti–Viet Nam song, "Bring Them Home." He also has been featured on numerous talk shows like Johnny Carson, Merv Griffin, and David Frost.

By 1967 the radical Right's attacks on Seeger and folk music were violent but lacked the immediacy of the 1963 Fi-Po resolution. Herbert Philbrick, a former FBI informer, did write a half-hearted attack on Seeger but concluded on a unique note: "It would be utterly insane to allege that modern folksinging is one great big Communist plot; or that folksinging is evil or subversive; or that 'all' folksingers are secret Communists, hiding behind the frets of their guitars." David Noebel, not heeding Philbrick's qualifier, returned to indict once again the *Fireside Book of Folk Music* in the *Christian Crusader*. On another occasion he labeled Columbia Records "the home of Marxist Minstrels," pointing to Pete Seeger, Malvina Reynolds, Bob Dylan, Len Chandler, Phil Ochs, and Joan Baez as purveyors of the Communist line. Despite these and other articles, by 1968 the focus of the Right was shifting rapidly to rock music, viewed as an extension of the folk music conspiracy.

Gabriel Almond, analyzing Communist propaganda, in *The Appeals of Communism,* suggests that radical literature exhibits two properties, the exoteric (external) and the esoteric (internal). The literature of the Right manifests these qualities. Real's and Noebel's treatment of contemporary singers invokes the imagery of dirty-unwashed-long-haired hippies. For example, in describing *Sing Out!,* Noebel argued that it extols death, seduction, misplaced love, ban the bomb, revolution, murder, desertion, illicit love, suicide, wife stealing, and parental disobedience, sins most Americans would generally oppose. The concern of the Right about the content of songs and the politics of folk entrepreneurs goes far beyond the common-sense viewpoint and is fundamentally esoteric.

Real sees folk songs as subversive, since they may contain the following messages: the need for peace, glories of the civil rights movement, individuals as victims of capitalism, criticism of so-called patriotic organizations like the American Legion and the Birch Society, and criticism of contemporary America. Moreover, the esoteric nature of the material is most pronounced when the topic of communism in America is approached. As noted, few if any of the articles dealing with folk music cite original data. The paramount source is the House Un-American Activities Committee. Rarely have the *Daily Worker, New Masses,* or *People's Songs Bulletin* been consulted, despite the fact that a great deal of objective evidence of the Communists' relationship to folk music is found in these publications. Due to reliance upon secondary sources much material is missed. For example, while some members of People's Songs Inc. were affiliated with the Communist party, many were not. Similarly, the fact that a person sings folk songs or publishes an article in *Broadside (NYC)* or *Sing Out!* does not make him a Communist. This fact the Right does not acknowledge. Moreover, accusations against the Beatles, Bob Dylan, and other public figures, while supporting the reality of the Right, do not increase its chances of recruiting members or eliciting outside support.

The utopian ideology of the radical Right, when applied to folk music, appears to appeal primarily to the radical consciousness of its constituency rather than to that of the common-sense world of the man on the street. Even in an area where some past Communist influence on folk music can be demonstrated, the Right has ignored this objective effect and constructed a monumental subversive plot. This plot, as described, is one generated by the supportive and complementary literature of the Right. Therefore, from this analysis we may conclude that Bell's view of the Left as ideologically isolated may also be applied to the Right.

While the radical consciousness of neither the Right nor the Left was pertinent to the common-sense world, several distinguishing differences between these world views are noteworthy. One of these differences is the Left's futuristic view of folk material. The Left maintained that folk music was the true genre of the masses. The masses, due to their "false consciousness," were simply not aware of this fact. It therefore became the cultural task of the Almanac Singers, People's Songs Inc., and People's Artists to educate the proletariat. These "cultural guerrillas" labored for many unsuccessful years, burdened with a dialectical vision and ideological orthodoxy.

The radical Right, conversely, looked back in time. The Right's objections to folk singers grew loudest long after the musical genre had been popularized and become part of the homogenized mass media. Beginning with its attack on the Weavers, the Right has been strongly opposed to popular music as having subversive elements, even though the Decca recordings of the group were totally apolitical.* In the 1960s the Right revived its charges of Communist subversion in popular music only when the actual political content of protest songs became nonideological. It appears that the Left was apt to advocate esoteric material as ideal for a mass audience, while the Right saw exoteric fare as fundamentally esoteric and not fit for popular consumption.

Interestingly, both ideological persuasions saw the mass media and their functionaries as tainted with evil. Stalinists and their supporters frequently parroted the dictum that Tin Pan Alley generated false class consciousness through popular music. The Right, as we have seen, perceived the mass media as attempting to create a Communist-inspired political consciousness. Both spectrums saw recording company executives as paid lackeys of some Machiavellian conspiracy. The Communist press attacked Tin Pan Alley for excluding the Almanac Singers while the Right verbally assaulted Columbia Records for not recording "Johnny Freedom" (Marty Robbins) and for promoting Bob Dylan, Pete Seeger, and Malvina Reynolds. Both movements seem to have missed the prime ingredient in their ideological fervor over folk music; that is, art for most people is not a weapon, nor is life a constant political struggle.

* The Weavers' political material was issued on the Hootenanny label, usually under the name of the lead singer and group, e.g., "Peter Seeger and Group." These records were sold by mail order and in some Communist bookstores. See *Sing Out! Hootenanny*, Folkways Records, FN 2513.

8

Epilogue: The Folk Music Revival and the New Protester

The historical antecedent for the so-called folk music revival was the ill-fated career of the Weavers. The Weavers, a name gleaned from a play by agitprop dramatist Gerhart Hauptmann, began at a Christmas Eve hootenanny staged in 1948 by People's Songs Inc., by then disintegrating. The participants were all active in PSI and three had been associated with the earlier Almanac House hootenannies. Pete Seeger and Lee Hays were founders of the prewar singing unit. As a teenager Fred Hellerman had attended the musical fests at Almanac House, and in 1947 he was accompanying Lee Hays's singing. Lee still had not learned to play an instrument. The fourth member of the Weavers was Ronnie Gilbert, a CBS secretary with an interest in folk music. Originally, the group exhibited many of the same traits associated with the Almanacs. Oscar Brand recalled, "They had great enthusiasm but little art. However, after singing a song a few times they would leave out all the discords and keep in some of the pleasant harmonies."

Following a hit and miss apprenticeship at various private parties and Stalinist gatherings, the Weavers were booked into Max Gordon's Village Vanguard on the basis of Pete Seeger's appeal to New York audiences. It was at the Village Vanguard, as show biz lore would have it, that they were discovered and signed to a Decca recording contract by arranger Gordon Jenkins. The remainder of the Weavers' choppy biography is now the lore of commercial folk singing. They recorded Leadbelly's "Goodnight Irene" and Woody Guthrie's Dustbowl piece

"So Long, It's Been Good to Know You" with the Gordon Jenkins orchestra. Both records made the Hit Parade, the Top Ten of its day. The Weavers' renditions of "Tzena, Tzena," "Wimoweh," and "Kisses Sweeter Than Wine" did equally well. However, in terms of both style and content this group was far removed from the enthusiastic and clean guitar-banjo interplay of the Almanacs. Violins collaborated with a large brass section to create the commercial sound desired by Gordon Jenkins. Although some of the Weavers' songs had a political history, they were totally inoffensive to those in search of entertainment. In two years the Weavers sold 4 million records for Decca. The few overt political pieces, such as "Hold the Line," a song commemorating Peekskill, were recorded on the Hootenanny label using the billing of "Pete Seeger and Chorus." On stage the Weavers no longer represented a class or a movement but, rather, formally attired professional musicians. *Time,* which had roundly condemned the Almanacs, praised the Weavers. True to form, *Sing Out!* was not nearly as impressed: "The Weavers would have sounded far better in the more vital and vibrant Hootenanny setting than they did in their formal evening attire on the Town Hall stage."

Several other *Sing Out!* reviews aimed at the Weavers cautioned the group for their inappropriate use of Negro material as well as for succumbing to bourgeois trappings. The application of the blacklist in 1952 curtailed both the successes and alleged excesses of the Weavers. The significance of the Weavers, as most popular music historians have noted, was not in their longevity. Rather, the Weavers established the economic truth that folk music, after proper orchestral polishing, was a salable commodity. Even more important, they reaffirmed the dreams and hopes of former Almanacs and People's Songsters that folk music was *the* music of America. The success of Harry Belafonte, who traced the Weavers' path from the Village Vanguard to Town Hall and national fame, only shored up this belief. Tennessee Ernie's version of the Merle Travis song "Sixteen Tons" further confirmed this conclusion. And all the while People's Artists and *Sing Out!* were vainly battling bill collectors, congressional investigators, and strange ideological vibrations emanating from the Kremlin.

Belafonte, despite his personal magnetism, which, perhaps more than his choice of musical genres, accounted for his success, in the mid-1950s was just another singer in the shadow of Elvis Presley. Elvis Presley was originally a country-music singer who incorporated black rhythm and blues into his singing style and songs. Like Belafonte's,

Harry Belafonte

Tennessee Ernie Ford

Presley's forte was his stage presence and personality. Everything Elvis the Pelvis did turned to gold. In the historical framework of the folk music revival Presley is a neglected but significant personality. He was the antithesis of the Weavers and the ever-present Gordon Jenkins. Originally, Presley sang a variant of the folk tradition in a simple and powerful manner minus an orchestra's conductors and arrangers. He made *déclassé* music respectable, at least to the youth of America. He also directed many young musicians away from their pianos to the guitars and other stringed instruments found in rock-a-billy bands. Most important, after this artistic set was implanted into the consciousness of both record producers and consumers, Presley was drafted into the Army, leaving an empty throne. Several logical successors—Jerry Lee Lewis, Carl Perkins, Gene Vincent, and Eddie Cochran—were taken out of contention due to public scandal, injury, or death. One of the potential but unsuccessful pretenders was English "skiffle" singer Lonnie Donegan, who recorded the Leadbelly classic "Rock Island Line" à la Presley. Donegan's American success was slight. During this period several other traditional folk songs were popularized in the rock 'n' roll genre—"Stagger Lee" by Lloyd Price and "C. C. Rider" by Chuck Willis. Nancy Wiskey's version of Elizabeth Cotton's "Freight Train" did relatively well on the Top Forty charts in 1957. None of these records had the success of the Weavers or even Belafonte. The disappearance of Presley and the record producers' attempts to find an acceptable substitute only fragmented the Top Forty audience on the bases of age and education.

Many college-age young adults who emulated Presley's mode of dress and screamed at his stage antics would not accept the host of artificially created substitutes such as Fabian, Frankie Avalon, and Paul Anka. Indeed, moving from the hop to the college milieu involved for some a change of life style in the late 1950s. On the campuses jazz, although drifting more into the esoteric refrains of McCann, Coleman, and Coltrane, was still popular. Folk music as Belafonte, the Tarriers, and the Weavers recorded it was a close second. The popularity of folk music on the nation's campuses during the 1950s was attributable to a great extent to the singular efforts of Pete Seeger, who cultivated his garden well. As a result of the blacklist and Seeger's contempt of Congress citation the banjo picker was limited to playing for progressive summer camps, left-wing groups, and politically tolerant colleges and universities. Here he continued the work the Almanacs had started, bringing folk music to the people. While it is impossible to gauge the number of converts Seeger made, he did keep the "little light shining."

There is no magic formula to determine the time of an idea or what becomes a hit. Consequently, most attempts at explaining the popularization of folk music in 1958 rarely transcend the simpleminded, time was right, Horatio Alger theory, which ignores the fact that *Sing Out!* was on the brink of bankruptcy and that Capitol Records took an admitted gamble by recording three clean-cut college men—David Guard, Bob Shane, and Nick Reynolds—who called themselves the Kingston Trio, after a Belafonte calypso song. The commerical folk music revival began in the United States with the Kingston Trio's rendition of the million-selling southern murder ballad "Tom Dooley." In a broad sense the Kingston Trio was the synthesis of the Weavers and Elvis Presley. They were overtly commercial, yet in their own way grass roots. Their musical arrangements were closer to Presley's than to those of Gordon Jenkins. Originally, their music was apolitical, rarely if ever treating controversial subjects.

Folk music, as we have seen, enjoyed sporadic bursts of popularity with the record-buying public. It was considered a novelty until the trio demonstrated to the record industry that it was still a salable commodity. In the record industry success always breeds emulation. Other record companies began signing folk entrepreneurs—the Limeliters, Brothers Four, the Travelers, Cumberland Three, *ad infinitum*—and the revival was in full swing. Guitars and banjoes became standard equipment for the average college student. After a time students were no longer content to merely memorize songs from Weavers or Kingston Trio records. Collections of Child and Sharp ballads and the works of the Lomaxes were çhecked out of libraries. *Sing Out!,* while debating the ideological efficacy of this new trend, found its subscription lists expanding and its advertising orders increasing.

The Times They Are a-Changin'

The college student of the 1950s has been popularly labeled a member of the Silent Generation. Some social observers have expanded this definition to refer to the "end of ideology," that is, the decade in which America turned its back on radical ideas, particularly Marxism. In the wake of the McCarthy period this characterization had considerable appeal. The only significant social dissent during the 1950s came from southern blacks who confronted *de jure* segregation in

Montgomery and Little Rock. Following the tradition of the labor colleges, the civil rights movement utilized such religious hymns as "We Shall Overcome" in its meetings and demonstrations. This musical tactic was adopted by the Student Nonviolent Coordinating Committee (SNCC) during its lunch-counter sit-ins in Greensboro, North Carolina, an event deemed by some the organizational birth of the new Left. The birth of the campus Left, according to other observers, occurred in the same year, 1960, when a group of pickets protested the appearance of the House Un-American Activities Committee. While sitting on the steps of the San Francisco City Hall, they sang such standard fare as "We Shall Not Be Moved." But they were moved, with water hoses. The musical fare of student protesters, regardless of geography or tradition, was of the 1930s.

The popular folk entrepreneurs offered little protest material. The Kingston Trio did record several satirical pieces such as "The MTA," about a commuter stuck on a train, and "The Merry Minuet," a parody on world politics. Both songs were entertaining but not particularly useful in any political sense. A group devoted to satirical songs, the Chad Mitchell Trio, appeared on the scene singing old temperance songs like "Away, Away with Rum" and "The Ballad of Lizzy Borden," which in part stated, "You can't kill your father up in Massachusetts." Both of the trios and their songs were great successes on the campus concert circuit. Following these rather successful attempts at social significance, the Kingston Trio finally recorded "Where Have All the Flowers Gone," an antiwar song by Pete Seeger. Peter, Paul, and Mary followed suit with the Seeger-Hays song "If I Had a Hammer," considered by some to be a civil rights piece. However, until the impact of Bob Dylan, protest songs rarely made their way into the mass media.

As the storm clouds of political discontent were forming in the black belt of the South and on some liberal campuses, *Sing Out!* and its editorial staff were pondering the significance of the revival. Alan Lomax upon his return from the United Kingdom in 1959 raised some rather disquieting issues in his *Sing Out!* article "The 'Folkniks'—And the Songs They Sing." As a folklorist Lomax contended that the folk singer had to "experience the feelings that lie behind his art." While several correspondents, particularly John Cohen of the New Lost City Ramblers, took great issue with Lomax, the question went on to haunt folk festivals for nearly half a decade. Indeed, the rural-worker uniform of many folkniks was in part a response to Lomax's dictum "to be folk, you live folk."

The Limeliters. Left to right: Alex Hassilev, Lou Gottlieb, Glenn Yarbrough.

A corollary to the Lomax position was the time-tested bugaboo of the Left, the question of commercialism. Originally, this topic was addressed on the basis of copyright abuses. Folk songs, it was argued, in many cases had no identifiable author and were generally in the public domain. When a commercial artist recorded a folk song, "who should benefit?" The case of "Tom Dooley" enraged a number of observers. Folklorist Frank Warner collected "Tom Dula" from a North Carolina farmer, Frank Proffitt. The Kingston Trio recorded the song and sold 3 million copies. Proffitt and Warner received nothing while the trio accrued all of the writing royalties. For many folk music fans this was an obvious case of exploitation. For the veterans of the People's Songs era this was yet another example of the machinations of Tin Pan Alley. But at the same time *Sing Out!* editorials were decrying the abuses of the revival, they were direct beneficiaries of it. In 1960 the circulation of *Sing Out!* doubled, and the smaller record companies—Elektra, Folkways, and Vanguard—became regular advertisers.

Protest songs were rare in *Sing Out!* Those that did appear reflected the 1940s and the topical songs of the British ban-the-bomb movement. In the correspondence columns of *Sing Out!* such writers as Pete Seeger and Malvina Reynolds pondered whether the United States could produce topical songs along similar lines. As Gordon Friesen, co-founder of *Broadside* (*NYC*), recalled, the debate involved many former Almanac Singers and the very issue raised by Alan Lomax; that is, does "being determine consciousness?" Pete Seeger, after visiting the British topical songwriters, and Sis Cunningham argued in *Broadside,* "How do we know that young people all over America may not be writing topical songs right now? It's just that we're not hearing about it. The big commercial music publishers and recording companies aren't interested in this sort of material. We may just be assuming that songs like this aren't being written and sung." Lee Hays countered with the old Almanac theory, one they constantly violated, that good topical songs must come from direct personal experience. Or, as Woody Guthrie once put it, "You can't write a good song about a whore-house unless you been in one." The more optimistic former Almanacs contended that the conditions of the times were such that some action must be taken. One did not have to die in a nuclear holocaust, they argued, to be opposed to war.

Ironically, the one source of support for the Seeger-Cunningham position was a songbook which lampooned the Almanacs and People's Songs Inc. In 1959 Dave Van Ronk and Richard Ellington published

The Bosses' Songbook, subtitled *Songs to Stifle the Flames of Discontent*. The title was taken from the Wobblies' pocket songbook *To Fan the Flames of Discontent*. The songs in the book were satirical but were directed at the ideology and personnel of the Old Left rather than the capitalist bosses. The Almanac Singers' favorite, "Hold the Fort," was changed to "Hold the Line":

> *There is a group in this here town*
> *That really goes too far.*
> *They've traded in their Ph.D.s*
> *For a folk guitar.*

CHORUS:

> *Sing a song for People's Artists,*
> *Balladeers unite!*
> *Buy your latest People's Songbook,*
> *There's a hoot tonight.*

> *Organize and fertilize*
> *And sing your little song.*
> *You are right on every issue,*
> *All the rest are wrong.*

Another song, titled "The Ballad of a Party Folk-Singer," was directed at Pete Seeger. Two verses are included here:

> *Well, they gave him his orders*
> *Up at Party Headquarters,*
> *Saying, "Pete, you're way behind the times.*
> *This is not '38; this is 1947.*
> *And there's been a change in that old party line."*

> *Their material is corny*
> *But their motives are the purest,*
> *And their spirit will never be broke,*
> *As they go right on with their great noble crusade*
> *Of teaching folk songs to the folk.*

The Bosses' Songbook aptly supported the contention that the folkniks of the 1960s were capable of writing topical songs. The anti-ideological tone of the collection, however, did not augur well for those envisioning another proletarian renaissance.

Despite the divergence of opinion, in February, 1962, 300 copies of *Broadside* were mimeographed at the total cost of $45. The magazine introduced itself as a bi-monthly and stated, "BROADSIDE may never publish a song that could be called a 'folk song.' But let us remember that many of our best folk songs were topical songs at their inception. . . . Old or new, a good song can only do good." One new song was "Talking John Birch Blues," a rather sophomoric piece by an unknown writer named Bob Dylan. The early issues of the mimeographed publication relied heavily upon traditional sources from the 1940s and, once again, the British pacifist and Marxist bards. Gordon Friesen wrote a series of articles dealing with the Almanac Singers, the first such series since Lee Hays's recollections in *People's Songs Bulletin* in 1948. With each succeeding issue *Broadside*'s dependence for material upon the Old Left decreased. The reason for this was the emergence of the so-called new politics and new radicals.

The new politics, like the folk music revival, began on the nation's campuses. The orientation of this new political entity was at best diffuse. Its major concern was full political participation or, as the Students for a Democratic Society labeled it, "participatory democracy." This included full civil rights and respect for human life. Indeed, as Keniston and Flacks have suggested, these ideals reflected the basic tenets of liberal democracy as outlined by Jefferson, Lincoln, and Franklin D. Roosevelt. What had to be done in the years of 1961 through 1963 appeared simple—right the wrongs. Consequently, the new radicals were primarily concerned with tactics. Mario Savio perhaps best summed up the orientation of political protesters: "There is a time when the operation of the machine becomes so odious, makes you so sick at heart that you can't take part, you can't even tacitly take part, and you've got to put your bodies on the gears and upon the wheels, upon the levers, and you've got to indicate to the people who run it, to the people who own it, that unless you're free the machine will be prevented from working at all." The new radicals were similar to the authors of *The Bosses' Songbook* in that ideology was for them passé and divisive. For the leftist of the pre–Viet Nam period social problems existed in and solutions were found in the realm of tactics rather than of ideology.

A good number of *Broadside*'s younger contributors supported this ethos. The topical song-writing boom mirrored the 1940s but con-

Phil Ochs

tained a twist of Thoreauvian individualism. The perceived style of life of rural folk and Dustbowl migrants was emulated. Trips were made to the northern branches of Woolworth's with guitars to protest the segregation of southern lunch counters. The Guthrie-Seeger tradition was invoked and filtered through a sense of individualistic or existential reality. Peter Krug, described as the "Bob Dylan of Berkeley," summarized this ethos:

> From this situation which has come to be called the Folksong Revival movement has grown another movement, shunning the "folkniks" for their strenuous insistence on authenticity and at the same time condemning the commercialists for their crass insipidness and lack of artistic principles. These young artists either modify existing traditional material to fit their needs of self-expression or create their own material in the folk mode.

As opposed to the Almanacs' ethic of anonymity, the new protesters asserted their individuality. Phil Ochs, one of the major musical polemicists of the revival, stated, "I'm only singing about my feelings, my attitudes, my views." Tom Paxton in an interview indicated that many of his songs were personal statements of discontent. He wrote "The High Sheriff of Hazard" because the lawman was a "bastard." Paxton further commented, "Every artist's first responsibility is to himself." Bob Dylan on a number of occasions indicated that his main responsibility was to himself and that protest songs were a means to an end, a way of launching his career. This is a far cry from the collective ethos of the proletarian renaissance where performers "sang everywhere for all sorts of causes" in order to change the social structure.

Despite the rejection of their ideological and organizational affiliations, such singers as Pete Seeger and Woody Guthrie were treated in print and in song as charismatic leaders. Contemporary writers— Tom Paxton, Phil Ochs, and Bob Dylan—idealized Guthrie and others in song.* Peter Krug provides one example of how Guthrie was deified by his successors:

> *I never knew him personally*
> *And yet I feel I've known him more intimately*

* See Phil Ochs's "Bound for Glory"; Tom Paxton's "Fare Thee Well Cisco"; Peter King's "The Man I Never Knew"; and Bob Dylan's "Song to Woody."

Tom Paxton

> *Than the silver-tongued preachers who called him their friend*
> *And used his affection as means to an end.*
> *Their secret derision couldn't trouble his mind,*
> *He was bound for a glory all of his own kind.*
> *He laughed all his laughter, he wept all his tears*
> *And he loved all his life, through his rich rolling years.*
> *He is a man I wish I'd known.*

("The Man I Never Knew")

With few exceptions revivalists canonized their folk-singing predecessors. Their response to Stalinist ideology was another matter. Dylan's refrain "I was so much older then, I'm younger then than now" is a repudiation of old ideologies. Phil Och's "Love Me I'm a Liberal" is equally irreverent:

> *Sure once I was young and impulsive,*
> *I wore every conceivable pin,*
> *Even went to Socialist meetings,*
> *Learned all the old union hymns.*
> *Ah, but I've grown older and wiser,*
> *And that's why I'm turnin' you in. . . .*

Despite the singers' lack of ideological orientation, they were heralded as "Woody's Children." Dylan particularly was lionized as the new white hope. The October, 1962, issue of *Sing Out!* featured Dylan on the cover and an article by Gil Turner, a co-editor at *Broadside,* which concluded, "Dylan's plans are simply to keep on singing wherever people want to hear him (but preferably not in night clubs) and putting down songs as fast as they come into his head." Increasingly, Bob Dylan's songs appeared in *Broadside,* songs like "Masters of War," "It's All Right," and "Blowin' in the Wind," which Peter, Paul, and Mary recorded for Warner Brothers. It sold over a million copies. Along with Dylan there appeared such topical songwriters as Phil Ochs, Tom Paxton, Mark Spoelstra, Peter LaFarge, Len Chandler, Buffy Saint-Marie, Eric Anderson, and many others. *Broadside* was originally their major vehicle of exposure. Most of them signed recording contracts with the smaller quality companies, such as Vanguard and Elektra, whose promotional facilities were meager at best.

When the complete history of the folk music revival is written, 1963 will no doubt be cited as its cultural and political zenith, with the Newport Folk Festival as its crescendo. According to *Billboard,* 1963 was the year of the hootenanny. ABC introduced a program by this name which immediately ran afoul of the New York folk scene by blacklisting Pete Seeger and the Weavers. Several motion pictures were scheduled to exploit the folk music revival, which was rapidly becoming a craze. A *Hootenanny* magazine appeared on the newstands. *Look, Life, Time,* and *Playboy* all ran feature stories on the "city-billy" phenomenon. The only Communist magazine to survive the stormy 1950s, *Mainstream,* ran a special "Woody Guthrie Issue."

As folk music was reaching unprecedented heights of popularity, the southern civil rights movement was also living through some of its finest hours. The confrontations at Albany and Birmingham between the Reverend Martin Luther King's Southern Christian Leadership Conference (SCLC) and the Student Nonviolent Coordinating Committee and the southern law enforcement agencies attracted national attention. Organizing drives in the black belt garnered considerable outside support which culminated in the triumphant march on Washington of 1963. Some of the supporters and participants were "New York folk-singers," as Phil Ochs portrayed them. Pete Seeger, Len Chandler, Tom Paxton, and many others traveled south that year to aid in the "cause of freedom." Like the Gastonia and Harlan County organizers, they brought back action songs and also the Freedom Singers, four young teenagers who sang for SNCC during the Albany campaign. The August 28th march on Washington, attended by nearly a million Americans, heard Joan Baez, Odetta, Bob Dylan, and Peter, Paul, and Mary lending their talents in support of equal voting rights. The civil rights struggle provided at least temporary common cause for nearly the entire folk music industry.

Another issue which solidified and gave impetus to the new protesters was the "Hootenanny" blacklist. As we have seen, People's Songsters were acutely aware of the power of the blacklist. They and many of their contemporaries were affected by its application. The banning of Pete Seeger and the Weavers from "Hootenanny," hosted by Jack Linkletter, was exposed by jazz critic Nat Hentoff in the *Village Voice*. His article was reprinted in both *Sing Out!* and *Broadside (NYC)*. In retaliation a number of folk entrepreneurs, led by Joan Baez, boycotted the program. The Folksingers Committee to Abolish Blacklisting, with Tom Paxton as its chairman, was formed. The committee sponsored letter-writing campaigns and organized pickets where-ever the Linkletter group appeared. The New York offices of ABC saw folk singers Hedy West, Lev Finschaef, and Jerry Silverman carrying signs reading "Let Our Pete Sing." The issue in many respects paralleled the "which side are you on" ethos of the HUAC days.* Many performers badly in need of public exposure, such as Tom Paxton and Phil Ochs, refused to appear on the TV show. It was desperate to use the talents of topical songwriters as well as Miss Baez and the Kingston Trio, who supported the boycott. Anyone appearing on the show immediately was branded a "fink." This reverse blacklist in time succeeded, since "Hootenanny" failed. The ruination of the show, however, was a mixed blessing because its overexposure of mediocre talent may have been the first nail in the coffin of the revival.

All of the social trends of 1963 merged in the revived folk festival at Newport, Rhode Island. The performers invited reflected the civil rights movement in the South, the topical song-writing school, traditional music, the Top Forty, and concert tour folk. The Freedom Singers, Bob Dylan, Pete Seeger, Jim Garland, Peter Paul, and Mary, and Joan Baez all came. So did sixty-five more pickers and singers and

---

* The "either-or" aspect of going on the show has been questioned by some. Don West, for one, in "Topical Songs and Folksinging, 1965," in *Sing Out!* 15 (Sept., 1965) , wrote, "The word I had was that Seeger actually encouraged singers to go on *Hootenanny*. His own brother did. So did Judy Collins." With the exception of Judy Collins, the New Lost City Ramblers, Theo Bikel, and Leon Bibb, the singers on the show were either discoveries or such Top Forty stars as the Limeliters.

an audience of 37,000 people.* *Broadside* presented its own topical song workshop, featuring protest songs old and new, American and English. Sam Hinton sang the People's Songs Inc. favorite, "Talking Atomic Blues," and Jim Garland performed his compositions "The Ballad of Harry Simms" and "I Don't Want Your Millions, Mister." Pete Seeger and the Freedom Singers musically recalled the integrity and victories of blacks in the South, but the true successes of this workshop were the new songwriters. Phil Ochs was an immediate star with "Talking Birmingham Jam." Tom Paxton impressed a considerable number of people with his antiwar song "The Willing Conscript" and the eulogy to those on the road, "Rambling Boy." Dylan, of course, lived up to his press clippings in his duet with Joan Baez, singing "With God on Our Side." Following the workshop the Committee to Abolish Blacklisting passed out for signatures 2,000 postcards addressed to ABC, protesting the hiring standards on the "Hootenanny" show. All the cards were signed; chairman Paxton exclaimed, "We could have had triple the number signed but hadn't money for more." The festival ended appropriately: the Freedom Singers linked arms with Peter, Paul, and Mary, Joan Baez, Bob Dylan, and Pete Seeger, all swaying together and singing "Blowin' in the Wind" and "We Shall Overcome."

As with the camp meetings of the 1820s, the festival was a reaffirmation of all that had come before. All of the strenuous, thankless hours at mimeograph machines and in little clubs now seemed worthwhile. The civil rights movement, in need of white northern allies, found some. Topical songwriters found a cause. People's Songsters, it appeared, had finally reached the people. Newport netted $70,000. *Sing Out!* and *Broadside* (*NYC*) published glowing reviews and accounts of the festival's events. The fall issue of *Sing Out!* had five topical songsters on the cover and an editorial by Irwin Silber which began, " 'Folk music is bigger than ever.' That's the word these days on Tin Pan Alley where a tremendous upsurge of interest in folk music has created a major revolution in American popular music." While condemning the overt commercialism of the "hootenanny craze," Silber concluded, "This is the time . . . to sing out the danger and the warning. . . . [The revival is] helping to create a new and vital American music with roots in the folk traditions we hold in common—a music which may help to bring to reality a better world than the human race has

* Vanguard Records has released many of the highlights of this historic gathering (VRS 9144–VRS 9149) .

Bob Dylan and Joan Baez

Courtesy of Manuel Greenhill
Folklore Productions

ever known." The same issue carried a twelve-page article by Gordon Friesen, with songs, on the new songwriters. *Broadside (NYC)* was no less enthusiastic. Josh Dunson praised the festival, particularly its workshops: "Topical music had shown its range and depth at Newport."

The aftermath of Newport was beneficial for nearly everyone except the Kingston Trio and the Saturday night revelers on "Hootenanny." At the festival folkniks were exposed to both the old and the new. Frank Proffitt, Clarence Ashley, Doc Watson, and many other country pickers exhibited what the "real thing" was all about. The *Broadside* contributors—Ochs, Paxton, Dylan—opened new vistas for many, including Joan Baez, who began to shift away from her renditions of Child ballads to the more contemporary songs of the young poets.

Engrossed in the euphoria generated by the Newport festival, the folk entrepreneurs of 1964 failed to comprehend the ramifications of the fact that they were now a segment of the mass culture. Although the editorial staff of *Sing Out!* repudiated the excesses of the hootenanny craze, they were the beneficiaries of it. The fact that Newport grossed $70,000 and drew 37,000 patrons clearly indicated that it was now part of popular music, and the music industry all too frequently devours its own. Folk entrepreneurs were now subject to the capricious tides of the *Billboard* charts and concert ticket sales. For the advocates of the people's music thesis it was a castle made of sand. Most of the folkniks who decried the commercialism of the Kingston Trio were introduced to folk music by "Tom Dooley." The same *aficionados* who insisted that Dylan was a member of the folk community would follow him into the world of rock a short year later. This was hardly the constituency necessary to build a new world or a movement.

The projection of the folk song genre into the mainstream of American popular music subjected its performers to new and previously unheard-of problems. As Newport and countless other folk festivals in 1963 and 1964 illustrated, the star system was becoming an integral part of the folk music scene. Of the 37,000 people who thronged to Newport, a vast majority came to see a particular artist or group. The 1964 Berkeley Folk Festival continued this trend; workshops of even the most esoteric nature were filled to capacity when attended by Joan Baez. Other workshops without Miss Baez found a few people in the midst of many empty chairs. This lesson was not wasted on the promoters of future folk festivals. In time a folk festival not featuring such name performers as Dylan, Baez, or Peter, Paul, and Mary could anticipate troubles at the box office. This obvious antithesis to the value structure of many folk entrepreneurs familiar with the Old Left tradition would evoke a bitter reaction in 1964.

As noted, one factor accounting for the folk song revival was the vacuum created in popular music by the conscription of Elvis Presley and the misfortunes of many of his imitators. In 1964 a quartet of long-haired Englishmen, the Beatles, recreated the adulation and mania which surrounded Presley during the "Hound Dog" and "Heartbreak Hotel" years. The impact of the Beatles upon American popular music requires little elaboration. Everything they sang sold. Once again record producers rushed to get on the bandwagon. *Sing Out!*, now with a circulation of over 20,000, generally ignored the Beatles and focused upon the successes of traditional singers on college campuses, the voter registration drives in the South, and the ever-rising star of Bob Dylan. *Broadside* (*NYC*) continued to publish excellent topical songs from the South and from an increasing number of young songsmiths.

The Beatles' popularity totally pervaded the music industry, but Dylan's albums continued to sell at an unprecedented pace for a protest singer. As rock historian Carl Belz has noted in his *Story of Rock*, ". . . he has never staggered the record industry in the way the Beatles have. Dylan's music possesses an artistic significance which is comparable to that of the Beatles . . . he has stimulated an audience commitment which is spiritually as deep, if not deeper, than that of Beatle fans." While he possessed a smaller following, Dylan's fans saw

him as the spokesman of a generation, the reincarnation of Woody
Guthrie, the musical great white hope of the Left. Dylan's early songs
certainly placed him in the Guthrie tradition but he was definitely not
Woody. Dylan totally lacked any strong ideological commitments. Unlike Woody, he was psychologically ill suited for a leadership role. He
was shy, retiring, and uncomfortable with success, as his stormy relationship with the press well illustrates. But he did what was necessary
to reach stardom. In contrast to Woody Guthrie, Bob Dylan became a
star, subject to all of the forces which impinge upon the famous.

In 1964 some folkniks denounced rock music as best suited for
their younger brothers and sisters. Others praised it as good for dances.
Many folk entrepreneurs privately endorsed rock as good music. Some
even performed parodies of rock songs during concerts. Joan Baez's
version of the Diamonds' "Little Darlin' " was a classic. Generally, the
folk-singing scene looked beyond Lennon and McCartney. Recording
artist and repertoire men did not share this public disinterest. Each
company tried to create some kind of American Liverpool sound. The
Beau Brummels' song "Laugh, Laugh" is an excellent case in point:
most listeners assumed that this San Francisco group was British. In
the summer of 1964 the Animals, a British group led by Eric Burdon,
released "The House of the Rising Sun" to the American market. It
was a commercial success, but many folkniks objected to the Animals
"desecration" of a song identified with Dylan. The song had appeared
on Dylan's first album and became a standard in folknik circles. Within
a year such American and English groups as the Turtles, the Byrds,
and Sonny and Cher would be recording Dylan songs, thus creating
what has been termed folk-rock.

By the fall of 1964 a number of dissenting voices were beginning
to be heard. Irwin Silber in a *Sing Out!* editorial warned against the
impact of the "American success syndrome" upon folk music: "Perhaps
the most disheartening symptom of it all has been the emergence of
the 'star system' in folk music . . . folk music has indeed reached a
level of popular acceptance that many of us could barely conceive 10
& 20 years ago. Whether America is any the better for it all is open to
question." Silber answered his own query, closing on the optimistic note
that folk songs had survived HUAC and consequently could overcome
success.

In the same issue two names familiar in left-wing circles appeared in the correspondence section. Moses Asch and Don West both
strongly objected to what Asch termed "the worship of the personality

cult." West noted, "Whether it is Elvis Presley, the Beatles, or a Dylan, the cash register must ring. And isn't that the sweetest music of all in our profit culture . . . I had hoped that SING OUT! might not succumb to the Madison Avenue ways and influences." These two voices from the past were not easily discounted. West was a founder of Commonwealth College and a labor organizer for many years. Moses Asch saved *Sing Out!* when it was on the verge of financial collapse and was a major stockholder in the magazine.

Newport 1964 appeared to lend credence to the Asch-West condemnation. The festival, which featured 228 performers in the span of three days, was described by one reviewer as being "a totally unmanageable circus because of its sheer size. Was the *meaning* slowly leaking out of the huge balloon?" Josh Dunson's *Broadside* review echoed this sentiment. Dunson complained that topical song singers were not given enough time to exhibit their wares. Dunson was equally disturbed by the positive reception accorded the Chad Mitchell Trio and the "watering down" of topical song material: "The year before Phil Ochs's 'Talking Birmingham Jam' was the most important song at the Newport workshop. This year there was no song, for instance, about the so-called 'White backlash' in the North, the Harlem riots . . . there was no direct confrontation with the most disturbing and meaningful events of this 'long hot summer.' "

While little consensus could be found about the total implication of Newport '64, there was little disagreement among the sages in New York that the folk revival had become too commercial and in the process had lost many of its inherent values. In short, its mentors had lost control of the folk music movement, as it was incorrectly labeled.* The culprit of the piece, not surprisingly, was Bob Dylan. The emperor, for many of his sponsors, had lost his clothes.

The Bob Dylan who appeared at Newport '64 was not the Guthrie model of years past. He was now a public personality. In his famous open letter to Dylan in *Sing Out!*, Irwin Silber outlined Dylan's new stature in highly negative terms: "I saw at Newport how you had somehow lost contact with people. It seemed to me that some of the paraphernalia of fame were getting in your way. You travel with an entourage now—with good buddies who are going to laugh when you

---

* The folk revival has incorrectly been termed a movement by many proponents, despite the fact that this phenomenon lacked many properties generally associated with a social movement. See Gary B. Rush and R. Serge Denisoff's, *Social and Political Movements*.

Bob Dylan

need laughing and drink wine with you and insure your privacy—and never challenge you to face everyone else's reality again."

Dylan's public demeanor no doubt violated Alan Lomax's dictum "to be folk, you have to live folk." It also underlined the fact that Dylan was no longer tied to the New York opinion-makers for further career building. This became particularly apparent in the area of politics. As we have seen, Dylan had been cast, by both himself and others, as the logical successor to Woody Guthrie. For example, the widely quoted story of Dylan's visits to the bed-ridden Dustbowl Balladeer appear to be the figment of a press agent's imagination. However, the donning of the mantle connoted one thing to the bearer, another to the bestowers. Without opening the Pandora's box of Dylan's early history in New York, it is sufficient to say that both he and his early enthusiasts profited from their associations. Nevertheless, in time he rejected the cry for justice metaphysic of music. Newport '64 was one evidence of this dissociation. *Another Side of Bob Dylan* was another. The two albums preceding *Another Side* were milestones in the art of protest songwriting. They contained "Blowin' in the Wind," "Masters of War," "Talking World War III," "Hattie Carroll," and many others. *Another Side* was just that—a long step away from the art is a weapon school. The liner notes included a statement by Dylan which aptly described his "new" orientation:

> i know no answers an no truth
> for absolutely no soul alive
> i will listen t no one
> who tells me morals
> there are no morals
> an i dream alot.

One song on the record, "My Back Pages," restated the theme that the ideologies of the past were history and an artist must chart his own course. The great white hope of folk consciousness had turned his back on it; in effect, he laughed in church.*

* It should be remembered that Dylan's new direction included some sociopolitical material but became progressively less overt and folkish.

The Rejection of Folk Consciousness

The striking aspect of the folk song revival after Newport '63 was the rejection of folk consciousness for a place in the popular music industry. This repudiation was both aesthetic and political. While folk consciousness was a form of esoteric communication, the evolution of folk-rock was a return to the familiarity theme. The socially conscious folkniks were products of the mass media. They were raised on the offerings of Elvis Presley, Pat Boone, and innumerable rhythm and blues quartets. Much of their original knowledge stemmed from the recordings and broadcasts of Belafonte and the Kingston Trio. Consequently, the folkniks' vision of the media was not necessarily hostile. They did not reject, as did the working-class intellectual of the 1940s, the offerings of mass media as obscurantist ploys. Nor did they necessarily desire the creation of a people's music. For them folk music was *already* part of popular music and subject to the structural nuances of the industry.

Their view, of course, differed greatly from the small, intimate gatherings at Almanac House or People's Songs Inc., where the collective was dominant. This differentiation has been aptly demonstrated by Marshall McLuhan in *Understanding Media: The Extrusions of Man,* where he outlines two types of media participation: "Hot media are, therefore, low in participation, and cool media are high in participation or completion by the audience." McLuhan illustrates this view by suggesting that radio is a hot medium and the telephone is cool, since radio does not require participation but the telephone demands the verbal interaction of conversation. A similar argument can be made regarding songs of persuasion in the proletarian renaissance and the material of the commercial revival.

In the late thirties the notion of mass singing and audience participation was stressed, and most songs accented the collective aspect of protest. For example, Woody Guthrie, in *People's World,* described a benefit held for migratory workers in New York City: "In several places the whole audience joined the singers and the theater rang like the hammer of a blacksmith . . . this . . . shows that songs can be useful." Bess Lomax Hawes, a member of the Almanac Singers, lamented to this writer that audience participation in UAW meetings in Detroit was confined to the "singing of 'Solidarity.' " The medium of transmission in the 1930s and 1940s was primarily face to face in an auditorium, meeting, or picket line. One index of this participation notion is the songbooks utilized during the period. Critics in *People's World* reported that they were "designed to solve the problem of those people who hum through songs at meetings with that 'I wish I knew the words' look on their faces!" The contents included Spanish Civil War songs, traditional labor hymns, Soviet songs, and others. The Almanac Singers, in appearances as well as in several albums, stressed the issue of labor and nonintervention. Their songs were directed at the social structure; that is, they voiced opposition to bosses and government policy with solutions of "organization" and "we won't go."

The revivalists exhibited the lack of continuity and the individualism generally associated with the mass media, of which many of them were a part. Phil Ochs and Bob Dylan disdained audience participation in their performances, and the structure of their songs excluded it. Their appearances at political affairs did not resemble those of the Almanac Singers, who described the structure of their songs as "saying the truth as simply as you can and repeat it as many times as it has to be repeated." The structure of most contemporary songs is patterned upon the lyric poem: long, rambling, and nonrepetitive. Some of Dylan's songs, such as "With God on Our Side," contain ten verses without a chorus. The key variable here follows McLuhan's argument of media; that is, the revival artists used the medium of recordings predominantly, as opposed to the collective mass meeting emphasis of the 1940s. Therefore, each long-playing record required ten or more selections. Equally, the marketplace prescribes a given frequency of record production which, in effect, saturates the mass culture with issues and individual statements of protest.

In comparing these two periods, one striking element is that the proletarian renaissance did not depend on the media. Woody Guthrie did not have an A and R man peering over his shoulder. Nor was it until the publication of *People's Songs Bulletin* in 1946 that a political folk magazine was sold in America. This mimeographed publication served for three years, to be replaced by *Sing Out!* During the revival *Sing Out!* was joined by a number of magazines glorifying the events and personalities of the movement. A similar phenomenon is found in the recording industry. Only Keynote, Disc Records, and Timely, followed by Folkways and Hootenanny, issued the products of the Almanac Singers, Leadbelly, etc. In the early sixties every American recording company marketed some folk and protest material.

The effect of this deluge was to create an underground Top Twenty reflective of the popular music format. One example is the

Peter, Paul, and Mary

career of "Blowin' in the Wind." Dylan recorded his composition, *Sing Out!* and *Broadside* published the words and music, and Peter, Paul, and Mary and other groups pressed the ballad. Other protest-oriented singers learned the song and performed it until a new album or song caught their fancy. So the life span of the composition is relatively short. It is significant that of the thousands of songs written during the revival, few if any have become standard fare. During the 1930s, however, songs from the Spanish Civil War, for example, showed considerable durability. Indeed, some songs of that period are still sung today. This media influence, coupled with ideology, may suggest two main differences in the orientation of adherents of urban folk singing.

Songs of persuasion can be classified on the basis of role or function. The first classification is the magnetic song; it appeals to the listener and attracts him to a specific movement or ideology. Within the ranks of adherents the propaganda song creates solidarity in the movement. Two basic elements are encased in this definition: external appeal and internal cohesion. For example, the classic "Which Side Are You On" accomplishes both with the following lines:

> *Don't scab for the bosses,*
> *Don't listen to their lies.*
> *Us poor folks haven't got a chance,*
> *Unless we organize.*

The other type of song of persuasion is rhetorical; it points to some social condition, describes the situation, but offers no ideological or organizational solution. The essence of this type of song is a statement of individual discontent rather than a cry for justice. Dylan's "Masters of War" and Phil Ochs's "Here's to the State of Mississippi" and "The Disgruntled Pacifist" are illustrative. Dylan's song, addressed to the military-industrial complex, can be summarized by one line: "I hope that you die and your death will come soon."

The songs of the proletarian renaissance stressed the "we are together" and "join a movement" ethos rather than that found in Dylan's statement. A comparison of the songbooks and recordings of the proletarian renaissance with those of three other periods revealed that a vast majority of the songs used by the Almanac Singers and the CPUSA were magnetic, stressing external and internal factors, whereas the material published in a contemporary topical song magazine was 77 percent rhetorical, emphasizing issue-oriented individual statements of discontent. Thus the proletarian renaissance can be characterized musically and structurally as collective-structural, as opposed to the individual event-oriented phenomena of the protest phase of the revival.

As Karl Mannheim suggests in his essay on generations, in *Essays on the Sociology of Knowledge,* age groups can be interpreted in the framework of location and societal conditions. He argues that rapid social change alters the perception of generational units. As the tempo of societal change increases, each generation incorporates parts of the past into a new cultural form. The musical statements of the 1960s assumed a hybrid form, based on the practices of the Left coupled with the values of the contemporary medium. The songs of the 1930s reflected the organizational and collective feelings of unity and power for social change. As Dunson suggests, "The songs came out of the unshakeable and immense feeling that the singer had discovered some truth, a plan that was going to make the world one of 'bread and roses.'" The Stalinist-oriented ballads of the time gave answers and solutions:

> *What can we do about it,*
> *To right this dreadful wrong?*
> *We're all going to join the union,*
> *For the union makes us strong.*

Dylan, the child of Guthrie during the revival, was sparked by disillusionment and dissent in the entelechy of this time. The essence of his material frequently was suggested by such immediate "outrages" shown him by the media as the murders of Emmett Till and Hattie Carroll. The tone of these songs also indicates that protest songs may be correlative with economic conditions. During the Great Depression work was glorified both in American interpretations of Marxian theory and in concrete reality. Stalinists and other political groups urged full employment; Socialist movements stressed the nationalization of economic institutions. Many of Woody Guthrie's writings speak of a "good job of work" and the role of Wall Street in preventing the attainment of this goal. The economic conditions of the decade, therefore, may be seen as engendering a form of class consciousness in the musical material.

In juxtaposition, the ethic of the revivalist may reflect the middle-class affluence of the 1960s, where the question of jobs or basic necessities of life is rarely raised. Rather, issues pointing to the imperfections of the social order are raised. Dylan's "Hollis Brown," a portrait of a coal miner, speaks of the plight of the rural dweller in the midst of plenty. Other songwriters have used the topics of environmental pollution, the Viet Nam war, and the issue of quality of life instead of the more economic dilemmas of the depression years.

Despite differences in world view, role of the media, and generations, the tools of social and political protest remain remarkably similar. Tactically, the notions of separatism, mobilization of the urban and rural poor, and other programs of the campus Left can be traced back to the Communist drives of the Third Period. A musical comparison of the Stalinists and the songsmiths of the 1960s suggests some similarities, but these are outweighed by differences based on ideology and media. It was over these differences that the final great debate regarding folk music raged.

One of the fundamental tenets of the proletarian renaissance was "thou shalt not go commercial." Guthrie, Seeger, and many others derided Tin Pan Alley and its products as unreal and obscurantist. Early editions of *Sing Out!* bristled with attacks upon Tin Pan Alley —the cultural Philistines—and those who associated with it. Even the Weavers were not immune to these attacks. Going commercial or selling out also had the ideological connotation of rejecting the art is a weapon philosophy. After all, the critics reasoned, why should the money changers allow themselves to be vilified by their own medium? The "thou shalt not go commercial" ethic pervaded the topical song-writing school as well.

During the revival Bob Dylan refused to appear on the Ed Sullivan program because of the censorship of "Talking John Birch Society." But this refusal occurred before his adoption of the art for art's sake position and the ensuing "Dylan controversy." This battle, which raged in the pages of *Sing Out!* and *Broadside,* highlighted the issues of aestheticism and social significance. In November, 1964, following the Newport festival, Irwin Silber published an "Open Letter to Bob Dylan," reminiscent of the thirties and forties, condemning the youthful singer for his lack of social concern. The editor of *Sing Out!* argued that Dylan had "somehow lost contact with the people" and that any honest statement dealing with the reality of the world must contain "protest." He concluded by pointing to commercialism's dilution of Dylan's material: "The American Success Machinery chews up geniuses at a rate of one a day and still hungers for more . . . through notoriety, fast money, and status, it makes it almost impossible for the artist to function and grow. It is a process that must be constantly guarded against and fought." Another proponent of the art is a weapon school compared Phil Ochs to Bob Dylan in *Broadside,* finding the differences between the two songwriters in "meaning vs. innocuousness, sincerity vs. utter disregard for the tastes of the audience, idealistic principle vs. self-conscious egotism."

The key to these assaults upon Dylan is that he had disregarded the dictum of social import because of the effects of the commercial world. Readers of *Sing Out!* and *Broadside* quickly took sides in the controversy. A majority of readers, as opposed to performers, supported Dylan's charting of these new waters, while many political traditionalists aligned themselves with Silber's position. Silber and his contemporaries in this polemic used a yardstick which applied to the proletarian renaissance but which had much less meaning in the context of the revival. As Dylan suggested, ". . . I'm not part of no movement. If I was, I wouldn't be able to do anything else but be 'the movement.' . . . I do a lot of things no movement would allow." Unlike his predecessors, Dylan was not obligated to an ideology, and the notion of selling out politically, it appears, was a minor consideration. For those committed to the tenet of social change, Dylan's actions were deviations from the norm. The radical Right, as previously shown, employed a similar rationale in extending their interpretations of the proletarian renaissance to the more recent commercial revival. For Silber and his compatriots Dylan was a sellout. On the political Right writers saw Dylan as owned by the Left. Both interpretations were incorrect.

Dylan's movement away from political material was compounded by his incorporation of the rock 'n' roll genre into his music. On July 25, 1965, Dylan appeared on the stage of the Newport Folk Festival as a "fierce Spanish outlaw" in a black leather jacket, holding an electric guitar in his hands. The Ribakoves described the audience reaction as hostile:

> The sight of the instrument infuriated the crowd. It was to them the hated emblem of rock 'n' roll, the tool of performers whose only aim was to take big money from dumb kids. In the hands of the man who had been their god, it was the symbol of the sell-out.
>
> Bob Dylan began to play and sing his strange, defiant verses. The audience . . . greeted the first two songs with a wall of silence.

At the end of the third . . . "Git rid of that guitar!" someone screamed—and the crowd applauded.

Dylan was driven from the stage. Reportedly, Pete Seeger stood back-stage with tears in his eyes. When Dylan returned, without the electric guitar, he sang "It's All Over Now, Baby Blue." For *Sing Out!* and Silber the song title was prophetic and appropriate.

On its fifteenth anniversay *Sing Out!* expanded the size of both its magazine and its distribution facilities. Contributing editor Pete Seeger optimistically wrote, "For many years we have been a cozy little group all to ourselves, congratulating ourselves on our exclusiveness. Now we are daring the dangers of the marketplace. We are daring to grow ten times as big as we ever were. . . . For now, for the first time, this magazine is going to be sold on the newsstands of America."

In the same anniversary issue Julius Lester reviewed Bob Dylan's *Highway 61 Revisited* album, condemning it for its "existentialist" orientation and for not being "where it's at." Without realizing it, Lester outlined the basic problem facing *Sing Out!:* defining social reality. From the editorial board of *Sing Out!* two positions emerged. Silber and Lester presented one view of Dylan and folk-rock while the purist, apolitical former editor of *Little Sandy Review,* Paul Nelson, championed the other. Nelson saw Dylan's work as being fundamentally a continuation of the folk music movement from "the Then to the Now." He accepted the fact that Dylan's defection from the traditional cry for justice orientation reflected social trends in America. The other position assumed that folk-rock was not socially significant or, properly, political. In Irwin Silber's words, "Perhaps our present world is too hip, too cool, too afraid of commitment, too intimidated at the thought of being square to pay proper attention to the memory of Joe Hill." Silber's view reflected both his disillusionment with the declining popu-larity of folk music and the rise of the drug-oriented hippie subculture and the New Left. Silber saw drugs as the new "opiate of the masses" and rock groups as "obscurantist influences" and purveyors of the "flippie" culture. In short, for the editor of *Sing Out!* his constituency was dwindling because of forces beyond his ideological framework. In time another affront to Silber's cry for justice stance came from an ally, Julius Lester.

Lester, as was the case with many black militants in the winter of 1966, had given up on working within the system. In a significant

The Beatles

Courtesy of Apple Records and Capitol Records

argument for black power, "The Many Children of Malcolm X," in *Sing Out!,* Lester concluded that the time of protest songs and singing was over. The gradualism of the Old Left was rejected: "Now it is over. The days of singing freedom songs and the days of combatting bullets and billy clubs with Love. We Shall Overcome (and we have overcome our blindness) sounds old, out-dated and can enter the pantheon of the greats along with the IWW songs and the union songs. As one SNCC veteran put it after the Mississippi March, 'Man, *the people are too busy getting ready to fight to bother with singing anymore.'* " As for the Love Generation and white allies, Lester discounted them: love is "always better done in bed than on the picket line and marches." Within the magazine, then, two positions vis-à-vis politics emerged: Nelson's advocacy of the aesthetic values of folk and rock music, as opposed to Lester's special pleading for black power, and Silber's Old Left militancy.

Irwin Silber, his political ideology reinforced by a visit to Cuba, resumed his attacks upon the forces of Marshall McLuhan, Timothy Leary, Joan Baez, "the mass arts," and a "new generation of pseudo-revolutionary hippies." Paul Nelson in his "Popoeuvres" column applauded the new new music and all the forces his editor saw as evil. In a column titled "Hammer and Popsicle" Nelson stated, "My favorite albums at the moment are the new ones by the Buffalo Springfield, the Kinks, the Jefferson Airplane, the Byrds and the Rolling Stones." Regarding the Airplane's album *Surrealistic Pillow*, Nelson saw the LSD-inspired "White Rabbit" as the most important song on the disk.

Meanwhile at the Berkeley campus of the University of California a student strike meeting was in progress when someone shouted, "Let's sing 'Solidarity Forever.'" According to one account, "No one seemed to know the words. Then from the back of the lecture hall, a hoarse voice shouted 'Yellow Submarine,' a song popularized by the Beatles. A thousand voices took up the song as the students floated from the building."

The internal ideological conflicts which raged in the editorial offices of *Sing Out!* were emphasized by the growing indebtedness of the publication. By the end of 1966 Dylan's "It's All Over Now" statement was becoming most obvious in the economic sphere. Folkniks were becoming hippies and rock freaks. The magazine had expanded its circulation and distribution just as the folk bubble had burst. As with People's Songs and People's Artists, the movements of the masses had been miscalculated. Dylan's Newport retreat proved a hollow and fleeting victory for folk music buffs and the mentors of *Sing Out!* Within the organization Irwin Silber became the obvious scapegoat for the economic misfortunes. Mixed into the attacks on the magazine's editor were personality differences as well as doctrinaire and political considerations. In response Silber, joined by co-owner Pete Seeger, relinquished his financial control of the magazine to eleven other people, including Izzy Young, Barbara Dane, and Paul Nelson. In the August–September, 1967, issue this realignment was announced. Silber remained editor while Seeger, Lester, and Nelson stayed on the editorial advisory board. This return to the structure of the People's Artists days of collective ownership was doomed to failure, since the ideological cohesion of the 1950s was absent. Unfortunately, the reorganization only heightened the internal conflicts.

In the fall of 1967 managing editor Ed Badeaux wrote a long-overdue obituary of the folk music revival, optimistically titled "The Spectacle Moves On." Badeaux's thesis explaining the decline was that the American middle class was incapable of coping with "unlettered music" and had therefore created a star system, foreign to folk music. The exigencies of the mass media and economic opportunism also accounted for the failure of folk music to become people's music. To counter these trends, the managing editor advocated a near-total return to the noncommercial clubs and hoots of the pre–Kingston Trio days:

"If this music, and along with it our personal identity, is worth preserving, we will not waste a great deal of time weeping over the Death of Folk Music. Rather we will join together, organize, and do what we must to keep our music healthy and kicking. The old methods have failed. Let's now find some new ones. The spectacle has moved on, but the real show is just beginning."

The show and the spectacle were indeed occurring in the acid-rock concerts at San Francisco's Fillmore Auditorium. However, the position of *Sing Out!*, as espoused by Lester and Silber, had not been altered by its new collective ownership. The issue following the re-organization message found Lester once again railing about the hippie subculture: "White youth dropped out into non-involvement. They were going to create their Levittowns of love, drugs and sex. Their music was wedded with colored lights filling the ceilings and walls of ballrooms while they danced in the midst of the sound and light, the aural and visual color creating a bubble around them, protecting them from what was outside. They were running while the world chose sides for Armageddon. Protest had failed, because it can be absorbed."

By the spring of 1968 *Sing Out!* was $12,000 in debt, and rumors of Irwin Silber's imminent withdrawal for a position with the Old Left–oriented *National Guardian* were voiced. The spring issue of the magazine confirmed these speculations. In an emotional statement the deposed editor announced the formation of a collective leadership at the magazine and concluded, ". . . the past belongs to the past. The times cry out for something new. New ideas, new people, new ways of looking at the world. I take it as part of the continuing vitality of *Sing Out!* that the kind of people who have involved themselves in its direction *are so much in touch with the world they live in—and so much committed to a sense of values which may be able to save this insane world yet.*"

Silber's closing sentence did not reflect the thinking of the collective leadership with its rainbow of ideologies and opinions. Indeed, despite Silber's rather myopic portrait of American social trends, he was an able administrator and editor with a sense of historical direction, however incorrect it proved to be. The ideological diffuseness of the editorial board became immediately apparent. One issue of the magazine contained ballads to Che Guevara and Ho Chi Minh coupled with three reviews of the Beatles' *Sgt. Pepper's Lonely Hearts Club Band* and a lengthy analysis of Bob Dylan's movie *Don't Look Back.*

With the exception of Nelson's material, this new emphasis upon rock music was awkward and unsophisticated in comparison to the columns of Richard Goldstein, Paul Williams, and Ralph J. Gleason, who specialized in this genre. Ironically, these attempts at contemporaneity alienated many die-hard folk enthusiasts, as letters to the editor and canceled subscriptions indicated.

The March–April, 1968, issue was the last of the expansion size. It contained forty-eight pages, exactly half the number of the fifteenth-anniversary issue. Reader discontent with the collective leadership became more apparent when Young, Nelson, and Lester issued the following statement: "In recent weeks, SING OUT! has received several letters requesting cancellation of subscriptions. . . . We have decided not to cancel any subscriptions. They were paid for and those who paid for them are going to get them. If they don't wish to read them, that is their business." The justification for this rather arbitrary position was that the magazine had to persevere in the midst of the "crisis in America."

The next edition, several months late in production, was smaller in size and exhibited even less sense of direction. For the first time publicly, Pete Seeger noted the problems of the publication: "The readers of this magazine should know: if SING OUT! can dig itself out of its present financial hole it will take the love and devotion of all. Some 12,000 bucks were lost in a *misguided attempt* to get the magazine sold on news stands. Now we are smaller, broker, and perhaps have fewer illusions about the realities of American journalism." Beginning with this issue, *Sing Out!* began to borrow styles from such magazines as *Crawdaddy*, a successful rock music journal, in the form of interviews with name performers—Janis Ian, Country Joe MacDonald, Bob Dylan, Roger McGuinn, and others. Despite these emulations the magazine's paid circulation had dropped from the peak, 24,258 (in 1966), to 13,362 by January, 1969. By the end of 1969 paid circulation was 11,611. Once again, as in the mid-1950s, appeals for money and the staging of benefits were interspersed with optimistic editorial statements. However, unlike the dark days of McCarthyism, the popularization of folk music was not a futuristic goal but now a memory of what had or could have been.

The major factor contributing to *Sing Out!*'s difficulties was perhaps best suggested by Irwin Silber in his statement of resignation. Failing to remain in touch with the world while being committed to a

Jefferson Airplane

"sense of values" was the American Left's Achilles' heel, particularly, as we have seen, in the realm of folk music. When *Sing Out!* writers were condemning folk-rock as "folk-rot" and acid-rock as "flippie" music, their youthful audience was buying Dylan, the Jefferson Airplane, the Byrds, and many others. When the magazine, like Lenin at the Finland station, attempted to catch up with the pop revolution, it was all over. In the process the editors lost many of the old ideological stalwarts who had read the publication before the Kingston Trio–Bob Dylan "glory days." Silber's retreat to the *National Guardian* perhaps best illustrates the decline of a cohesive ideological position and the total Balkanization of the *Sing Out!* editorial policies.

From a dusty flatbed truck to a concert stage, from Gastonia to Newport, from Ella May Wiggins to Bob Dylan, the three-decade relationship between folk music and political ideology was a stormy one. During the early years of the Almanac Singers, People's Songs, and People's Artists the folk entrepreneurs took shelter in their isolation, at the same time decrying it. Someday, they mused, folk song would have its day in the sun as people's music. When Joan Baez was featured on the cover of *Time*—the American signal of a successful artist—folk music had indeed become popular music. The *Zeitgeist* of the folk revival was far removed from the utopian dreams of the Almanacs and People's Songsters. In 1968 Pete Seeger wrote the following lines:

> *No song I can sing will make Governor Wallace change his mind.*
> *No song I can sing will take the gun from a hate-filled man. . . .*
> ("False from True")

In a more contemporary sense Lennon and McCartney best sum up this entire work:

> *. . . if you go carrying pictures of Chairman Mao,*
> *You ain't going to make it with anyone anyhow. . . .*
>
> ("Revolution")

Selected Discography
of American
Protest Songs

Almanac Singers, Pete Seeger and Chorus. *Talking Union and Other Union Songs.* Folkways Records (FH 5285).
Broadside at Newport. Vanguard Records (VRS 9144).
The Broadside Singers. Broadside Records (BR 303).
Broadside. Vol. 4. Broadside Records (BR 306).
Dylan, Bob. *Another Side of Bob Dylan.* Columbia Records (CS 8993).
———. *Bringing It All Back Home.* Columbia Records (CS 9128).
———. *The Freewheelin' Bob Dylan.* Columbia Records (CS 8786).
———. *The Times They Are a-Changin'.* Columbia Records (CS 8905).
Elliott, Jack. *Songs of Woody Guthrie.* Prestige Records (13016).
Foster, Pat, and Dick Weisman. *Documentary Talking Blues.* Counterpoint/Esoterics (550).
Friedland, Bill, and Joe Glazer. *Ballads for Sectarians.* Labor Arts (2).
———. *Songs of the Wobblies.* Labor Arts (3).
Glazer, Joe. *Image of Freedom: 20 Years of the CIO.* Sound Studio (FO8P 1690).
———. *Songs of Joe Hill.* Folkways Records (FA 2039).
———. *Songs of Work and Freedom.* Washington (WR 460).
———. *We Dared to Dream.* Sound Studio (JO8P 2721).
Greenway, John. *American Industrial Folksongs.* Riverside Records (RLP 12-607).
———. *Great American Bum.* Riverside Records (RLP 12-619).
———. *The Songs and Stories of Aunt Molly Jackson.* Folkways Records (FH 5457).

———. *Talking Blues*. Folkways Records (FH 5232).

Gunning, Sarah Ogan. *Girl of Constant Sorrow*. Folk-Legacy Records (FSA 26).

Guthrie, Woody. *Ballads of Sacco and Vanzetti*. Folkways Records (FH 5485A).

———. *Bound for Glory*. Folkways Records (FA 5485A).

———. *Dustbowl Ballads*. RCA Records (LPV 502).

———. *Sing Out*. Sing Out Records (1A and B).

———. *Talking Dust Bowl*. Folkways Records (FA 2011).

———. *Woody Guthrie Library of Congress Recordings*. Elektra Records (EKL 271/272).

Hootenanny at Carnegie Hall. Folkways Records (FN 2512).

Hootenanny Tonight. Folkways Records (FN 2511).

Houston, Cisco. *Songs of the Open Road*. Folkways Records (FA 2480).

———. *Songs of Woody Guthrie*. Vanguard Records (VRS 9089).

ILGWU Local 91 Chorus. *We Work—We Sing*. New York Cloak Makers Joint Board (CB 772).

Kingston Trio. *Time to Think*. Capitol Records (ST 2011).

Lieberman, Ernie. *Goodbye Mr. War*. Americord (ALP 101).

MacColl, Ewan, and Peggy Seeger. *The New Briton Gazette*. Folkways Records (FW 8732).

The March on Washington August 28, 1963. Council for United Civil Rights Leadership Record.

Mitchell, Chad. *Best of the Chad Mitchell Trio*. Kapp Records (KL 1334).

New Lost City Ramblers. *Songs from the Depression*. Folkways Records (FH 5264).

Ochs, Phil. *All the News That's Fit to Sing*. Elektra Records (EKL 269).

———. *I Ain't Marching Anymore*. Elektra Records (EKL 287).

———. *Phil Ochs in Concert*. Elektra Records (EKL 310).

Paxton, Tom. *Ain't That News*. Elektra Records (EKL 298).

———. *Outward Bound*. Elektra Records (EKL 317).

———. *Ramblin' Boy*. Elektra Records (EKL 277).

Rome, Harold. *A Touch of Rome*. Heritage Records (H 0053).

Seeger, Pete. *American Industrial Ballads*. Folkways Records (FH 5251).

———. *Broadside Ballads. Vol. 2*. Broadside Records (BR 302).

———. *Gazette. Vol. 1*. Folkways Records (FN 2501).

———. *Gazette. Vol. 2*. Folkways Records (FN 2502).

———. *I Can See a New Day*. Columbia Records (CL 2257).

————. *Love Songs for Friends and Foes.* Folkways Records (FA 2453).

————. *Rainbow Quest.* Folkways Records (FA 2454).

————. *We Shall Overcome.* Columbia Records (CL 2101).

————. *With Voices Together We Sing.* Folkways Records (FA 2452).

————, Woody Guthrie, Lee Hays, and Peter Hawes (Almanac Singers). *The Soil and the Sea.* Mainstream Records (S 6005).

————, and Group: Ernest Busch and Thallmann Chorus. *Songs of the Spanish Civil War. Vol. 1.* Folkways Records (FH 5436).

Sing Out! Hootenanny. Folkways Records (FN 2513).

Spoelstra, Mark. *Five and Twenty Questions.* Elektra Records (EKL 283).

Swingle, John. *American Songs of Peace.* Century Records (C 31164).

Travelers. *A Century of Song.* Arc Records (A 261).

United Farm Workers Organizing Committee. *Viva la Causa!* Thunderbird Records (TR 00001).

Weavers. *The Weavers' Greatest Hits.* Decca Records (DL 75169).

West, Hedy. *Old Times and Hard Times.* Folk-Legacy Records (FSA 32).

Selected Bibliography

A. Books

Aaron, Daniel. *Writers on the Left*. New York: Harcourt, Brace and World, 1961.

Ames, Russell. *The Story of American Folk Song*. New York: Grosset and Dunlap, 1955.

Asch, Moses, ed. *American Folksong*. New York: Oak Publications, 1961.

———, and Alan Lomax, eds. *The Leadbelly Songbook*. New York: Oak Publications, 1962.

Bernstein, Irving. *The Lean Years: A History of the American Worker, 1920–1933*. Boston: Houghton Mifflin, 1960.

Brand, Oscar. *The Ballad Mongers*. New York: Funk and Wagnalls, 1962.

Browder, Earl. *Communism and Culture*. New York: International Publishers, 1941.

Cattell, David T. *Communism and the Spanish Civil War*. New York: Russell and Russell, 1965.

Chaplin, Ralph. *Wobbly*. Chicago: University of Chicago Press, 1948.

Chase, Gilbert. *America's Music*. New York: McGraw-Hill, 1955.

Cole, Wayne S. *America First: The Battle against Intervention 1940–1941*. Madison: University of Wisconsin Press, 1953.

Communist Seeger Sings. Los Angeles: Citizens Committee of California, 1964.

Cooke, Alistair. *A Generation on Trial: U.S.A. v. Alger Hiss.* New York: Alfred Knopf, 1952.

Dies, Martin. *The Trojan Horse in America.* New York: Dodd, Mead, 1940.

Draper, Theodore. *The Roots of American Communism.* New York: Viking Press, 1957.

Dreiser, Theodore. *Harlan Miners Speak.* New York: Harcourt, Brace, 1932.

Dunson, Josh. *Freedom in the Air.* New York: International Publishers, 1965.

Egbert, Donald D., and Stow Persons, eds. *Socialism and American Life,* vols. 1 and 2. Princeton, N.J.: Princeton University Press, 1952.

Fast, Howard. *Peekskill USA.* New York: Civil Rights Congress, 1951.

Finkelstein, Sidney. *The Composer and the Nation.* New York: International Publishers, 1960.

———. *How Music Expresses Ideas.* New York: International Publishers, 1952.

———. *Jazz: A People's Music.* New York: Citadel Press, 1948.

Foster, William Z. *History of the Communist Party of the United States.* New York: International Publishers, 1952.

Gates, John. *The Story of an American Communist.* New York: Thomas Nelson and Sons, 1958.

Greenway, John. *American Folksongs of Protest.* Philadelphia: University of Pennsylvania Press, 1953.

Guthrie, Woody. *American Folksong.* Ed. Moses Asch. New York: Oak Publications, 1961.

———. *Born to Win.* Ed. Robert Shelton. New York: Macmillan, 1965.

———. *Bound for Glory.* New York: E. P. Dutton, 1943.

———. *California to the New York Island.* New York: Oak Publications, 1960.

Guttman, Allen. *The Wound in the Heart: America and the Spanish Civil War.* New York: Free Press, 1962.

Harap, Louis. *Social Roots of the Arts.* New York: International Publishers, 1949.

Hentoff, Nat. *Peace Agitator: The Story of A. J. Muste.* New York: Macmillan, 1963.

Himelstein, Morgan. *Drama Was a Weapon.* New Brunswick, N.J.: Rutgers University Press, 1963.

Howe, Irving, and Lewis Coser. *The American Communist Party: A Critical History.* Boston: Beacon Press, 1958.

Ives, Burl. *Wayfaring Stranger.* New York: McGraw-Hill, 1948.

Jackson, Bruce, ed. *Folklore and Society*. Hatboro, Pa.: Folklore Associates, 1966.

Kampelman, Max. *The Communist Party versus the CIO*. New York: Praeger, 1957.

Kornbluh, Joyce, ed. *Rebel Voices: An I.W.W. Anthology*. Ann Arbor: University of Michigan Press, 1964.

Kornhauser, Arthur, Robert Dubin, and A. M. Ross, eds. *Industrial Conflict*. New York: McGraw-Hill, 1954.

Landis, Arthur H. *The Abraham Lincoln Brigade*. New York: Citadel Press, 1967.

Lasswell, Harold, and Dorothy Blumenstock. *World Revolutionary Propaganda*. New York: Alfred Knopf, 1939.

Lawless, Ray M. *Folksingers and Folksongs in America*. New York: Duell, Sloan, and Pearce, 1960.

Lens, Sidney. *Radicalism in America*. New York: Thomas Crowell, 1966.

Lloyd, A. A. *The Singing Englishman*. London: Workers' Music Association, n.d.

Lyons, Eugene. *The Red Decade*. Indianapolis: Bobbs-Merrill, 1941.

MacDougall, Curtis D. *Gideon's Army*, vol. 2. New York: Marzani and Munsell, 1965.

Matusow, Harvey. *False Witness*. New York: Cameron and Kahn, 1955.

Miller, Merle. *The Judges and the Judged*. Boston: Beacon Press, 1952.

Mitchell, H. L. *Oral History of the Southern Tenant Farmers Union*. Mimeographed. Oral History Project. New York: Columbia University Press, 1956–1957.

Morris, James O. *Conflict within the AFL: A Study of Craft versus Industrial Unionism 1901–1938*. Ithaca, N.Y.: Cornell University Press, 1958.

Nelson, Steve. *The Volunteers*. New York: Masses and Mainstream, 1953.

Noebel, David A. *Communism, Hypnotism and the Beatles*. Tulsa, Okla.: Christian Crusade Publications, 1965.

———. *Rhythm, Riots, and Revolution*. Tulsa, Okla.: Christian Crusade Publications, 1966.

Oliver, Paul. *Blues Fell This Morning*. New York: Horizon Press, 1960.

Pope, Liston. *Millhands and Preachers*. New Haven, Conn.: Yale University Press, 1942.

Poulin, A., Jr., and David A. DeTurk, eds. *The American Folk Scene*. New York: Dell Books, 1967.

Qualtar, Terence H. *Propaganda and Psychological Warfare*. New York: Random House, 1962.

Record, C. Wilson. *The Negro and the Communist Party*. Chapel Hill: University of North Carolina Press, 1947.

Reuss, Richard A. *A Woody Guthrie Bibliography 1912–1967*. New York: Guthrie Children's Trust Fund, 1968.

Ribakove, Sy and Barbara. *Folk-Rock: The Bob Dylan Story*. New York: Dell Books, 1966.

Rolfe, Edwin. *The Lincoln Battalion*. New York: Random House, 1939.

Schmidt, Karl M. *Henry A. Wallace: Quixotic Crusade*. Syracuse, N.Y.: Syracuse University Press, 1960.

Schneider, David M. *The Workers' (Communist) Party and American Trade Unions*. Baltimore: Johns Hopkins Press, 1928.

Selznick, Philip. *The Organizational Weapon: A Study of Bolshevik Strategy and Tactics*. New York: Free Press, 1960.

Shannon, David A. *The Decline of American Communism*. New York: Harcourt, Brace, 1959.

Siegmeister, Elie. *Music and Society*. New York: Critics Group Press, 1938.

———. *Music Lover's Handbook*. New York: William Morrow, 1943.

Slonimsky, Nicolas. *Music since 1900*. New York: Norton, 1937.

Sokolov, Y. M. *Russian Folklore*. New York: Macmillan, 1950.

Stavis, Barrie. *The Man Who Never Died*. New York: Haven Press, 1951.

Stegner, Wallace. *The Preacher and the Slave*. Boston: Houghton Mifflin, 1950.

Tippett, Tom. *When Southern Labor Stirs*. New York: Jonathan Cape and Harrison Smith, 1931.

Warren, Frank A. *Liberals and Communism: "The Red Decade" Revisited*. Bloomington: Indiana University Press, 1966.

Wilgus, D. K. *Anglo-American Folksong Scholarship since 1898*. New Brunswick, N.J.: Rutgers University Press, 1959.

B. Articles

The following abbreviations are used: *DW* for *Daily Worker; M&M* for *Masses and Mainstream;* NM for *New Masses; PSB* for *People's Songs Bulletin; PW* for *People's World; SO* for *Sing Out!; SW* for *Sunday Worker; WW* for *Western Worker*.

Aarons, Leroy F. "FBI Checks Folk Songs—Then Mum's Word." *Washington Post,* Nov. 6, 1965.

Adams, Camilla. "Woody Guthrie: Man or Myth." *Broadside,* 71 (June, 1966), 7–9, 10.

Adams, Frederick. "Folk Songs of the People." *DW,* Jan. 30, 1937, p. 9.

Adohmyan, Lahn. "What Songs Should Workers' Choruses Sing?" *DW,* Feb. 7, 1934, p. 5.

Allen, Gary. "That Music: There's More to It Than Meets the Ear." *American Opinion,* 12 (Feb., 1969), 49–62.

Almanac Singers. "Songs of Work, Trouble, and Hope." *PW,* Oct. 28, 1941, p. 5.

"Almanac Singers: Four Young Men with a Lot to Sing." *PW,* Aug. 1, 1941, p. 5.

"Almanac Singers Star on CBS 'We the People.'" *PW,* Jan. 6, 1942, p. 5.

"The 'Almanacs' Part, but Keep on Singing." *DW,* Jan. 8, 1943, p. 7.

"The Almanacs Sing of, by, and for the People." *DW,* Nov. 10, 1942, p. 7.

"American People's Heritage Marx and Lincoln." *SW,* Feb. 11, 1940, p. 7.

Ames, Russell. "Protest and Irony in Negro Folksong." *Science and Society,* 14 (Summer, 1950), 193–213.

Auerbach, Jerold S. "Southern Tenant Farmers: Socialist Critics of the New Deal." *Labor History,* 7 (Winter, 1966), 3–18.

Barden, J. C. "Pete Seeger." *High Fidelity,* Jan., 1963, pp. 51–54.

"Behind the Barbed Wire: Songs of the Concentration Camps Recorded to Aid Exiled Writers." *DW,* June 20, 1941, p. 7.

Belz, Carl. "Popular Music and the Folk Tradition." *Journal of American Folklore,* 80 (Apr.–June, 1967), 130–142.

"Benjamin Franklin: Advocate of People's Music." *SO,* 1 (May, 1950), 8–9.

Bittner, Egon. "Radicalism and the Organization of Radical Movements." *American Sociological Review,* 28 (Dec., 1963), 928–940.

Blitzstein, Marc. "Music and the People's Front." *DW,* Apr. 13, 1938, p. 7.

Botkin, B. A. "Paul Bunyan Was OK in His Time." *NM,* Apr. 23, 1946, p. 13.

Bratt, George. "From Cow Pastures to Picket Lines." *PW,* Sept. 27, 1939, p. 5.

Breit, H. "Talk with Alan Lomax." *New York Times Book Review,* July 23, 1950, p. 12.

"Burl Ives Sings a Different Song." *SO,* 3 (Oct., 1952) , 2.

Calmer, Alan. "The Wobbly in American Literature." *NM,* Sept. 18, 1934, pp. 21–22.

Carmon, Walt. "Songs from Sea, Field and Camp." *DW,* Apr. 30, 1928, p. 5.

"The Children of Bobby Dylan." *Life,* Nov. 5, 1965, pp. 43–50.

"CIO Radio Show Is Oasis on Business Owned Air." *DW,* Feb. 11, 1947, p. 11.

Claiborne, Robert. "Folk Music of the United States." *SO,* 2 (Oct., 1951) and (Nov., 1951) , 8–9, 16.

———. "Music in Review." *DW,* Nov. 19, 1946, p. 11.

Cohen, John. "In Defense of City Folksingers." *SO,* 9 (Summer, 1959) , 32–34.

" 'Come All You Poor Workers,' She Sang to the Harlan Miners." *DW,* June 4, 1941, p. 7.

"The Composer's Collective of New York." *DW,* Mar. 5, 1936, p. 5.

Cowley, Malcolm. "Kentucky Coal Town." *New Republic,* March 2, 1932, pp. 67–68.

Crane, Marjorie. "The People Sing." *PW,* Sept. 12, 1941, p. 5.

"Crisis in Music." *DW,* July 25, 1936, p. 7.

Davis, Henry. "The Almanac Singers: Recordings of 'The Ballad of October 16' and Other Songs." *NM,* May 27, 1941, pp. 29–30.

Denisoff, R. Serge. "Dylan: Hero or Villain." *Broadside,* 58 (May, 1965) , n.p.

———. "Folk Music and the American Left: A Generational-Ideological Comparison." *British Journal of Sociology,* 20 (Dec., 1969) , 427–442.

———. "The Proletarian Renascence: The Folkness of the Ideological Folk." *Journal of American Folklore,* 82 (Jan.–Mar., 1969) , 51–65.

———. "Protest Movements: Class Consciousness and the Propaganda Song." *Sociological Quarterly,* 9 (Spring, 1968) , 228–247.

Dorson, Richard. "Folksong and the NDEA." *Journal of American Folklore,* 75 (April–June, 1962) , 163.

Eisler, Hans. "The Composer in Society." *DW,* Dec. 5, 1935, p. 5.

———. "Reflections on the Future of the Composer." *Modern Music,* 12 (June, 1935) , 180–186.

Feld, Naomi. "The American People's Chorus Says: Singing Is a Form of Battle." *DW,* Dec. 28, 1942, p. 7.

Ferkis, Victor C. "Political and Intellectual Origins of American Radicalism, Right and Left." *Annals,* 144 (Nov., 1962) , 3–11.

———. Populist Influences of American Facsism." *Western Political Quarterly,* 10 (June, 1957), 350–373.

Field, Arthur J. "Notes on the History of Folksinging in New York City." *Caravan,* 7 (June-July, 1959), 7–14, 17.

Finkelstein, Sidney. "Festival and Folk Song." *M&M,* July, 1948, p. 93.

Flexner, Jean A. "Brookwood." *New Republic,* Aug. 5, 1925, pp. 287–289.

Flynn, Elizabeth Gurley. "A Visit to Joe Hill." *Solidarity,* May 22, 1915, p. 1.

"Folk Singers in Original Revue Tonight." *DW,* May 15, 1941, p. 7.

"Folksongs and the Top 40—A Symposium." *SO,* 16 (Mar., 1966), 12–21.

Foster, Joseph. "Hans Eisler: Revolutionary Composer." *DW,* Mar. 1, 1935, p. 5.

"Four Almanacs Washed Up as OWI Singers." *New York Times Herald,* Jan. 6, 1943, p. 1.

Frank, Richard. "Negro Revolutionary Music." *NM,* May 15, 1934, pp. 28–29.

"Free World 'Hoot': Music in Action." *DW,* Oct. 22, 1946, p. 11.

Friedrich, Carl J. "Poison in Our System." *Atlantic Monthly,* 167 (June, 1941), 668.

Friesen, Gordon. "Almanac Singers: End of the Road." *Broadside,* 15 (Nov., 1962), n.p.

———. "Aunt Molly Jackson." *DW,* Jan. 10, 1942, p. 7.

———. "Open Door at Almanac House." *Broadside,* 7 (June, 1962), n.p.

———. "Winter and War Come to Almanac House." *Broadside,* 8 (June, 1962), n.p.

———. "Woody Guthrie: Hard Travellin." *Mainstream,* Aug., 1963, pp. 4–11.

———. "Woody Works on His Book." *Broadside,* 9, 10 (July, 1962), n.p.

Gannes, Harry. " 'Roosian Reds' and the Kentucky Coal Strike." *DW,* Feb. 4, 1932, p. 4.

Garland, Jim. "It Seems to Me." *SO,* 16 (Nov., 1966), 10–15.

Garlin, Sender. "Constant Reader." *DW,* Feb. 20, 1942, p. 7.

Garrett, George. "Radio and Labor." *NM,* Nov. 23, 1943, p. 30.

"Geer, Woody, in Anti-War Songs Tonight." *SW,* Nov. 10, 1940, p. 7.

"Get Ballots with Ballads." *SO,* 3 (Sept., 1952), 4–5.

Gleason, Ralph J. "Surrounded by 'Subversive Music.' " *San Francisco*

Sunday Examiner and Chronicle, Nov. 14, 1965 *(Datebook)*, p. 23.

Gleason, Ralph J. " 'The Times They Are a-Changin' ': The Changing Message of America's Young Folksingers." *Ramparts,* Apr., 1965, pp. 36–48.

Gold, Mike. "Change the World." *DW,* various dates from 1933 to 1946.

———. "It's an Unbeatable Army That Sings of Freedom." *PW,* July 8, 1941, p. 5.

———. "Mike Gold Sneaks In a Plug." *DW,* Apr. 5, 1946, p. 13.

———. "Paean to Pete Seeger and American Music." *PW,* Feb. 8, 1959, p. 7.

"A Great Rebel Passes On." *SO,* 10 (Dec.–Jan., 1961), 31–32.

Green, Archie. "American Labor Lore: Its Meanings and Uses." *Industrial Relations,* 4 (Feb., 1965), 51–68.

Greenway, John. "Woodrow Wilson Guthrie (1912–1967)," *Journal of American Folklore,* 81 (Jan.–Mar., 1968), 63.

Guthrie, Woody. "Folk-Song—Non Politickled 'Pink.' " *SO,* 2 (May, 1952), 10.

———. "My Constitution and Me." *SW,* June 19, 1949, pp. 3, 12.

———. "People's Songs." *SW,* Mar. 13, 1946, p. 7.

———. "Real Folk Songs Are Pretty Rare." *DW,* Sept. 26, 1940, p. 7.

———. "They Stage a Benefit for Okies." *PW,* Mar. 14, 1940, p. 5.

———. "Tom Joad Ballad." *PW,* May 16, 1940, p. 5.

———. "Wandering Singer Explains the Meaning of His Jazz." *DW,* Jan. 15, 1947, p. 11.

———. "Woody, Dustbowl Troubadour, Sings Songs of Migrant Trails." *PW,* Apr. 19, 1940, p. 5.

———. "Woody Says He's a Proletarian, Proud of It." *DW,* Apr. 11, 1940, p. 7.

———. "Woody Sez: A New Columnist Introduces Himself." *PW,* May 12, 1939, p. 4.

———. "Woody's Folks to Make Music for Sharecroppers Blowout." *PW,* Apr. 4, 1941, p. 5.

Haize, L. "Singing for Victory." *SW,* Aug. 15, 1948 (Section 2), pp. 1, 10.

Hatchard, Charles. " 'Music Unifies Workers,' Says Eisler Describing Experiences in Europe." *DW,* Oct. 7, 1935, p. 5.

Hayes, Al. "Paterson Strikers Get a Ballad." *DW,* Nov. 26, 1935, p. 5.

Hays, Lee. "Almanacs: Part II." *PSB,* 3 (Nov., 1948), 9.

————. "Cisco's Legacy." *SO,* 11 (Oct.–Nov., 1961), 4–5.

————. "Concludes Almanacs History." *PSB,* 3 (Dec., 1948), 9.

————. "History of Almanac Singers." *PSB,* 3 (Sept., 1948), 9–10.

————. "Let the Will . . ." *NM,* Aug. 1, 1939, p. 15.

————. "Simon McKeever at Peekskill." *SW,* Sept. 18, 1949 (Section 2), p. 5.

Hentoff, Nat. "The Odyssey of Woody Guthrie." *Pageant,* Mar., 1964, pp. 103–108.

"Hill-Billy Songs." *DW,* Mar. 17, 1937, p. 7.

"History of the Workers Music League." *Worker Musician,* Dec., 1932, p. 6.

"Hootenanny Features Singing Convention Stars." *DW,* July 30, 1948, p. 13.

Howe, Irving. "New York in the Thirties." *Dissent,* 8 (Summer, 1961), 241.

Huck, Susan. "Why Is Rock Music So Awful?" *Review of the News,* Feb. 11, 1970, pp. 17–24.

"Illustrious History of Hootenanny." *DW,* July 6, 1946, p. 11.

James, Thelma. "Folklore and Propaganda." *Journal of American Folklore,* 61 (Oct.–Dec., 1948), 311.

"Jam Session, Almanac Singers at Writers, Artists Spring Frolic." *DW,* May 17, 1941, p. 7.

"Jim Garland, Kentucky Striker Tells Story of Simms' Murder." *DW,* Feb. 16, 1932, p. 4.

Landau, Felix. "People's Songs—First Year." *PSB,* 2 (Feb.–Mar., 1947), 2, 15.

Larkin, Margaret. "Ella May's Songs." *Nation,* Oct. 9, 1929, pp. 382–383.

————. "Story of Ella May." *NM,* Nov., 1929, pp. 3–4.

————. "We'll Never Let Our Union Die." *DW,* Sept. 14, 1938, p. 7.

Lass, Roger. "Art of the Urban Folksinger." *Caravan,* Oct.–Nov., 1958, pp. 20–23.

————. "Chronicle of the Urban Folksinger." *Caravan,* Mar., 1958, pp. 11–17.

Levine, Ben. "Enjoyable Concert Offered by Folk Say Group and AYD." *DW,* May 18, 1948, p. 12.

Lewis, George. "America Is in Their Songs." *DW,* Mar. 24, 1941, p. 7.

Lloyd, A. L. "Guerrilla Songs of Greece." *NM,* Jan. 30, 1945, pp. 29–30.

————. "Songs of Tito's Partisans." *NM,* May 30, 1945, pp. 26–29.

————. "Street Singers of the French Revolution." *SO*, 13 (Summer, 1963), 25–31.

Lloyd, Jessie. "Ella May, Murdered, Lives in Her Songs of Class Strife." *DW*, Sept. 20, 1929, pp. 1, 3.

Lomax, Alan. "The 'Folkniks'—And the Songs They Sing." *SO*, 9 (Summer, 1959), 30–31.

————. "A New Folk Community Composed of Progressives, Anti-Fascists and Union Members." *New York Times Magazine*, Jan. 26, 1947, pp. 16, 41, 42.

————. "Songs of the American Folk." *Modern Music*, 18 (Jan.–Feb., 1941), 137–139.

Lowenfels, Lillian. "One Million Americans Have Heard Almanacs." *DW*, Sept. 2, 1941, p. 7.

McCall, Martin. "New Singers Present Popular and Folk Songs." *DW*, May 2, 1939, p. 7.

MacColl, Ewan. "The Singer and the Audience." *SO*, 14 (Sept., 1964), 16–20.

McGrath, Thomas. "Poetry: Form and Content." *NM*, July 16, 1946, p. 21.

McHenry, Beth. "Lee Hays and His Buddies Hit the Picket Line Again." *DW*, May 13, 1946, p. 13.

————. " 'No Pasaran' in New York City." *DW*, Sept. 6, 1937, p. 7.

Malraux, André. "Art, Popular Art, and the Illusion of the Folk." *Partisan Review*, 10 (Oct., 1950), 489.

Marrs, Ernie. "The Incompleat Woody." *Broadside*, 40 (Feb., 1964), n.p.

Martin, Marty. "Blind Sonny Terry: A People's Artist." *DW*, July 22, 1946, p. 11.

————. "GI Folksay on the Political Front." *DW*, Aug. 31, 1946, p. 11.

————. "People's Songs for Political Action." *DW*, Aug. 2, 1946, p. 16.

"Maurice Sugar." *DW*, July 8, 1938, p. 7.

"Minstrel with a Mission." *Life*, Oct. 9, 1964, pp. 61–68.

Mitchell, Louise. "Songs They Sing at Show Time for Wallace." *SW*, May 23, 1948, p. 7.

Nevins, Nathan. "Red Song Book." *Worker Musician*, Dec., 1932, p. 8.

"New Music League." *DW*, Feb. 10, 1936, p. 5.

"New Theatre School Planned in Arkansas." *SW*, June 9, 1940, p. 7.

Noebel, David A. "Columbia Records: Home of the Marxist Minstrels." *Christian Crusader*, Mar., 1967, pp. 18–20, 28.

————. "Suffer Little Children." *Christian Crusader,* Feb., 1967, pp. 7–9.

"Oscar Brand Joins Witch Hunt Hysteria." *SO,* 2 (Nov., 1951), 2, 16.

"Out of the Corner." *Time,* Sept. 25, 1950, pp. 59–60.

"OWI Plows Under the Almanac Singers." *New York Times,* Jan. 5, 1941, p. 9.

Page, Myra. "Miner's Ballad Songs." *DW,* Jan. 11, 1931, p. 4.

"People's Songs Group Fights Canadian Book Seizure." *DW,* June 18, 1948, p. 13.

Philbrick, Herbert A. "Subverting Youth with Folksinging," in Kenneth W. Ingwalson, ed., *Your Church Their Target.* Arlington, Va.: Better Books, 1966, pp. 167–177.

"Preamble." *Unison,* 1 (May, 1936), 1.

Quin, Mike. "Seeing Red." *WW,* May 14, p. 7; June 22, 1936, p. 5; July 8, 1937, p. 5.

Radosh, Ron. "Commercialism and the Folk Song Revival." *SO,* 8 (Spring, 1959), 27–29.

Real, Jere. "Folk Music and Red Tubthumpers." *American Opinion,* 7 (Dec., 1964), 19–24.

Redfield, Robert. "The Folk Society." *American Journal of Sociology,* 48 (Jan., 1947), 239–308.

Reuss, Richard A. "The Ballad of 'Joe Hill' Revisited." *Western Folklore,* 22 (July, 1967), 187–188.

————. "The Roots of American Left-Wing Interest in Folksong." *Labor History* (forthcoming).

Reynolds, Malvina. "A Ribbon Bow." *SO,* 13 (Summer, 1963), 15–17.

Robbin, Ed. "Three Squares: Woody Pops Up." *PW,* Feb. 14, 1940, p. 5.

Robbins, Bert. "Josh White and His Guitar: Blasting Jim-Crow with Song." *DW,* Sept. 25, 1941, p. 7.

Rolfe, Edwin. "Red Song Book Is Out: Music and Words for Workers." *DW,* Nov. 5, 1932, p. 4.

"Roll the Union On." *Fortune,* Nov., 1946, pp. 183–184.

Rosenfeld, Paul. "Folk Music and Culture Politics." *Modern Music,* 17 (Oct.–Nov., 1939), 18–24.

Rubin, Bernard. "Broadway Beat." *DW,* Apr. 8, 1949, p. 13.

Russell, Don. "They Sing Hard-Hitting Songs That Belong to the People." *DW,* Aug. 14, 1941, p. 7.

Sand, Carl (pseud.). "The Internationale." *DW,* Oct. 31, 1934, p. 5.

————. "Organizing Worker's Bands." *DW,* Nov. 7, 1935, p. 5.

———. "Songs by Auvilles Mark Step Ahead in Workers' Music." *DW,* Jan. 15, 1935, p. 5.

Schumacher, Brent. "From Western Union Picket Line Comes Songs of Victory." *PW,* Oct. 6, 1939, p. 5.

———. "There's a Daily Drama of Solidarity on the Western Union Picket Line." *PW,* Nov. 30, 1939, p. 5.

Seay, S. S. "Folksinger Arrested in Highlander Frame-Up." *SO,* 9 (Winter, 1959–1960), 44–45.

Seeger, Charles. "On Proletarian Music." *Modern Music,* 11 (Mar.– Apr., 1934), 120–127.

Seeger, Pete. "How 'Hootenanny' Came to Be." *SO,* 5 (Autumn, 1955), 32–33.

———. "Johnny Appleseed, Jr." *SO,* 17 (June–July, 1967), 47.

———. "Leadbelly," in Moses Asch and Alan Lomax, eds., *Leadbelly Songbook.* New York: Oak Publications, 1962, p. 7.

———. "Library of People's Music." *SO,* 1 (July, 1950), 6, 11.

———. "People's Songs and Singers." *NM,* July 16, 1946, pp. 7–8.

———. "Remembering Woody." *Mainstream,* Aug., 1963, pp. 27–33.

———. "Whatever Happened to Singing in the Unions." *SO,* 15 (May, 1965), 28–31.

———. "Woody Guthrie—Some Reminiscences." *SO,* 14 (July, 1964), 25–29.

———, and Irwin Silber. "A Menace to Nation's Songs." *DW,* May 31, 1948, p. 8.

"Seeger Conviction Reversed." *SO,* 12 (Summer, 1962), 72.

Seghers, Anna. "The Tasks of Art." *NM,* Dec. 19, 1944, pp. 9–10.

Seligson, Lou. "Labor's Highlander School Brings Democracy to the Deep South." *PW,* Nov. 28, 1939, p. 5.

"Seven Kentucky Miners Join Party and Tell Reason Why." *DW,* Feb. 18, 1932, p. 3.

Seymour, Ann. "Growth of American Music." *DW,* Feb. 17, 1946, p. 14.

———. "Josh White Says: 'Music Is a Mighty Sword against Discrimination.'" *DW,* Jan. 15, 1947, p. 11.

Siegmeister, Elie. "Americans Want American Music." *Etude,* Jan., 1944, pp. 28, 54.

———. "The Future of American Music." *DW,* Oct. 13, 1939, p. 7.

Silber, Irwin. "Fan the Flames." *SO,* 17 (Dec.–Jan., 1967–1968), 55.

———. "He Sings for Integration." *SO,* 10 (Summer, 1960), 4–7.

———. "Hootenanny on TV." *SO,* 13 (Summer, 1963), 2.

———. "Male Supremacy and the Folk Song." *SO*, 3 (Mar., 1953), 4–5, 11.

———. "Peekskill USA." *SO*, 1 (May, 1951), 4.

———. "Peggy Seeger—The Voice of America in Folksong." *SO*, 12 (Summer, 1962), 4–8.

———. "People's Songs." *SO*, 1 (July, 1950), 8–9.

———. "Pete Seeger—Voice of Our Democratic Heritage." *SO*, 4 (May, 1954), 4–5.

———. "Racism, Chauvinism Keynote US Music." *SO*, 2 (Nov., 1951), 6–7, 10.

———. "Sing a Labor Song." *SO*, 1 (Apr., 1951), 6, 15.

———. "Song Pirates Fly Skull and Bones over Tin Pan Alley." *SO*, 2 (June, 1952), 6–7, 11.

———. "Woody Guthrie: He Never Sold Out." *National Guardian*, Oct. 14, 1967, p. 10.

Sillen, Samuel. "Battle in Search of a Hymn." *NM*, May 19, 1942, pp. 22–23.

" 'Singability': War Songs to Be Tried Out by Music Experts." *DW*, Nov. 11, 1942, p. 7.

"Singing Army Backed by a Singing Nation." *DW*, Dec. 20, 1941, p. 7.

"Singing the Songs of the Working People." *SW*, Jan. 28, 1940, p. 7.

Small, Sasha. "Fighting Songs for Workers' Children." *DW*, Aug. 12, 1933, p. 4.

———. "200 Artists Aid Oklahomans." *DW*, Jan. 1, 1941, p. 7.

Smith, Vern. "Folk Ballads and Fighting Songs." *DW*, Nov. 10, 1927, p. 4.

"Song with a Purpose." *PW*, Apr. 16, 1940, p. 5.

"Stay out of War." *PW*, June 12, 1941, p. 5.

Stegner, Page. "Labor History in Fact and Song." *Caravan*, June–July, 1960, pp. 8–16.

Stegner, Wallace. "Joe Hill, the Wobblies' Troubadour." *New Republic*, Jan., 1948, pp. 20–24, 38–39.

Stekert, Ellen. "Cents and Nonsense in the Urban Folksong Movement: 1930–1966," in Bruce Jackson, ed., *Folklore and Society*. Hatboro, Pa.: Folklore Associates, 1966, pp. 153–168.

Summers, Scott. "Cooling Off the Cold War with Folk Songs." *SO*, 12 (Feb.–Mar., 1962), 23.

Swift, L. E. (pseud.) "The Auvilles' Songs." *NM*, Feb. 5, 1935, p. 28.

Tamony, Peter. " 'Hootenanny'—The Word, Its Content, and Continuum." *Western Folklore*, 22 (July, 1963), 165–170.

"There's Solidarity in People's Song." *PW*, May 23, 1941, p. 5.

Tilkin, Anita. "Campaign Song Has Done Much in US History to Influence People's Vote." *DW*, Oct. 5, 1938, p. 7.

———. "Folklore in Balladry." *DW*, Dec. 23, 1938, p. 7.

"The Time of the Lists." *SO*, 4 (Jan., 1954), 2, 11.

Tisa, John. "Unionist Condemns Guthrie's Article." *SW*, Feb. 1, 1948, p. 8.

Tracy, Hugh. "Music as an Agent of Political Expression." *SO*, 13 (Summer, 1963), 45–49.

Truzzi, Marcello. "Folksongs on the Right." *SO*, 13 (Oct.– Nov., 1963), 51–53.

———. "The 100% American Folksong: Conservative Folksongs in America." *Western Folklore*, 28 (Jan., 1969), 27–40.

"Two Composers on War Songs." *NM*, July 7, 1942, p. 22.

"The Un-Americans Retreat." *SO*, 2 (Apr., 1952), 2, 11.

"The Un-American Subpoenas." *SO*, 2 (Mar., 1952), 2.

"Urge Workers to Set Up Music Groups." *DW*, Apr. 17, 1932, p. 4.

"Welcome Home Hootenanny for Youth Delegates." *DW*, Sept. 9, 1947, p. 11.

Westby, David L. and Richard G. Braungart. "Utopian Mentality and Conservatism: The Case of the Young Americans for Freedom." Paper presented at the annual meetings of the American Sociological Association, Aug. 30, 1967, San Francisco.

White, Josh. "I Was a Sucker for the Communists." *Negro Digest*, Dec., 1950, pp. 26–31.

Wilgus, D. K. "All Is Not Nonsense and Hard Cash." *SO*, 11 (Feb.– Mar., 1961), 26.

———. "Folk Song and Democracy." *Gifthorse*, 1949, pp. 19–20.

Wilson, Edmund. "Frank Keeney's Coal Diggers," in *American Earthquake*. Garden City, N.Y.: Doubleday, 1964, pp. 310–327.

Wimberly, Lowry Charles. "Hard Times Singing." *American Mercury*, 31 (June, 1934), 197.

Wolfe, Paul. "The 'New' Dylan." *Broadside*, 53 (Dec., 1964), n.p.

Wolff, William. "For Cisco Houston—The End of the Road." *SO*, 11 (Oct., 1961), 8–13.

———. "The Songs, Dances, and Ballads of Our America." *DW*, July 1, 1939, p. 7.

————. "A Texas Worker Writes a New American Folk Song." *PW*, Oct. 20, 1939, p. 5.

Wood, Robert. "Oklahoma Robin Hood." *DW*, Sept. 8, 1936, p. 7.

"Workers Music League." *NM*, Oct., 1931, p. 31.

Wright, Richard. "Huddie Ledbetter, Famous Negro Folk Artist, Sings the Songs of Scottsboro and His People." *DW*, Aug. 12, 1937, p. 7.

"Youth Theatre to Take Part in Almanac Singers Ballad Program." *DW*, Mar. 27, 1941, p. 7.

Index

A

Adams, Frederick, 51

Adohmyan, Lahn, 39, 42; and New Singers, 51

"Ain't I Right," 148

Allen, Lewis, 66

Almanac House, 78

Almanac Singers: and folk consciousness, 70–71; accused of disloyalty, 71, 92–94, 129; origins, 71–74; personnel, 74; structure, 75; Detroit unit, 75, 91; choice of name, 77; "anonymity movement," 76; as "people's artists," 77–78; summer tour, 78, 85; "hoots," 79; Stalin-Hitler pact, 81; support of APM, 81; antiwar songs, 82–85; impact of German invasion of USSR, 85; prowar songs, 86–92; brief successes, 89–90; Rainbow Room incident, 90; dissolution, 91–93; Red baiting, 92–94; assessment of, 93–97; relationship to CPUSA, 95–97; contribution to

folk revival, 97–98; contrasted to PSI, 99–105

American Federation of Labor (AFL), 28

Americanization as culture, 50

American League Against War and Fascism, 128

American Music League. See Workers Music League

American Music League Festival, 51

American Peace Mobilization (APM), 81, 92

American People's Chorus, 66

"American success syndrome," 172

American Workers' Chorus, 38

American Youth for Democracy, 55

Anderson, Eric, 167

Andrews Sisters, 88

Animals, the, 172

"Anonymity movement," 76

Anti-Communist songs, 147

"Any Bonds Today," 88

Arent, Arthur, 60

Asbel, Bernie, 103

Some other books published by Penguin
are described on the following pages.

Walter and Miriam Schneir

INVITATION TO AN INQUEST
Reopening the Rosenberg "Atom Spy" Case

A carefully documented review of the twentieth century's most controversial espionage case. Walter and Miriam Schneir devoted years of research to the events leading up to the 1953 execution of Julius and Ethel Rosenberg — convicted of spying for the Soviet Union. In these pages, the Schneirs re-create not only the trial but also the moral climate that surrounded it. The questions they ask throw a new light on the workings of American justice: Were the Rosenbergs tried in the press rather than in the courts? Were their accusers untrustworthy? Were they convicted without proper evidence in an atmosphere of terror? Were they guilty? "A vital social document. . . ."—*The Nation*

Richard J. Walton

COLD WAR AND COUNTERREVOLUTION

This is a radical re-evaluation of President John F. Kennedy's foreign policy. Basing itself squarely on the available evidence, *Cold War and Counterrevolution* reveals that Kennedy was a hawkish counterrevolutionary whose vigorous anticommunism prevailed over his sympathy for the oppressed peoples of the world. Although he had political skill and several great achievements to his credit, Kennedy's chief legacy was the miscalculations of Cuba, Berlin, and Vietnam. As this courageous book makes clear, it is not too early to subject that legacy to strict historical scrutiny.

Lewis Yablonsky

ROBOPATHS

The robopaths are the people who pull the triggers at My Lai, Kent State, and Attica, make policy in Washington . . . and live next door. Dehumanized by regimentation, bureaucratization, and indiscriminate violence, they are rapidly increasing in modern society. What can be done? Yablonsky doesn't claim to have the final answers, any more than Charles Reich or Alvin Toffler. Like them, however, he believes that we must persist with the questions.

THE HIPPIE TRIP

A look at the hippie movement of the 1960s. Lewis Yablonsky spent many months studying the hippies in their own environment. He found them to be a varied group who include "pure" hippies, drug addicts, people with severe emotional disturbances, and a miscellany of hangers-on and tourists. *The Hippie Trip* covers them all and goes on to explore a way of life based on "love," spiritually free sex, dope as a religious sacrament, and a new work ethic.

Richard Fairfield

COMMUNES USA
A Personal Tour

An exciting personal report on the American communal movement. Richard Fairfield has had five years' experience with communes and the people in them. Hippies, utopians, self-proclaimed messiahs, anarchists, traditional Christians, and dropouts from suburbia attempting group marriage are all covered in this unique book. To Fairfield, a commune is "an arrangement of three or more persons among whom the primary bond is some form of sharing"—and the sharing can take in anything from work to sex. In most communes, he says, honest and successful efforts are being made to create new ways of life. Alone in contemporary writing, *Communes USA* offers a truly intimate view of this growing, but little-known, sub-culture. Illustrated with photographs.

Edited by Thomas C. Wheeler

THE IMMIGRANT EXPERIENCE

Nine deeply personal narratives—especially written for this book by immigrants or close descendants of immigrants—express "the anguish of becoming American." The contributors are Mario Puzo, Jade Snow Wong, Harry Roskolenko, William Alfred, Eugene Boe, Jack Agueros, Czeslaw Milosz, John A. Williams, and Alan Pryce-Jones—all talented writers who bring to life the Italian, Chinese, Jewish, Irish, Norwegian, Puerto Rican, Polish, Black, and English points of view. Crowded with unforgettable portraits of various ethnic ways of life, these pieces say something important not only about Americanization but also about America itself. "It is a good book, rich in variety and tone —nine very different voices describing old dreams and failures, new adventures and hopes."—*New York Times Book Review.*